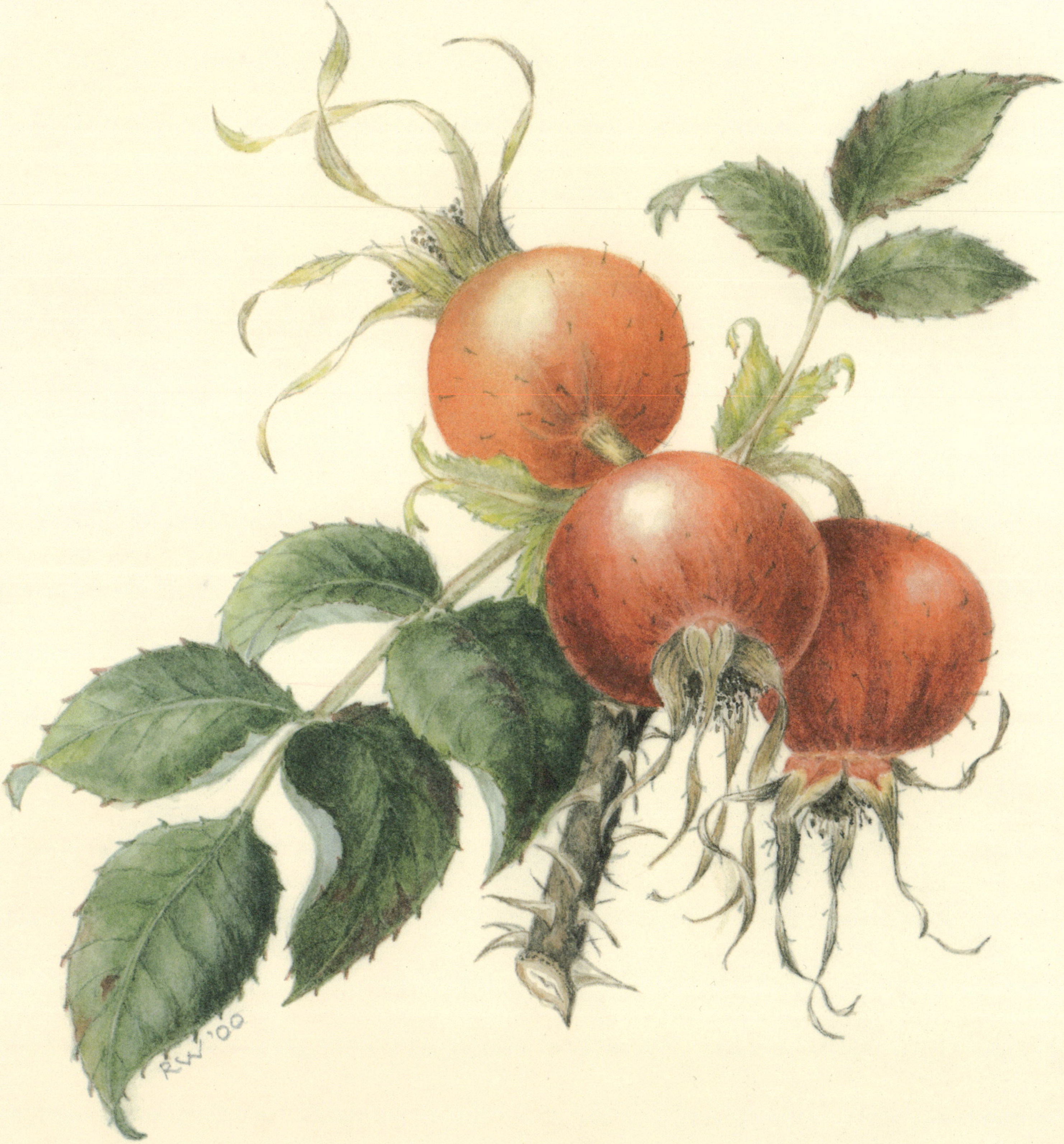
RW '00

£18

Flower Paintings
from the
Apothecaries' Garden

Contemporary Botanical Illustrations from
Chelsea Physic Garden

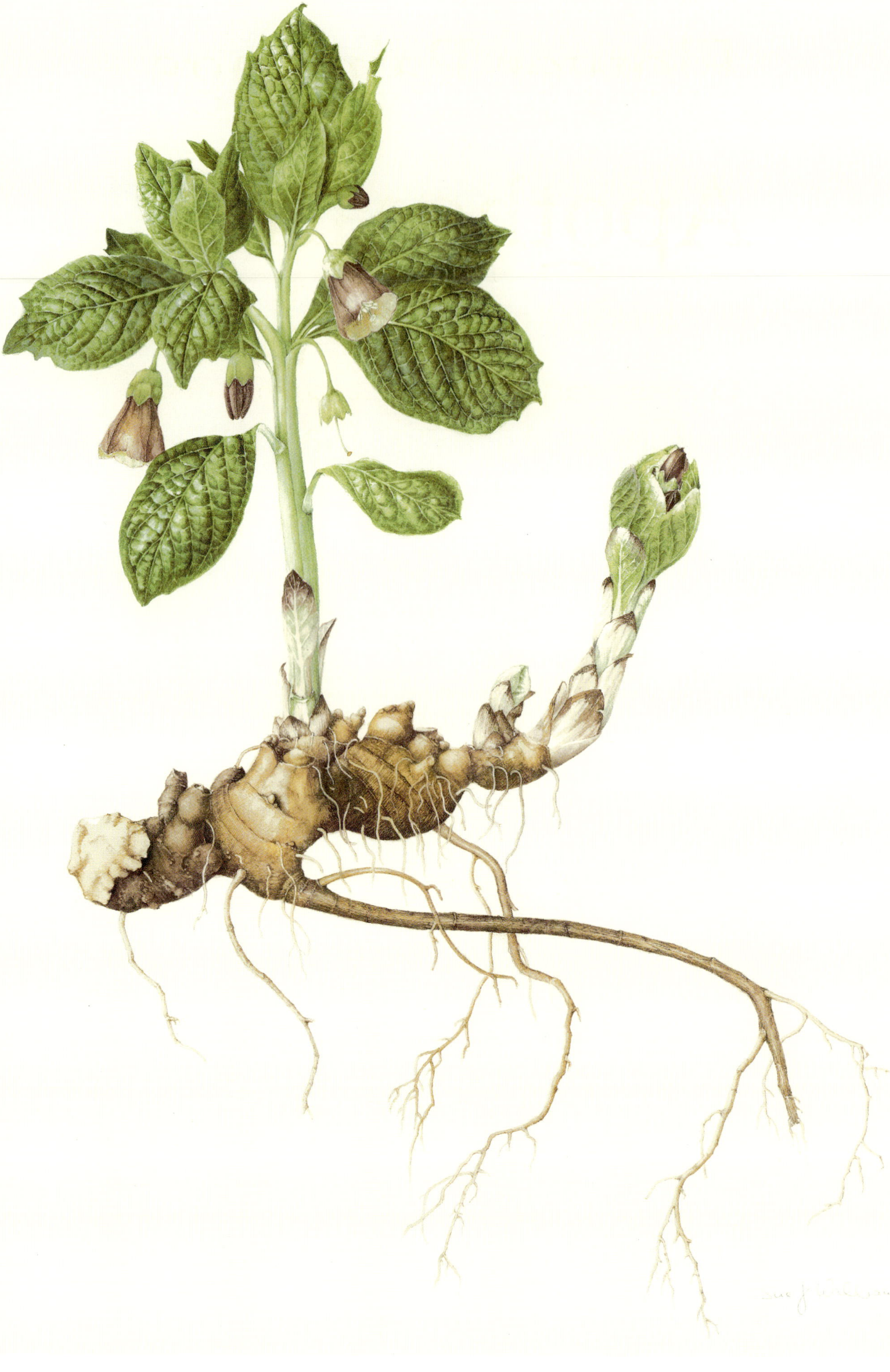

Flower Paintings from the Apothecaries' Garden

Contemporary Botanical Illustrations from Chelsea Physic Garden

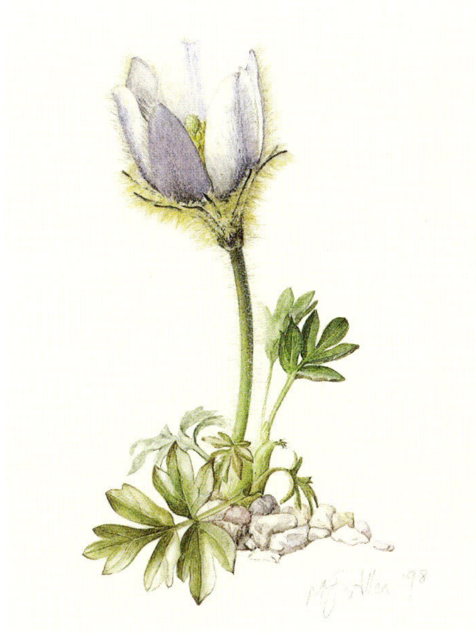

Andrew Brown

ANTIQUE COLLECTORS' CLUB

ISBN 1 85149 503 7

Frontispiece: *Scopolia carniolica,* Sue Williams

British Library Cataloguing-in-Publication Data
A catalogue record for this book is available from the British Library

Printed in Spain
for the Antique Collectors' Club Ltd., Woodbridge, Suffolk

Contents

Preface

Chelsea Physic Garden was set up by the Worshipful Society of Apothecaries in 1673 to train their apprentices to distinguish plants with healing properties from those which are poisonous but look almost identical. Apart from plant collecting and making herbarium specimens, the apothecaries relied on illustrated herbals and floras to expand their knowledge. Today, with the aid of genome sequencing equipment, botanists can very nearly determine a plant's identity by its DNA without ever looking at a growing plant. Yet artists still strive to capture the natural beauty of the plants growing in this remarkable botanic garden which has become London's oldest outdoor classroom.

Sir Hans Sloane, whose statue watches over the Garden, was a notable collector of botanical art and helped the struggling artist Elizabeth Blackwell. Between 1737 and 1739 Blackwell was given access to the Garden in order to illustrate its plants and record their uses. Her book, *The Curious Herbal*, to which Sloane subscribed, was the most comprehensive set of figures of medicinal plants in colour of its day. Indeed, it raised enough money for her to extricate her husband Alexander from debtors' prison. Sadly, it was not long before this ill-fated man once more fell foul of the authorities, this time in Sweden where he was eventually executed.

Sloane was just one of many enlightened individuals connected with Chelsea Physic Garden who have valued botanical art. The Chelsea Physic Garden Florilegium Society continues this worthy tradition with the publication of *Flower Paintings from the Apothecaries' Garden* as part of its tenth anniversary celebrations. Each plant is portrayed with such precision and detail that it can be recognised and distinguished from another species. What also excites me is that these are real plants shown with all their imperfections.

On behalf of the Trustees of Chelsea Physic Garden, I would like to thank the Honorary President of the Florilegium Society, Anne-Marie Evans, its Honorary Patron, Dr Phillip Cribb, Chairman, Dr Andrew Brown and Honorary Vice-chairman, Gillian Barlow as well as all the members of the Society who have made possible this publication. We are also grateful to the members of the selection panel: Mr Barry Ambrose, Dr Phillip Cribb, Dr David Frodin, and Head Gardener, Mark Poswillo for their dedication in deciding which illustrations are accepted for this priceless collection. *Flower Paintings from the Apothecaries' Garden* is a true celebration of talent and professionalism as well as a glorious legacy for future generations.

Rosie Atkins
Curator, Chelsea Physic Garden
January 2005

Foreword

The florilegium as a concept has a long history, proceeding as it does from the earliest attempts in the seventeenth century to depict plants for their uniqueness and individual character alone, quite apart from any medicinal, iconic or religious significance they may have, and to do this accurately in the light of the steadily expanding science of botany. In some ways, one can view florilegia as part of the curiosities movement, where items were collected for their rarity or novelty. New plants brought back from newly-discovered lands were thus collectable and the sure way of recording their distinctiveness beyond their natural season or life cycle was to have their portrait painted.

The appropriateness of Chelsea Physic Garden for the creation of a twenty-first century florilegium can hardly be bettered both in terms of its links with the development of botany as a science and its pedigree of associated botanical artists over three centuries.

The Chelsea Physic Garden Florilegium Society is composed of a restricted number of botanical artists who propose to themselves the task of painting the portraits of those plants which currently flourish in the Physic Garden. Members' paintings are selected yearly by the curator and a panel of judges who stress the importance of botanical accuracy.

The Society's first Chairman, Margaret King, established its firm foundation and high standards which continue to thrive today. The idea of groups of individuals who set about illustrating plants of a specific garden has since gathered momentum and several such societies are now blossoming here and in the USA.

Anne-Marie Evans
Honorary President, Chelsea Physic Garden Florilegium Society

Introduction

In the following pages are displayed fifty-six paintings of plants currently cultivated at Chelsea Physic Garden. Each artist who has at least one painting in the Garden's archive is represented. Inevitably, the artists have differing outputs of finished paintings. Some are retired, some combine career and family commitments, some are working artists, others have demanding careers in fields with no connection to painting. In selecting images for this book it has been our intent to show as wide a range of species as possible.

Not all the plants illustrated have pharmaceutical uses for, despite its origins, the Physic Garden has long been a botanic garden, not just an apothecaries' garden. For each species a short account is given of the plant's uses, pharmaceutical or otherwise. Where appropriate, information about the plant's cultivation in the Physic Garden is also included. Names of plants and families are given according to *The Plant Book* (2002).

Each artist was asked to supply a biographical note to accompany their painting. This collection of biographies demonstrates a wide variety of background, career and artistic experience amongst the artists. This variety has inevitably led to a diversity of painting style but this, as the illustrations show, has not stood in the way of producing an archive of the highest quality and consistency. Indeed, the diversity of artistic style can only be seen as an enriching force.

In reading the text it will become obvious that many names of people and institutions appear repeatedly. At the Physic Garden the personalities include William Curtis who was Demonstrator and *Praefectus Horti* from 1772 to 1777. After resigning, Curtis published *Flora Londinensis* (1775–1798) in which he documented all the species growing within a ten-mile radius of London. He also started in 1787 what later became universally known as *Curtis's Botanical Magazine*, which is still being published. Amongst the plant name authorities (the names printed, often in an abbreviated form, after the plant's specific name) there frequently appear 'Miller'and 'Lindl.' (for Lindley). The first is Philip Miller who was Gardener for almost fifty years from 1722 to 1770. Apart from his gardening abilities he is renowned for the *Gardeners Dictionary*, a massive folio, first published in 1731, which ran to twelve editions. John Lindley was *Praefectus Horti* and Professor of Botany from 1836 to 1853. Lindley was an extremely productive botanist, teacher and writer, perhaps best known for his studies of the orchid family, especially those species being introduced from the British Empire and tropics in general.

In our own time, and beyond Chelsea, the name of Dr Shirley Sherwood as a patron of the skill of the botanical illustrator is known world-wide. In amassing her personal collection of paintings and drawings, in exhibiting them around the world, in lecturing and organising painting masterclasses, Dr Sherwood has overseen a renaissance in this field of artistic endeavour over the past fifteen years. Her collection has been displayed in two sumptuous publications, *Contemporary*

Botanical Artists (1996) and *A Passion for Plants* (2000). She has given generously of her time and advice to so many artists, at a very personal level, often in their own studios. Many of the contributors to this volume have benefited from her input and enthusiasm to support artists by buying their work.

The Hunt Institute for Botanical Documentation at Carnegie Mellon University in Pittsburgh, USA, is perhaps the world's greatest repository of botanical illustrations. The Institute regularly holds an International Exhibition at which the work of living artists is displayed. Its series of exhibition catalogues, with their artists' biographies and illustrations of works of art, serve as a near-complete record of what is being achieved in this field in modern times. As ever, it is the people of an institution who determine its success and at 'the Hunt' it is the Curator of Art, James J. White who has become a friend of so many organisations and individuals outside the USA and who has been such a great champion of artistic endeavour. Many of our members at Chelsea have benefited from James White's infectious enthusiasm.

In preparing this book to celebrate the tenth anniversary of the Chelsea Physic Garden Florilegium Society and all that it has achieved during that time, I have been helped by very many people. I thank each of them. Every artist, each of which has responded promptly to requests for information about themselves. Rosie Atkins, the Curator, for her support for the project and for her preface. Gillian Barlow, the Society's Vice-Chairman, for the immense pains taken to ensure the correct conservation and accurate recording of the archive on behalf of both the Society and the Garden, and for her brief history of the Society. Dr Phillip Cribb, for his genuine interest and support of the Society as its Honorary Patron, and for his essay on the role of botanical illustration today. Anne-Marie Evans, teacher *extraordinaire*, for her foreword, but more particularly, for being a major source of inspiration for artists and for the generation of the Society. David Nunn, a pharmaceutical scientist, who compiled much of the information about the uses of the plants. Mark Poswillo, Head Gardener, and his team, for collecting the specimens for the artists and providing information about plants as they are grown in the Garden.

Andrew Brown
Chairman, Chelsea Physic Garden Florilegium Society

The role of botanical illustration today

Botanical illustration is considered by many to be a left-over pastime from the Victorian era. However, it not only continues in botanical institutes worldwide, but has received a stimulus in recent times from the increasing number of practitioners attracted to it. Foremost amongst its promoters has been the Chelsea Physic Garden Florilegium Society. Their success with displays at the Royal Horticultural Society's shows and the Hunt Botanical Institute has stimulated similar groups to form at other botanic gardens in the British Isles. Of course, botanical illustration has never gone away and has been fostered by institutes such as the Royal Botanic Gardens at Kew and Edinburgh, and at the Natural History Museum, for many years.

The question is often posed as to why botanical illustration has not been superseded by colour photography. The botanical illustrator not only produces a likeness of the habit of the plant and its flowers, but can also include on the same illustration details which the camera cannot capture and that enable any competent botanist to distinguish that species from any other. Using living plants or herbarium material from a variety of localities, the illustration can also include details of infra-specific variation, often ignored or overlooked in descriptions. As such, the illustration becomes a critical part of the materials that aid accurate identification and naming of plants. Comparative plates, illustrating the same feature, e.g., leaf, stamen or fruit, from closely related species, have always been a particularly useful method for assisting identification. Illustrated keys have also been successfully used in a number of recent field guides.

Thus, botanical illustrations are critical for scientific work, not only taxonomic, but over a range of disciplines from horticulture and agriculture to ecology and conservation. The misidentification of plants can have serious consequences, e.g., in plant-based traditional medicine where misidentification can kill.

The majority of botanical illustration for scientific publications is still undertaken in black and white, rather than colour. At Kew, nine out of every ten illustrations are in black and white. These are used to illustrate articles in scientific journals, floras, field guides, and popular horticultural books. However, coloured illustrations are still published in some quantity, particularly for botanical monographs and for *Curtis's Botanical Magazine*, founded in 1787 and the longest surviving magazine published with colour illustrations. A good illustration can save hundreds of words in descriptions and keys.

Overall, the demand for good botanical illustration has not slackened, rather it has increased in recent years, because as printing costs have fallen it has become possible to include more illustrations.

Between 1755 and 1760 Philip Miller published fine coloured illustrations by G.D. Ehret, J.S. Mueller, R. Lancake, J. Bartram and W. Houstoun for his *Figures of the most beautiful, useful and uncommon plants described in the Gardeners Dictionary*. Thus Chelsea Physic Garden can justifiably claim to have been amongst the earliest institutes in the country to have fostered botanical illustration and a group of botanical artists. Its Florilegium Society, following in a long and proud tradition, has attracted many talented artists. Their work, reflecting the many, various and often rare plants grown today at this historic garden, is published here as a collection for the first time. Three and a half centuries after the publication of Philip Miller's work, it is both an advertisement for a wonderful garden and its collections, and a window for the talent of a dedicated and inspired association of artists.

Phillip Cribb
Deputy Keeper of the Herbarium
Royal Botanic Gardens, Kew
Honorary Patron, Chelsea Physic Garden Florilegium Society

Chelsea Physic Garden Florilegium Society – A brief history

The Chelsea Physic Garden Florilegium Society was founded in 1995 with the primary aim of recording in paintings and drawings the plants growing in the Physic Garden. Work would be donated to the Garden's archive, subject to selection by committee, for the use and benefit of the Garden.

In November 1994 Margaret King put her idea to the Curator, Sue Minter, for the formation of a society of botanical artists working to record the plants growing in the Physic Garden. The Curator and Trustees gave their permission to go ahead. Margaret King became the founder Chairman and Wendy Alexandra Page became the founder Honorary Secretary. They formulated a Set of Rules by which the Society is still run. The nucleus of the Society was a small number of students who had just completed the first Certificate of Botanical Illustration course to be offered by the English Gardening School, directed by Anne-Marie Evans, who was made Honorary President of the Society.

Anne-Marie Evans suggested the name 'Florilegium Society' and this was approved. Margaret King and Wendy Page co-opted Dr Barbara McLean to become the Society's Scientific Adviser. In 1995 Anne-Marie Evans wrote: 'Whereas the florilegia of the seventeenth century were created to portray the beauty and novelty of those plants brought back from the expanding colonies, the modern florilegium may be seen as a conservation tool, instrumental in recording for posterity collections of plants within a chosen garden. Although Chelsea Physic Garden has played a central role in the development of botanical painting in the UK and abroad, as yet no florilegium of its content has been produced.'

The Society's first Honorary Patron was the inspiring and remarkable Professor William Stearn, whose wide-ranging scholarship he so generously shared. The Society is honoured that, following William Stearn's death, his mantle was taken on by Dr Phillip Cribb, Deputy Keeper of the Herbarium at Kew Gardens. His dynamism and constructive advice and guidance will help develop the worth and standing of the Society's future work.

The primary aim remains the portrayal of the Garden's entire plant collection. As there are more than 5000 plant names listed, current members are still merely laying the foundations of a vast project! From the members' annual submission of paintings and pen-and-ink drawings, work is selected by an independent panel to maintain highest standards. Nearly 200 watercolours and 120 drawings have been accepted at the time of writing. All plant material is grown in the Garden. Herbarium specimens are also prepared to accompany each illustration. The Head Gardener and his team continue to instruct and help members, willingly providing both cuttings and advice when requested.

When a painting Member of the Society has had three works selected by the

Curator's selection committee for inclusion in the archive, the Member then becomes a Fellow of the Society.

The Society fulfils its second aim — 'to further general awareness of this exacting method of portraying plants' by occasional exhibitions of the paintings. The Society showed paintings of plants associated with Philip Miller, Gardener from 1722 to 1770, at the Royal Horticultural Society London Show in January 1999. This exhibit was awarded a Gold Medal. In 2000 the Society showed paintings at the Hunt Institute, with which we have a warm relationship through its Curator of Art, James J. White, our enthusiastic Honorary US Patron. Some thirty-five members of the Society are independently represented in the Hunt Institute's collection. The Society has also exhibited as a group in Munich and London. Many members are successful artists exhibiting worldwide. Some have Royal Horticultural Society medals to their credit. Where this is so, the awards are listed after the artist's biographical note. Some teach botanical illustration and some produce scientific illustrations to support academic botanical publications at Kew. Nineteen are represented in the celebrated collection of Dr Shirley Sherwood, whose travelling exhibitions have created a large discerning public for this art.

As our work is donated for the benefit of the Garden, it is gratifying that our drawings are used to illustrate the Annual Report and several Garden booklets on specific aspects of the plant collection. The Society has published several books on technical botany and illustration techniques to aid artists and support both the work of the Society and the Garden.

We aim to help promote florilegia worldwide. Our advice has been accepted in the formation of four new societies to date, based at the Brooklyn Botanic Garden, New York, Sheffield Botanic Gardens, the Eden Project and Hampton Court, just outside London. Advice is sought for other reasons too. In 1998 Margaret King was asked which institution might conserve a collection of 500 paintings of fungi by renowned Japanese artist Michiko Kobayashi (who had indicated that all her extant paintings were to be put in her coffin at her death so that they might be cremated with her). Margaret King approached Sir Ghillean Prance, the Director of the Royal Botanic Gardens at Kew, who enthusiastically embraced the idea of saving the collection. The outcome was that in June 2000 the artist gifted her paintings in person to Kew.

The Society grows from strength to strength: may the next decade be as exciting as the first.

Gillian Barlow
Honorary Vice-Chairman
Keeper of the Archive, Chelsea Physic Garden Florilegium Society

List of Plates

The plates are arranged alphabetically by Latin name of the plant depicted. Each plate is accompanied by a text in which the medicinal, culinary or other uses of the plant are discussed and aspects of its cultivation in the Physic Garden are summarised where possible. Then follow notes about the artist.

29	*Eryngium giganteum*	Jane Leycester Paige
30	*Gaultheria procumbens*	Valerie Bolas
31	*Geum pyrenaicum*	Kate Evans
32	*Glaucium flavum*	Jenevora Searight
33	*Hoheria lyallii*	Angie Girling
34	*Ipomoea lobata*	Barbara McLean
35	*Jasminum nudiflorum*	Monica McAllen
36	*Liquidambar orientalis*	Lesley Catchpole
37	*Magnolia grandiflora*	Margaret Stones
38	*Morus alba*	Sarah Gould
39	*Muscari botryoides*	Wendy Alexandra Page
40	*Olea europaea*	Mariella Baldwin
41	*Paulownia tomentosa*	Janet Callender
42	*Penstemon heterophyllus*	Peggy Dawe
43	*Phlomis tuberosa*	Valerie Bradburn
44	*Platycodon grandiflorus*	Masako Sasaki
45	*Pulsatilla vernalis*	Martin Allen
46	*Punica granatum*	Joanna Craig-McFeely
47	*Punica granatum*	Caroline Hervey-Bathurst
48	*Quercus coccifera*	Kay Rees-Davies
49	*Ribes americanum*	Shirley-Ann Nunn
50	*Romneya coulteri*	Elisabeth Sherras Clark
51	*Rosa* 'Scabrosa'	Ruth Woakes
52	*Salvia discolor*	Barbara Clemence
53	*Saxifraga paniculata*	Loveday Gabriel-Best
54	*Scopolia carniolica*	Sue Williams
55	*Tulipa urumiensis*	Diana Everett
56	*Vicia faba* 'Crimson Flowered'	Judi Stone

Abelmoschus esculenta (L.) Moench
Family – Malvaceae

Ainslie Ensom

Best known as the vegetable okra, its other common name is lady's fingers. It is a plant of the Old World tropics taken to North America and the West Indies by slaves.

The plant is cultivated for its fruit, a pod about three inches long and rich dark green in colour. It requires a warm temperate climate but will grow in northern climates in hot summers. It succeeds best in cooler climates if protected by a greenhouse or polythene tunnel.

Abelomoschus is a member of the mallow family and has flowers similar to the hibiscus. It was at one time named *Hibiscus esculentus*. The roots contain much mucilage, which, after drying, grinds to a white powder said to be superior to traditional marsh mallow. Extracts from the plant are used in herbal medicine as an antispasmodic. In Egypt the seeds are chewed as a stomachic, nervine and breath sweetener. They are also used as an aphrodisiac. In India, infusions of the pods are used to treat urinogenital problems as well as chest infections.

About the artist

Ainslie Ensom was born in 1947 and after taking her Advanced Levels she received a Diploma in Art and Design in Fashion and Textiles from Ravensbourne College of Art and Design in London. In 1995 she gained a Distinction in the Diploma in Botanical Painting at the English Gardening School.

Ainslie's first career was almost twenty years of designing and making hand-printed and embroidered silk clothes for a designer boutique. Latterly she has given herself to botanical illustration both at Chelsea Physic Garden and the Eden Project. She is a member of the Eden Project Florilegium Society, The Society of Floral Painters and the American Society of Botanical Artists. She has exhibited in London, Wales, Sweden and the Hunt Institute. Her work is held in private collections, the Eden Project, Cornwall and the National Museum and Gallery of Wales, Cardiff.

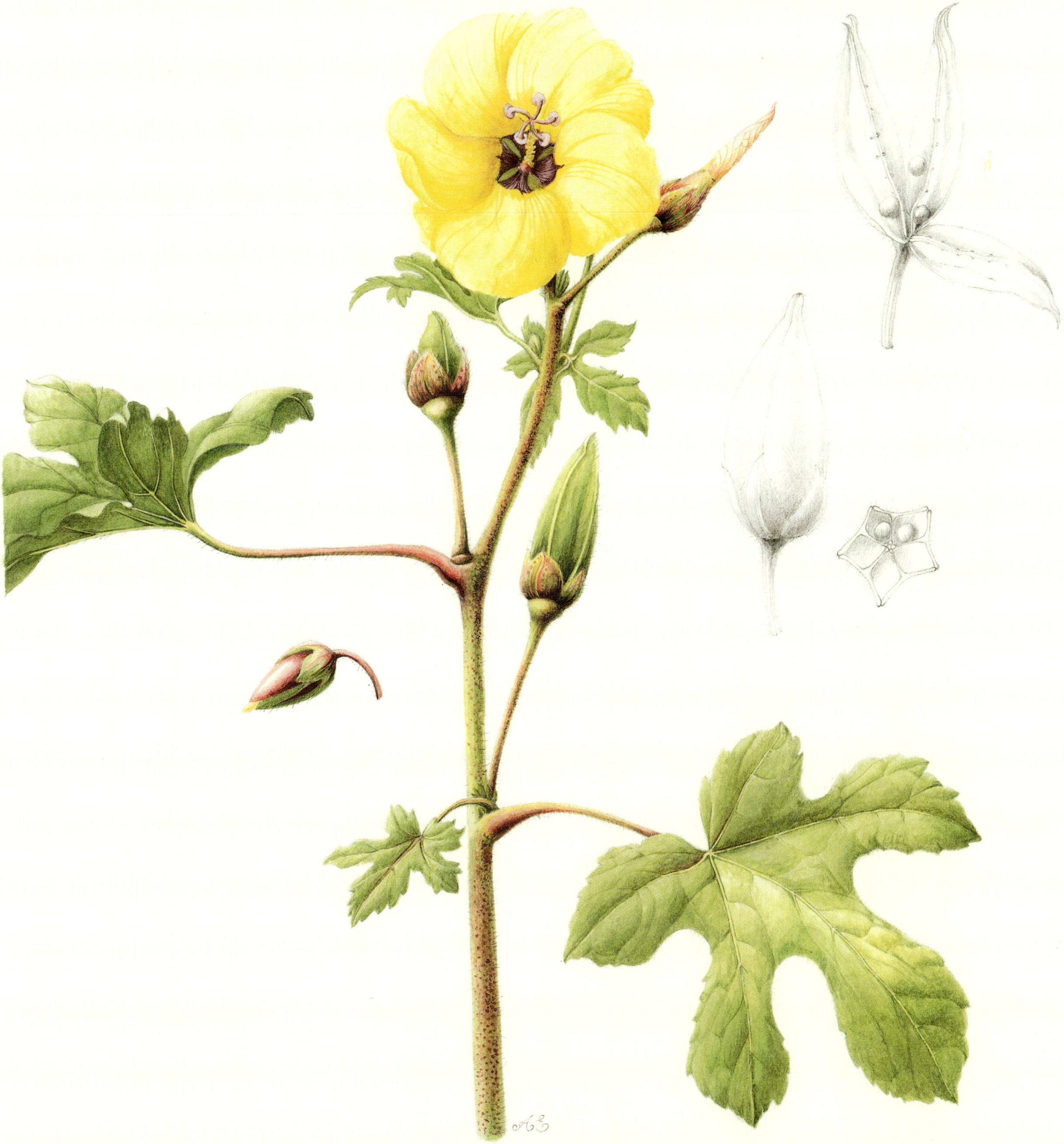

Acanthus dioscoridis L.
Family – Acanthaceae

Helen Allen

Acanthus mollis, known as bear's breeches, and *A. spinosus* are well known to British gardeners. The leaves and roots of *A. mollis*, which contain significant quantities of tannin and mucilage, are used to treat dislocated joints and burns. The use of the roots to treat burns was known to the Greek physician, Dioscorides (First century AD) and the epithet for *A. dioscoridis* reflects this 2000 year-old association. *Acanthus dioscoridis* is native to Turkey, Iran and Iraq.

About the artist

Helen Allen, born 1948, trained as a textile designer at the University of Leeds. After graduating she studied for a Postgraduate Certificate in Education at Homerton College, Cambridge. After several career changes Helen studied botanical illustration at the English Gardening School at Chelsea Physic Garden.

Helen took up the post of Course director of the one-year Botanical Design course at the English Gardening School in 2001. She will become Course Director of the one-year diploma course in Botanical Illustration on Anne-Marie Evans' retirement from the school.

Helen's work is held both in the archive of Chelsea Physic Garden and the Hunt Institute. Helen has exhibited at the Ebury Galleries, London, at four shows, at the Ursus Gallery in New York, the Hunt Institute, and twice at the National Botanic Garden for Wales.

Helen was commissioned by the League of Friends of the Royal London Homoeopathic Hospital to paint an illustration of *Calendula officinalis*. This painting was presented to HM the Queen in celebration of the hospital's 150th anniversary.

Her work has been used to illustrate articles in the magazines *Country Life* (1999) and *House and Garden* (2003). Helen is a member of the working group in preparing a florilegium of the plants in the gardens of Highgrove and is also a Fellow of the Chelsea Physic Garden Florilegium Society.

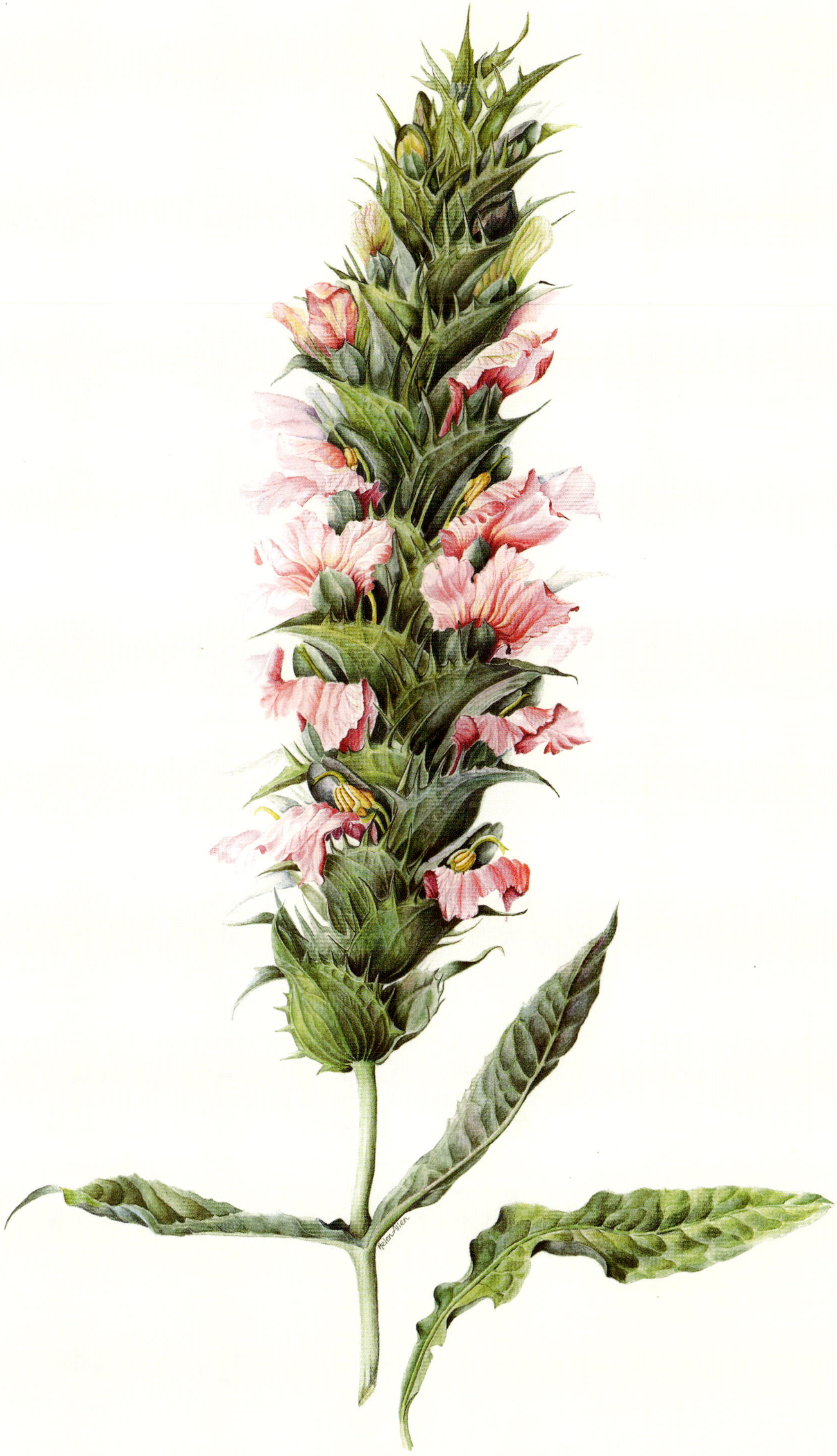

Ajuga reptans L. (pink form)
Family – Labiatae

Julia Trickey

The common name for *A. reptans* is bugle. It grows wild in woodlands throughout England and is generally distributed from Europe to Iran. The flowers are usually violet-blue, but pink or white forms are occasionally found. The Physic Garden material is derived from a pink form collected from woodland near Buckler's Hard in Hampshire. At one time it was regarded as a remedy for gout and jaundice as well as being good at healing wounds. It was also formerly used for staunching haemorrhages.

About the artist

Julia always enjoyed drawing and painting as a child and went on to study visual communication at Bath Academy of Art in the early 1980s. Painting in a realistic style was not encouraged and she left having spent much of her final year designing posters, booklets and studying typography. Having worked for several years as a graphic designer Julia discovered botanical illustration when her children were small. She enrolled on an adult education course run by Bromley council, and she immediately felt at home, having discovered a way of combining the two interests of art and plants. When the course tutor, Judi Stone, moved on in 2003, Julia took over teaching the classes for Bromley as well as setting up two classes for Croydon council. Julia joined the Chelsea Physic Garden Florilegium Society in 2002. She has work held in private collections world-wide. Having moved to Bath in the summer of 2004, she is now a member of the Bath Society of Botanical Artists.

RHS medals: Silver Gilt 2001, 2004

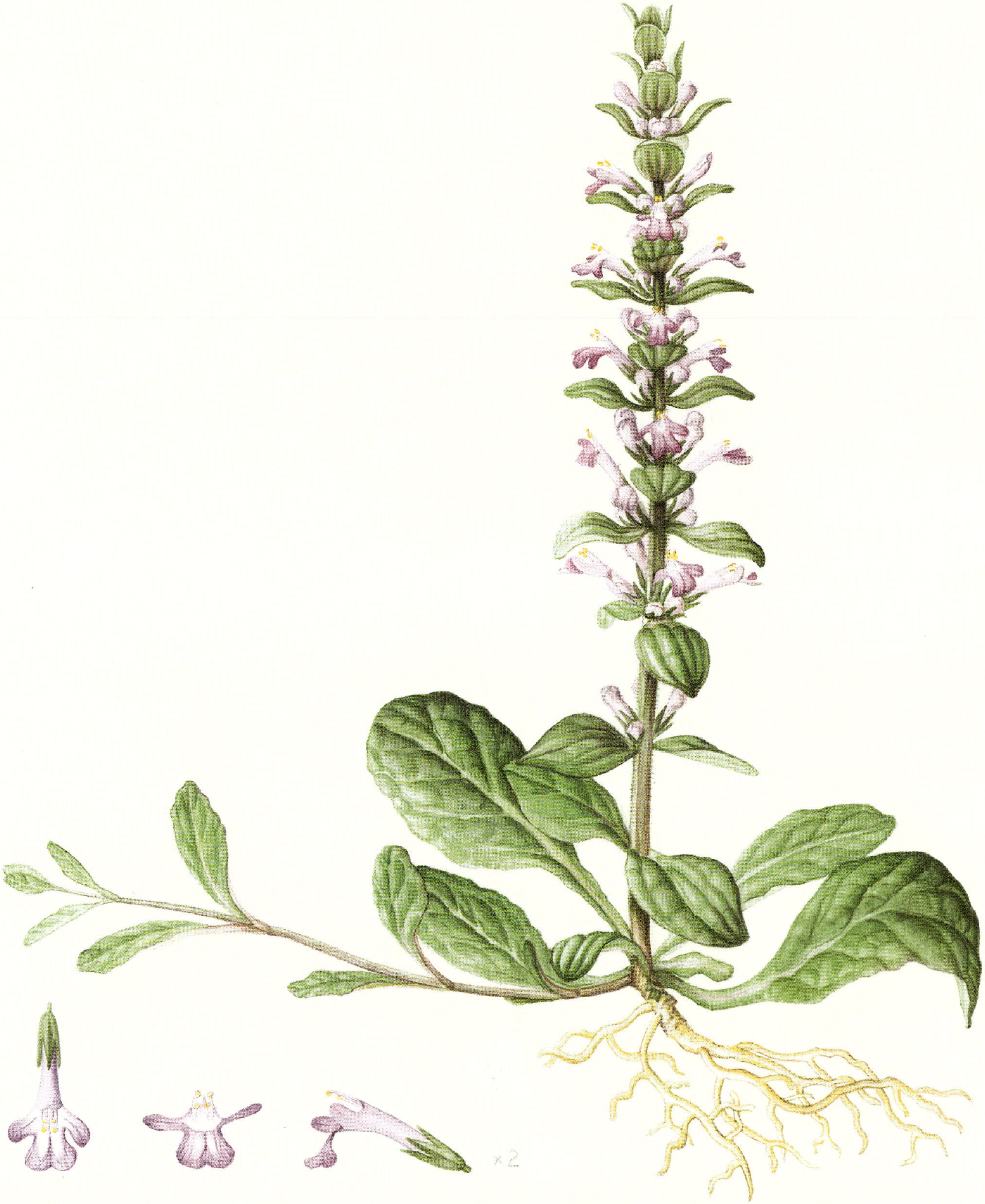

AJUGA REPTANS (PINK FORM)

Julia Trickey

Allium tuberosum Rottler ex Sprengel
Family – Alliaceae

Andrew Brown

Allium tuberosum, from southeast Asia, is known by the common names of Chinese chives, oriental garlic or cuchay. The genus *Allium* consists of nearly seven hundred species and includes chives, garlic, onions and shallots. All have a distinct pungent odour resulting from the presence of organic sulphur compounds and are reputed to have a wide range of medicinal properties, ranging from antibacterial and antifungal activity to the reduction of cholesterol. Work published in the USA lists over 500 chemical constituents identified in *Allium sativum*.

About the artist

Andrew Brown was born in 1948. He read Botany at Oxford University and did research for a PhD in palynological vegetational history at Cambridge University. He taught biology in independent schools for twenty-nine years whilst developing his skills as a botanical illustrator, something that he had wanted to do from childhood. In 2001 he retired from teaching to become an illustrator and is now working as a part-time freelance artist for the Royal Botanic Gardens, Kew. He has no formal training in illustration techniques and ascribes his ability to inheritance of skills from two grandfathers who were both competent amateur artists.

He has held solo exhibitions of botanical illustrations at the Footstool Gallery at St John's, Smith Square, at Westminster School and Wolfson College, Oxford. His work is held in many private collections, and a set of twenty-two illustrations of the flora of the Brooks Range, Alaska, is held by the Hunt Institute where they were displayed in a two-man show in 1995. He has taken part in group shows at the Kew Gardens Gallery and at the Hortus Gallery in Chelsea.

Apart from his pen and ink scientific drawings for Kew and the illustrations he has produced for Chelsea Physic Garden, Andrew has illustrated the *Flora of Oxfordshire* (1998) and provided illustrations for BBC *Wildlife Magazine* and *Curtis's Botanical Magazine*. His work has been selected for inclusion in the Highgrove Florilegium which is being created under the umbrella of the Prince of Wales's Charitable Foundation and which will celebrate and record in a permanent way the flora in the garden at Highgrove.

He is the current Chairman of the Chelsea Physic Garden Florilegium Society.

RHS medals: Gold 1992, 1994, 1997, 1999, Silver Gilt 1991, 1992, 2002

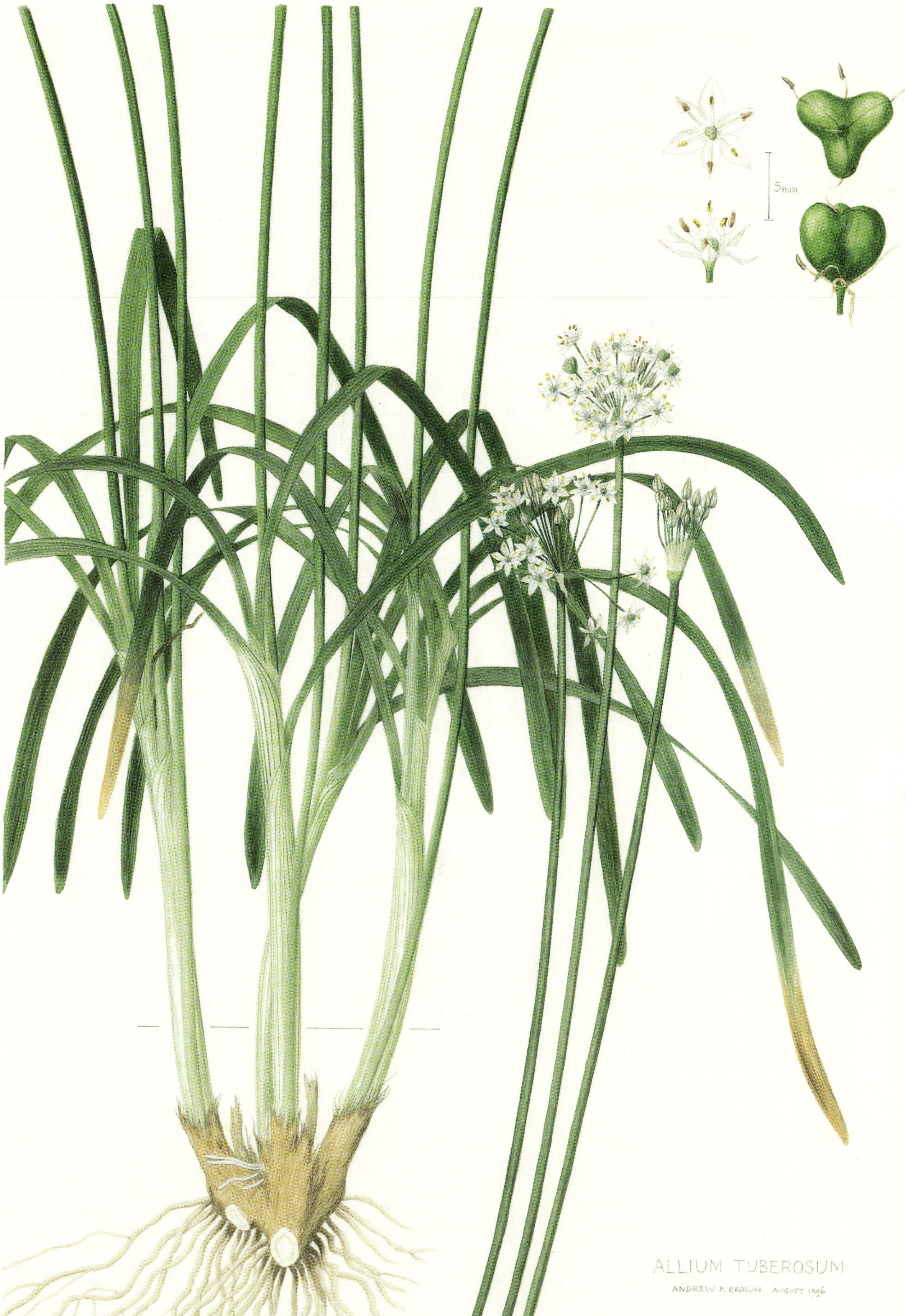
5mm
ALLIUM TUBEROSUM
ANDREW P. BROWN AUGUST 1996

Aloe humilis (L.) Miller
Family – Aloaceae

Pauline Dean

Aloes are indigenous to eastern and southern Africa but have spread to the Mediterranean and they reached the West Indies in the sixteenth century. The juice of aloes is drained from transversely cut leaves and concentrated by natural evaporation or the application of gentle heat. Medicinal aloes were known as Barbados or Socotrine aloes, their prime use being as a purgative. In recent years the best known species is *Aloe vera* which is widely advertised as an ingredient in cosmetic skin preparations. Work published in the USA details use of this species in thirty different countries, its uses ranging from anti-tumour activity to plant growth inhibition. Advocates for the use of common names for plant identification might wish to note that, in India alone, twenty-eight common names have been used for *Aloe vera*.

About the artist

Pauline Dean, a resident of Guildford, tutored botanical art courses at Wisley Gardens for eleven years to 2002. She has taken an individual stand and exhibited and sold her work at three Chelsea Flower Shows. Solo exhibitions include The Botanic Garden, Geneva in 1999 and previously at the Guildford House Gallery.

Her illustrations have been regularly published in scientific journals and horticultural books. She designed the three winter plates in the RHS Collectors' series, with Royal Worcester, and also the 1996 Chelsea Flower Show plate. In 2001 Pauline was commissioned by the Mayor of Guildford for a painting of the new *Clematis* 'Eleanor of Guildford', with pencil detail of the famous Guildford clock.

Pauline featured in *The Tortworth Chestnut* – one of the BBC 2 series *Meetings with Remarkable Trees.*

Her book *Pauline Dean – A Portfolio of a Botanical Artist* was published in September 2004. It includes a short autobiography and contains fifty-six full page colour Illustrations of some of her work, one of which, *Pinus* x *holfordiana* won 'Best in Show' at the American Society of Botanical Artists and Horticultural Society of New York's Annual Exhibition in 2001.

Her paintings are in private and public collections world-wide. Nowadays she works largely to commissions.

RHS medals: Gold 1989, 1991 (twice), 1993, 1995, 1999, 2001, 2002.

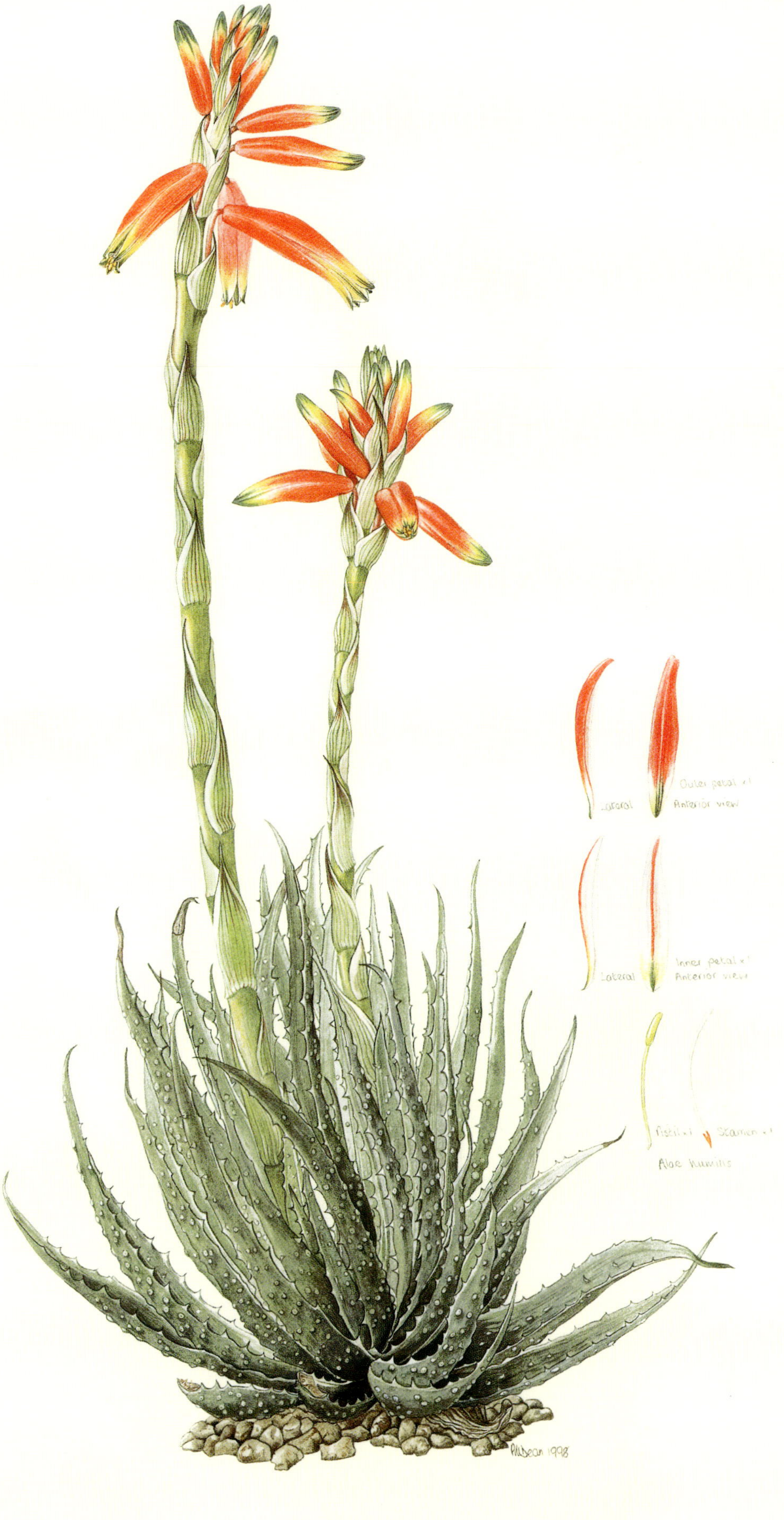

Aloe humilis - Cape S Africa

Argemone mexicana L.
Family – Papaveraceae

Gillian Barlow

Argemone mexicana is native to the southern United States, the West Indies and central America. It has a number of common names besides Mexican poppy, one of which is devil's fig. John Gerard's *Herbal* (1597) also refers to it as 'the golden thistle of Peru'. He refers to the fig-like fruit as being 'full of sharpe and venemous prickles, that whosoever had one of them in his throat, doubtless it would send him packing to heaven or to hell.'

Like most poppies it has a latex-like sap which, along with the seeds and aerial parts, is used in herbal medicine as a pain killer. The fresh latex is also recommended for cold sores and warts and is used as a yellow dyestuff in Peru.

About the artist

Gillian Barlow is the daughter of a botanist and developed a natural love of plants and nature from her father and from early school Nature Study lessons. After leaving school, she first studied painting and drawing at the Slade School of Art, London and later went to the University of Sussex to read Art History, hoping to continue painting thanks to the student grant. She gained both BA and MA, and took a postgraduate teaching certificate course, specialising in gallery and museum lecturing rather than in art teaching. Although she did not take up this work at the time, she has now been teaching at the Wallace Collection in London for some years, presenting small watercolour workshops for adults, mostly with flower-based themes, relating to paintings and other works of art displayed at the Museum. Since 1997 she has taught on the English Gardening School's One Year Botanical Illustration Diploma course, based at Chelsea Physic Garden, and also gives short courses of her own devising, there and with groups elsewhere.

Gillian's main occupation since leaving school has been painting, supported first by sign-writing, then for the past fifteen years by work as a Herald painter at the College of Arms in London. She exhibited in Britain, India, and especially in America, and she was represented by Blond Fine Art. While living in New York, and needing to support herself, in 1985 Gillian started painting flower portraits and paintings of shells, which were sold to decorators' clients. This was successful enough to finance other painting activities, which took precedence. However, on returning to London, botanical painting quickly became her main concern. An early public showing was as one of several artists shown at the Linnean Society in 1990. Some works were bought by the Hunt Institute in 1992, and again in 1996.

Gillian participated in the CPGFS' Gold Medal exhibit of plants associated with Philip Miller in January 1999. Her first major solo exhibition of botanical art took place in 1995, at Spink, London. She has exhibited widely in group shows, both here and abroad, and has work at the Hunt Institute, the British Council, RBG Kew, RHS Orchid Archive, Vassar College New York and in many private collections. Gillian has worked as assistant to the RHS Orchid Committee's principal artist for many years, her interest in orchids being encouraged by Dr Henry Oakeley. She has produced illustrations for the original *Plantsman* magazine, the *New Plantsman*, and *Curtis's Botanical Magazine* many times in the past fifteen years.

RHS medals: Gold 1994, 1997, Silver Gilt 1991

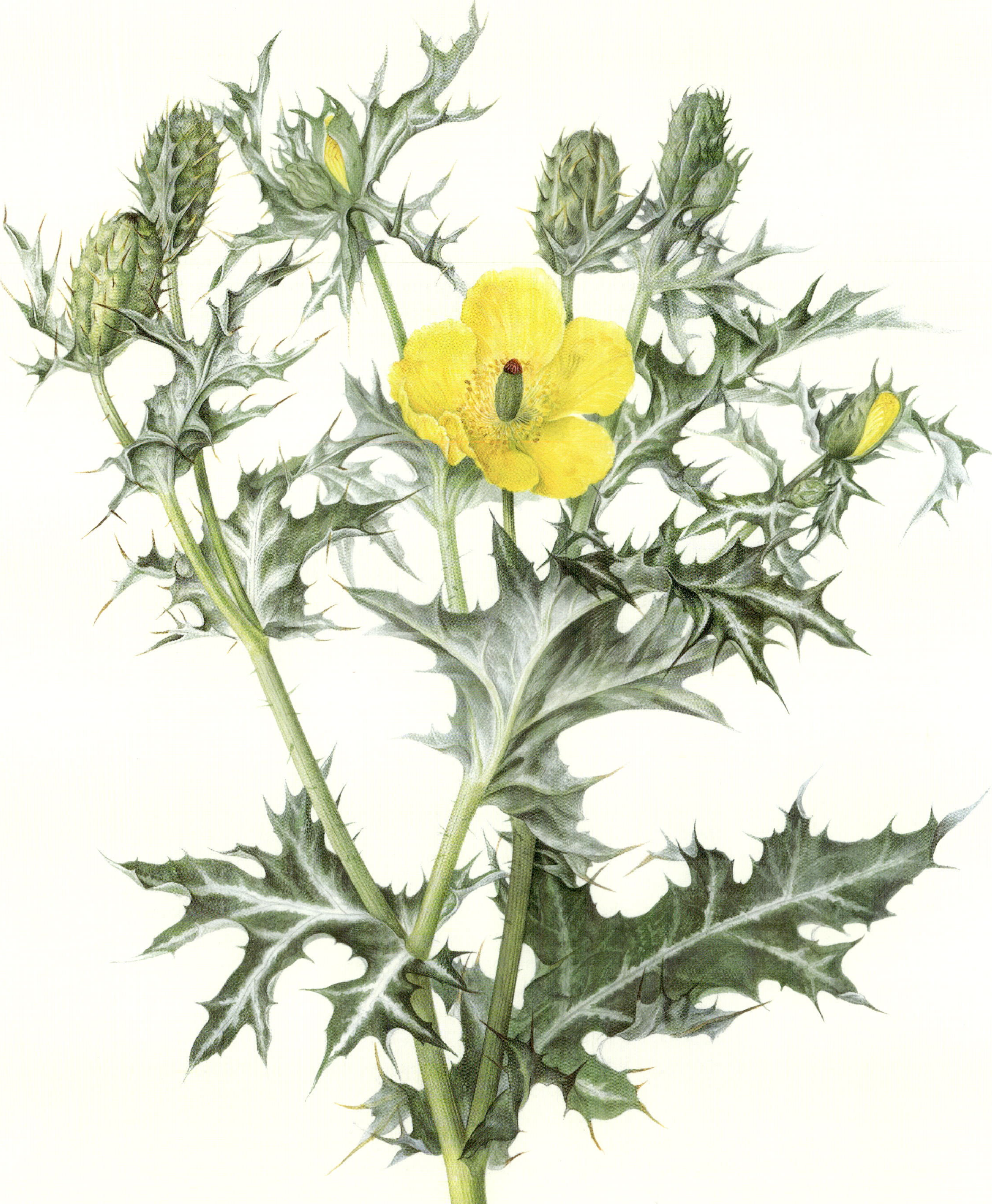
GB'99

Arum italicum Miller
Family – Araceae

Sally Pinhey

Philip Miller is the authority for naming this plant. It is native to the Mediterranean area of southern Europe, extending outwards to the Canary Islands and eastward as far as Cyprus. To attract pollinating insects the spadix gives out a quantity of heat sufficient to be sensed by touching the plant. This phenomenon also occurs with the arum that grows wild in British hedgerows, *A. maculatum*. This species is also known by the common names cuckoo pint, lords and ladies and starchwort. The tuberous root has a high starch content and was used in Elizabethan times to stiffen ruffs. On the Isle of Portland in Dorset the starch was at one time processed to produce a food known as Portland arrowroot or Portland sago. The juice of the raw root was described by Gilbert White (1720–1793) as 'remarkably warm and pungent'. The raw root is poisonous, containing crystals of calcium oxalate which cause itching and burning of the skin. The fruits are also poisonous.

About the artist

Sally Pinhey was born in Woking in 1946, educated in English boarding schools and qualified as a social worker at Exeter University in 1968. She married a Naval Officer and after short careers in social work and personnel management, she continued to develop her early artistic skills while looking after her two young children at home in Dorset. She was based in Italy from 1987–90, studying the fruits and flowers of the Mediterranean. Painting these and archaeological landscapes formed her style. From 1983 to 2000 she held regular solo exhibitions in Cornwall, Dorset, Wiltshire, Sussex, London and Italy.

She is a full member of the Association of Illustrators, the Chelsea Physic Garden and the Eden Project Florilegium Societies, and is passionate about providing plant illustrations for scientific archives.

Coming to teaching through art therapy, she developed her own system for teaching basic drawing skills, parallel to those of Dr Betty Edwards of California. She has been the Botanical Art instructor for Kingston Maurward College since 1998, and tutored courses at the Eden Project in Cornwall from 2000 to 2003. Her 'How to Draw' courses at The Springhead Trust near Shaftesbury have run since 1997. She was an invited demonstrator at 'Art in Action' in 2002 and 2003.

She has illustrated three books: her father's *Nigerian Memoirs* (1994), *Pears* by Jim Arbury (Fruit Superintendent at RHS Wisley) (1997) and *Plums* also by Jim Arbury (2002). Each of the fruit books contains over fifty varieties with flowers and cross sections. In 2003 her work *Egdon Heath* was bought by The House of Lords for the Fielden House building. She runs a company which publishes and markets her own designs. She is involved in her local community, serving as a magistrate and singing in the church choir.

RHS medals: Silver Gilt 1997, 1999, Silver 1992, 2001, 2005

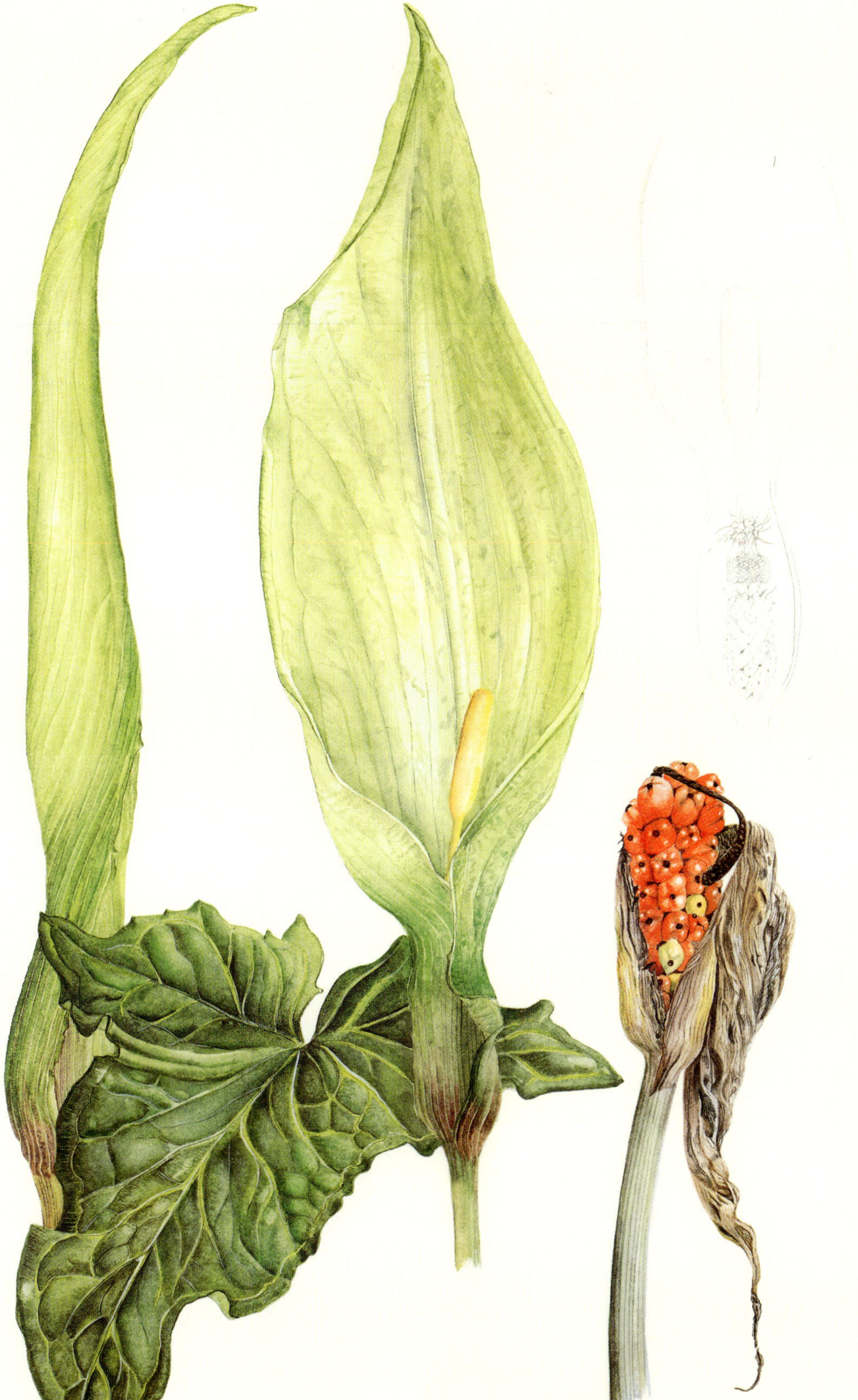

Arum italicum

Asarina procumbens Miller
Family – Scrophulariaceae

Gillian Constable

Asarina procumbens was named by the Chelsea Gardener Philip Miller. This plant has also been known as *Antirrhinum asarina*. It is a low growing plant suitable for rockeries. It self-seeds freely. The plant is indigenous to southern France and northeast Spain.

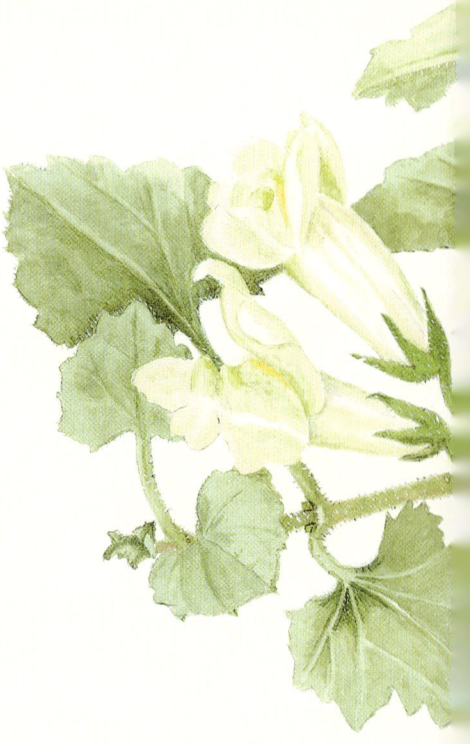

About the artist

Gillian Constable was born and grew up in London about three kilometres from the Chelsea Physic Garden. She had a strong interest from an early age in both wild and garden flowers, and natural history in general. A visit to the Chelsea Flower Show was sometimes fitted in after school. At school she hated art and managed to drop it when fourteen to do extra needlework. She loved the technical forms of art encountered in geography, biology and even maths, but painting a 'windy day' with big brushes, powder paint and rough grey paper did not provide any form of pleasure.

She studied mathematics, specialising in statistics, as an undergraduate at St Andrews University and as a graduate at Sheffield University. The planned year at Sheffield became thirty years and for twenty-five of these years she lectured in Probability & Statistics at the University. She became aware of courses in Botanical Illustration in the Adult Continuing Education Department when occasional displays of the students' work were held in the University Library. These displays made her yearn for time to devote to looking closely at plants and attempting to capture their beauty in pencil and paint. Early retirement in 1996 enabled her to escape to freedom and botanical illustration.

Gillian studied Introductory Botanical Illustration with Valerie Oxley and, later, she undertook Sheffield University's Certificate course, also tutored by Valerie Oxley.

Successful completion of the Certificate coincided with a move to Dorset where Gillian rapidly made many new friends through botanical illustration. She now organises and tutors a group in the Sherborne area, and, with a friend, has organised a number of workshops, courses and exhibitions. In 2002 she gained full membership of the Society of Floral Painters and in 2004 membership of the Chelsea Physic Garden Florilegium Society. She has exhibited at a number of venues in southern England and Sweden and she also had two paintings in the *Flora of Dorset* 2004 calendar.

Gillian's other interests include bird and butterfly watching, the latter as part of a long-term ecological study near her home. She also has particular love of fungi.

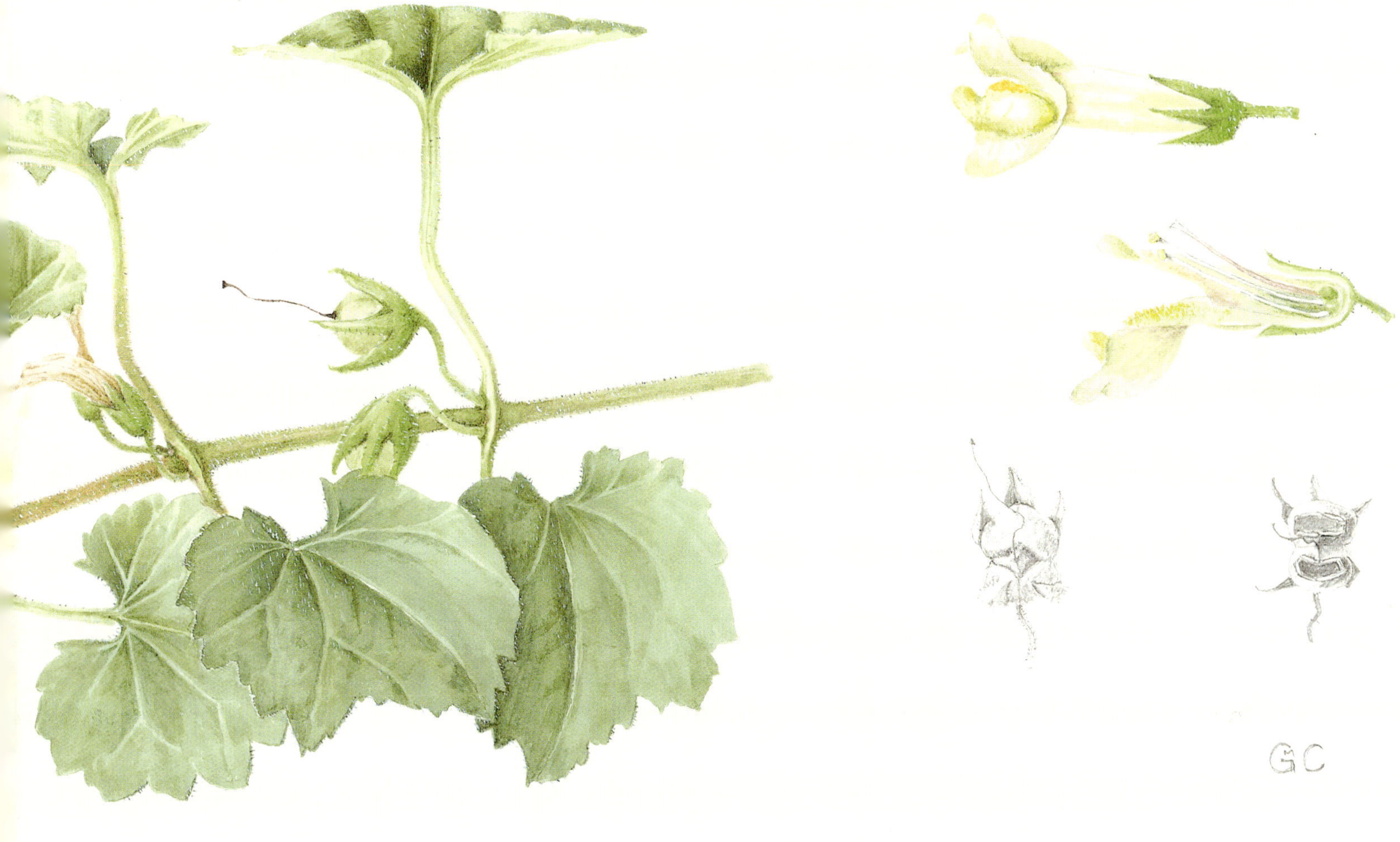
GC

Athamanta turbith (L.) Brot.
Family – Umbelliferae

Margaret Hatherley-Champ

The genus *Athamanta* takes its name from Mount Athamas in Sicily. The species of this genus favour screes and rocky montane habitats. *Athamanta turbith*, native to the southern Carpathians, Balkan peninsula and northeast Italy, is only available from one nursery in the UK. The Physic Garden plants are derived from seed from St Petersburg Botanic Garden. A related species also cultivated in the Physic Garden, *A. cretensis*, grows wild in the mountainous areas of France and Germany. A similar plant, *Meum athamanticum*, also known as baldmoney or spignel, may be found wild in northern England and Scotland. *M. athamanticum* was formerly cultivated for its edible roots and for medicinal use. *Athamanta meum* is listed as growing in the Chelsea Physic Garden in 1772.

About the artist

Margaret was born in 1941. After raising a family and a successful secretarial career she took early retirement and started attending various botanical courses, culminating with the one year Diploma course in Botanical Painting at the English Gardening School in 2001.

Margaret's skill and enthusiasm led her to gain a licence from the Director of Royal Palaces to start the Hampton Court Palace Florilegium Society of which she is the Founder Chairman.

Margaret particularly enjoys the challenge of painting small plants with complicated structure, resorting to the use of strong magnifying glasses, a microscope and lots of patience.

She has exhibited both in London and her home county of Essex and she now teaches botanical painting for local art groups.

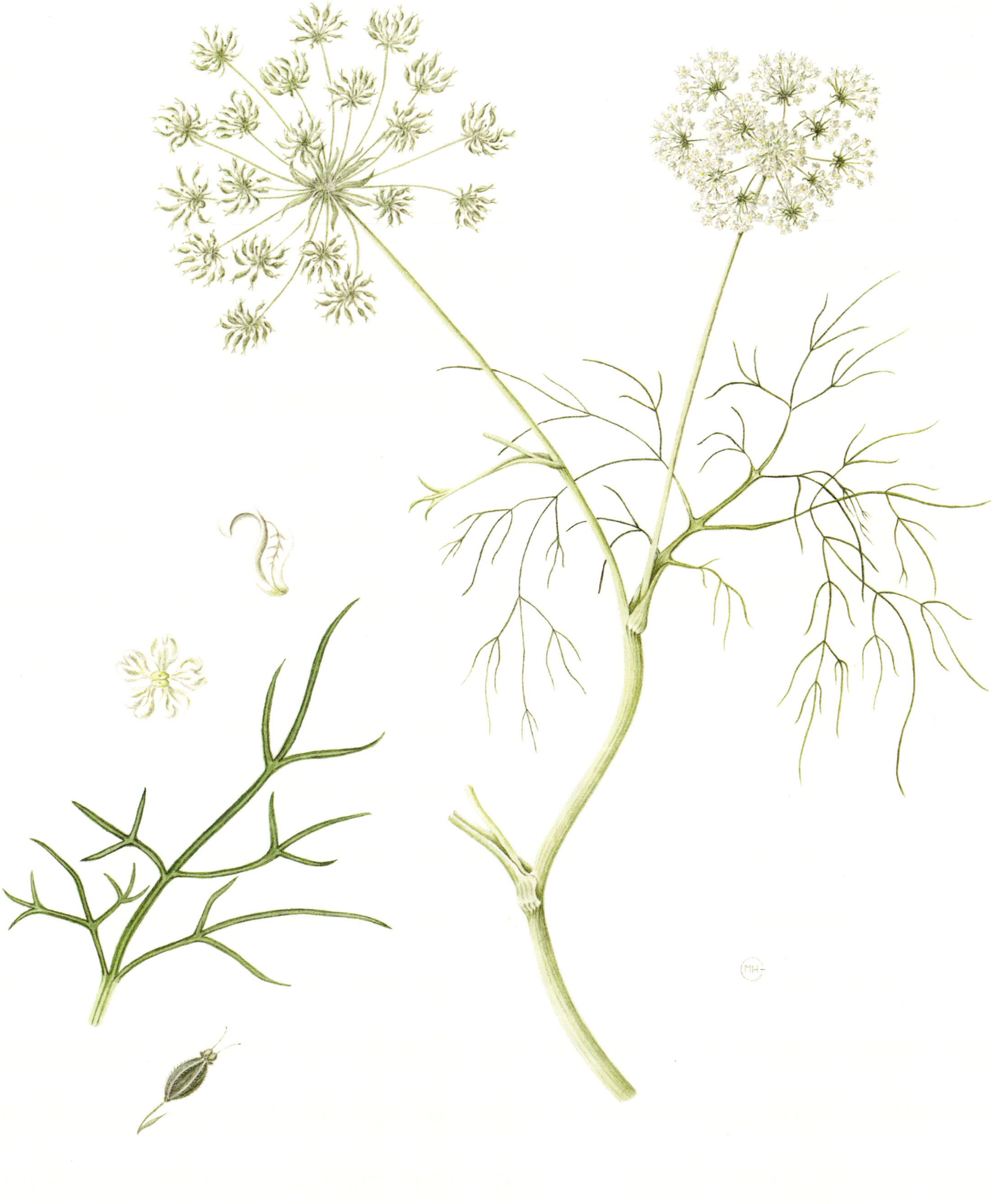

Athamanta turbith

Atropa belladonna L.
Family – Solanaceae

Judith Hillelson

Commonly known as deadly nightshade, all parts of the plant are poisonous. The shiny black berries are particularly attractive to children. The plant grows on chalky soil and can be found wild in southern England. Native to Eurasia and the Mediterranean region, it has been cultivated in England, Europe and the United States of America for medicinal purposes. In the Physic Garden it grows best in the shade provided by the yew, *Taxus baccata*, itself an important drug plant (source of taxol, used against ovarian cancer). The chief medicinal constituent of *Atropa belladonna* is hyoscyamine, older leaves also have a significant content of atropine. Atropine, when instilled into the eye, dilates the pupil and the name belladonna relates to its use by Venetian women to enhance the attractiveness of their eyes.

The first *British Pharmacopoeia* (1864) contained monographs for atropia (an alkaloid obtained from the root), belladonna (the leaves and fresh branches) and belladonna radix (the root, stated to be imported from Germany). The medicinal preparations associated with these monographs included an ointment, liniment, a plaster and tincture (an alcoholic solution). By the mid-1950s there were some eighteen preparations of belladonna dispensed regularly by pharmacists. However, in 2002 prescribing advice issued to doctors stated that belladonna alkaloids were outmoded for treating bowel disorders, any clinical virtues being outweighed by atropinic side effects. Preparations of atropine for injection and use in the eye were still approved.

About the artist

Born in New York City, Judith studied Art at Hunter College and then went to Tufts University where she took a BSc and a Certificate course in Occupational Therapy. Since coming to England Judith has worked with her husband running a photographic press agency and photo library.

She has done several intensive courses in Botanical Illustration at West Dean College, the Horniman Museum and Morley College. Judith has taken part in exhibitions over the past twenty years and showed her watercolour paintings of *Fuchsia* at the Royal Horticultural Society.

RHS medal: Silver 1996

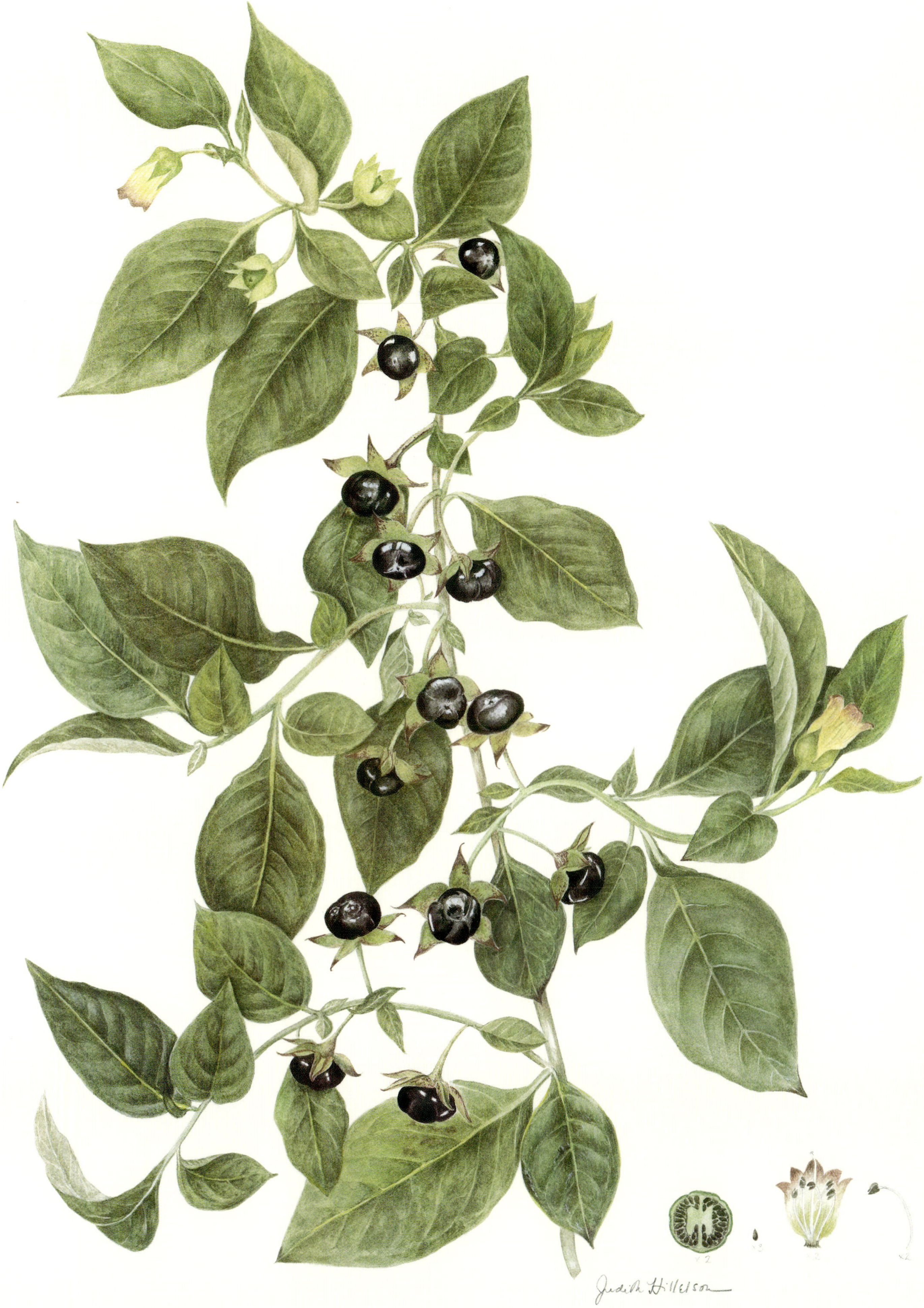
x 2
x 3
x 2
x 2
Judith Hillelson

Berberis canadensis Miller
Family – Berberidaceae

Jane Bruce

Berberis canadensis is native to the Allegheny Mountains of eastern America and is very similar to the European *B. vulgaris*. The berries and the bark of the European berberis are used in herbal medicine to relieve gallbladder pain and have benefit in a number of digestive system problems. The fruits of *Berberis*, known as barberries, have been used for culinary purposes such as jellies or the French speciality *confiture d'epine vinette*. The roots have also been used to dye wool and leather.

About the artist

Born in 1947, over a twelve year period Elizabeth Jane Bruce studied life drawing at Exeter College of Art, etching at both Somerset and Gloucestershire College of Art and Design and botanical illustration at the English Gardening School.

She has exhibited watercolours and etchings nine times, both in the west country and at the National Army Museum. Jane has shown her botanical illustrations also on nine occasions, including the RHS, the Hunt Institute and the Ebury Galleries, London.

Apart from in the Chelsea Physic Garden archive, her work is held by the Hunt Institute and in many private collections. Her work has been used to illustrate articles in the magazines *Country Living*, *The Garden* and *Homes and Gardens*.

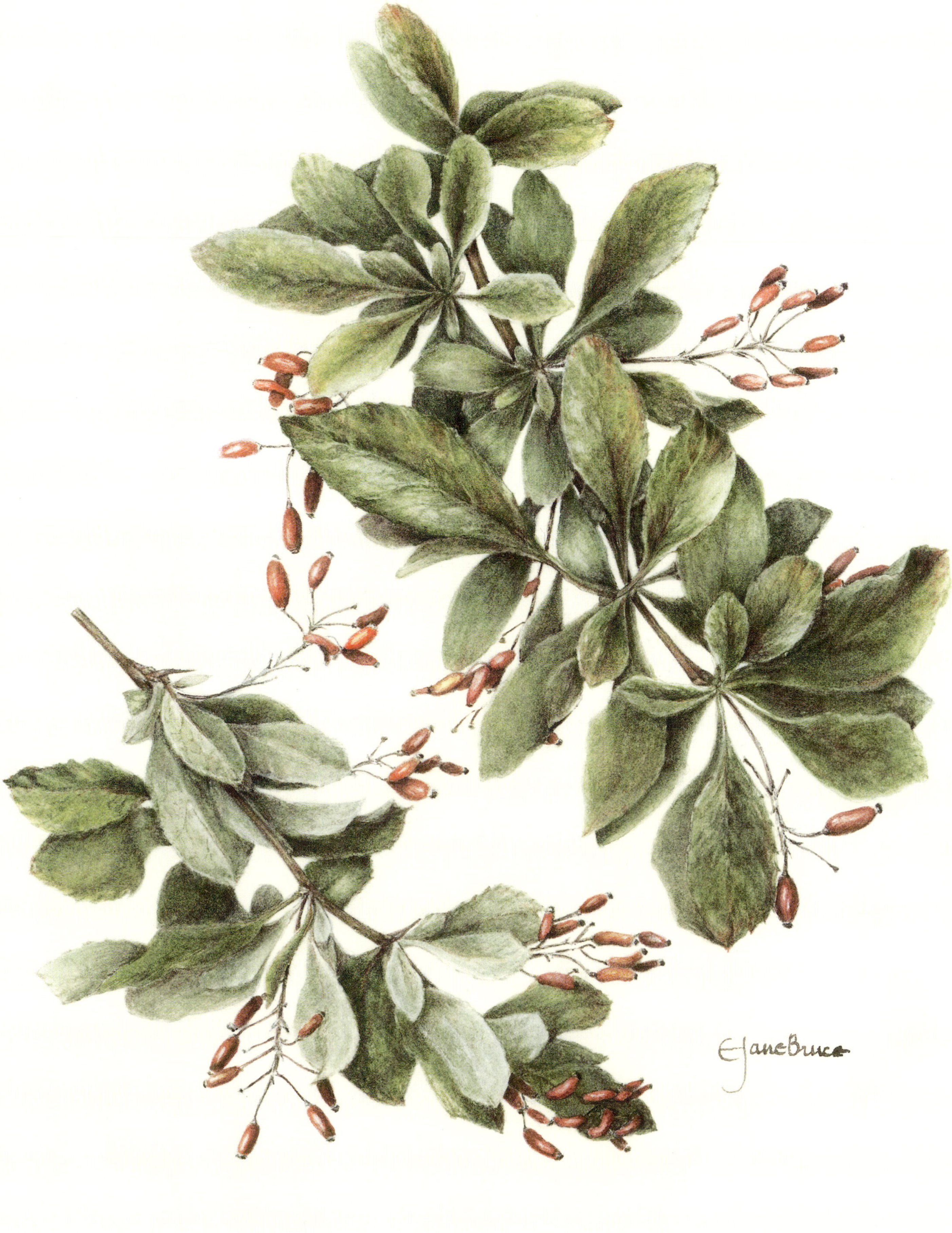
EJaneBruce

Callistemon phoenicius Lindl.
Family – Myrtaceae

Sally Crosthwaite

Plants of the Australian genus *Callistemon* are known as bottle brushes. The first bottle brush was introduced into the UK by Joseph Banks in 1789. This was *C. citrinus*, the red form that is widely grown by UK gardeners. While the red forms are most usually seen, both white and pale yellow are available. The bird-pollinated flowers have long showy stamens with a dot of yellow pollen at the end. The name of the genus is derived from the Greek words *kalos* and *stemon* and, when literally translated, mean beautiful stamens.

About the artist

Sally Crosthwaite was awarded a Distinction on the Diploma Course on Botanical Illustration at the English Gardening School in 1995 and she became a Founder Member of the Chelsea Physic Garden Florilegium Society. Sally took part in the group exhibit of plants associated with Philip Miller which was awarded an RHS group Gold Medal in January 1999.

Sally's tulip and fruit paintings appear on sixteen Carolyn Sheffield porcelain plates and four of her tulips on a Limoges dinner service. Her work has been acquired by the Royal Botanic Gardens, Kew and the Hunt Institute.

Her work features in several books, among them *The Origin of Plants, Arte e Botanica, La Tulipa* and twenty-seven illustrations in the *National Gardens Scheme Book* 2001. Her work is also featured in one chapter of *The Art of Botanical Painting*, published in association with the Society of Botanical Artists of which Sally is a member.

Sally was one of three botanical artists selected to take part in a programme filmed by Channel 4 TV at the 1999 Chelsea Flower Show. She has exhibited extensively in group exhibitions at home and abroad including the USA, Munich, Sweden and Tasmania and her work is held in private collections in the USA, Germany, Denmark, Sweden and France.

RHS medals: Gold 2001, Silver 1998

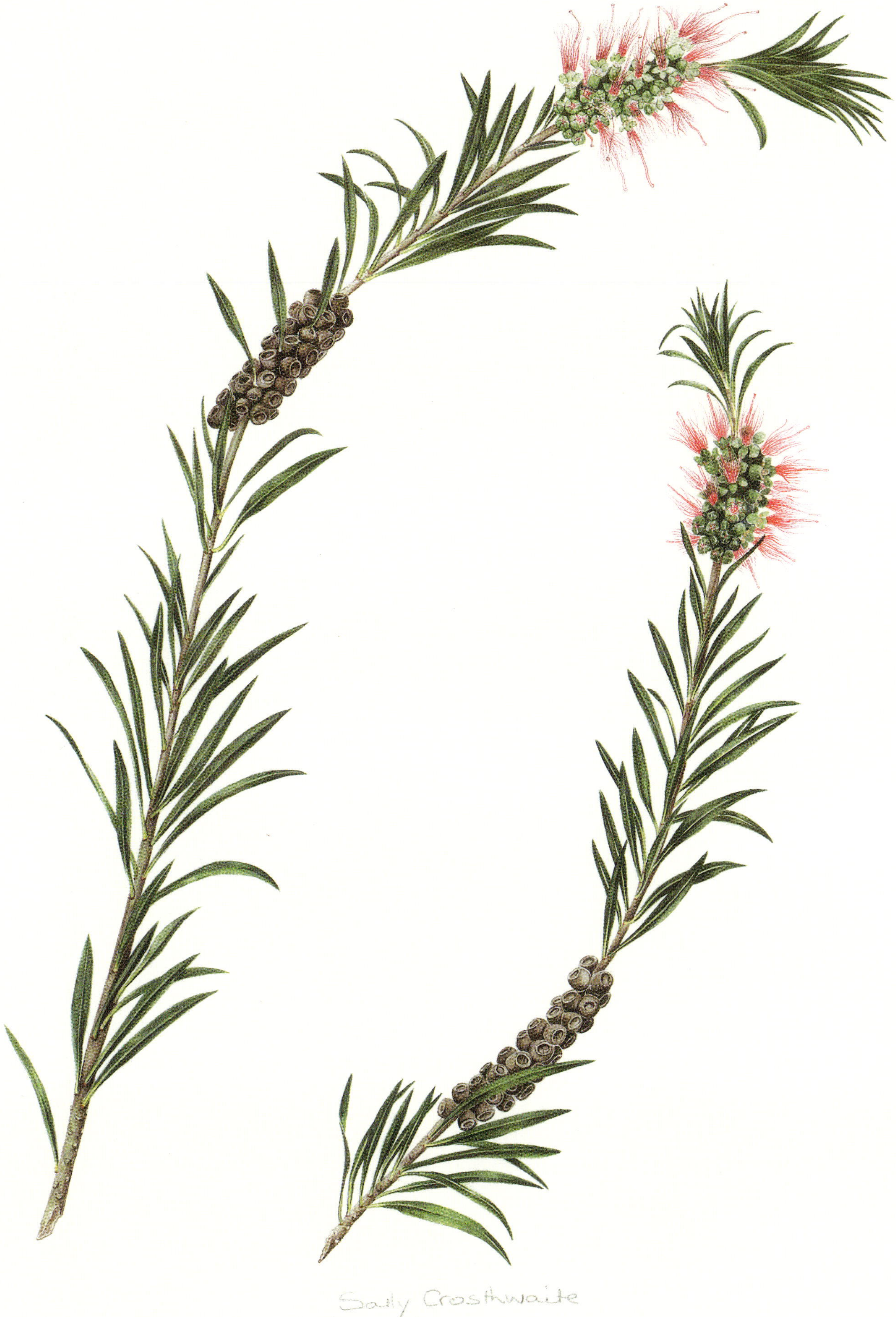
Sally Crosthwaite

Camellia sinensis (L.) Kuntze
Family – Theaceae

Mally Francis

This plant is the prime source of the England's favourite beverage, tea. Tea is grown in China, India, Sri Lanka and elsewhere. Tea is prepared from hand-picked leaf buds and very young leaves. It is available as black or green tea, the dark colour of black tea developing as a result of fermentation during the processing of the leaves after picking. Green tea is unfermented. The main active constituents of tea are caffeine and tannins. Tea is used as a stimulant, diuretic and astringent. The stimulant properties are due to the caffeine, the astringency arises from the tannins. Tea is drunk in most countries of the world and is believed to have been drunk in China prior to 2000 BC. The wild distribution of the plant is uncertain, but is probably western China.

About the artist

Mally's formal tuition as a botanical artist commenced in Leicester in 1987 under Anne-Marie Evans and she subsequently attended several refresher courses.

Mally joined the Chelsea Physic Garden Florilegium Society in 1995 and her first submission was selected for the summer exhibition at the Hunt Institute. She became a Fellow in 2001. Since 1997 she has lived in Cornwall, within The Lost Gardens of Heligan.

In 1998 Mally spent a year working to commission to illustrate the plants in the book *Heligan Wild* which covers a year of nature in The Lost Gardens. The paintings were exhibited for sale at The Museum of Garden History in London and at the Veryan Galleries, Cornwall. Since then she has been commissioned by Heligan Gardens to paint more of their plants, including a Cornish Red rhododendron, currently under threat from the fungus *Phytophthora ramorum.*

Mally specialises in the traditional form of botanical illustration applying artists' watercolours to highest quality hot-pressed paper or vellum with a very fine sable brush. All subjects are painted from life.

In her large private studio Mally holds short residential courses and one-day-a-week courses in botanical illustration which are suitable for beginners and for more experienced artists. In 2000 she founded and became chairman of the Eden Project Florilegium Society which has aims similar to those of the Chelsea Physic Garden Florilegium Society. She organises and tutors botanical painting courses for the Friends of Eden.

In 2000 Mally exhibited at the Ebury Gallery in Chelsea, London, during the Chelsea Flower Show. She now regularly exhibits her own work in Cornwall and in 2004 held an exhibition of her work and that of her group at Heligan.

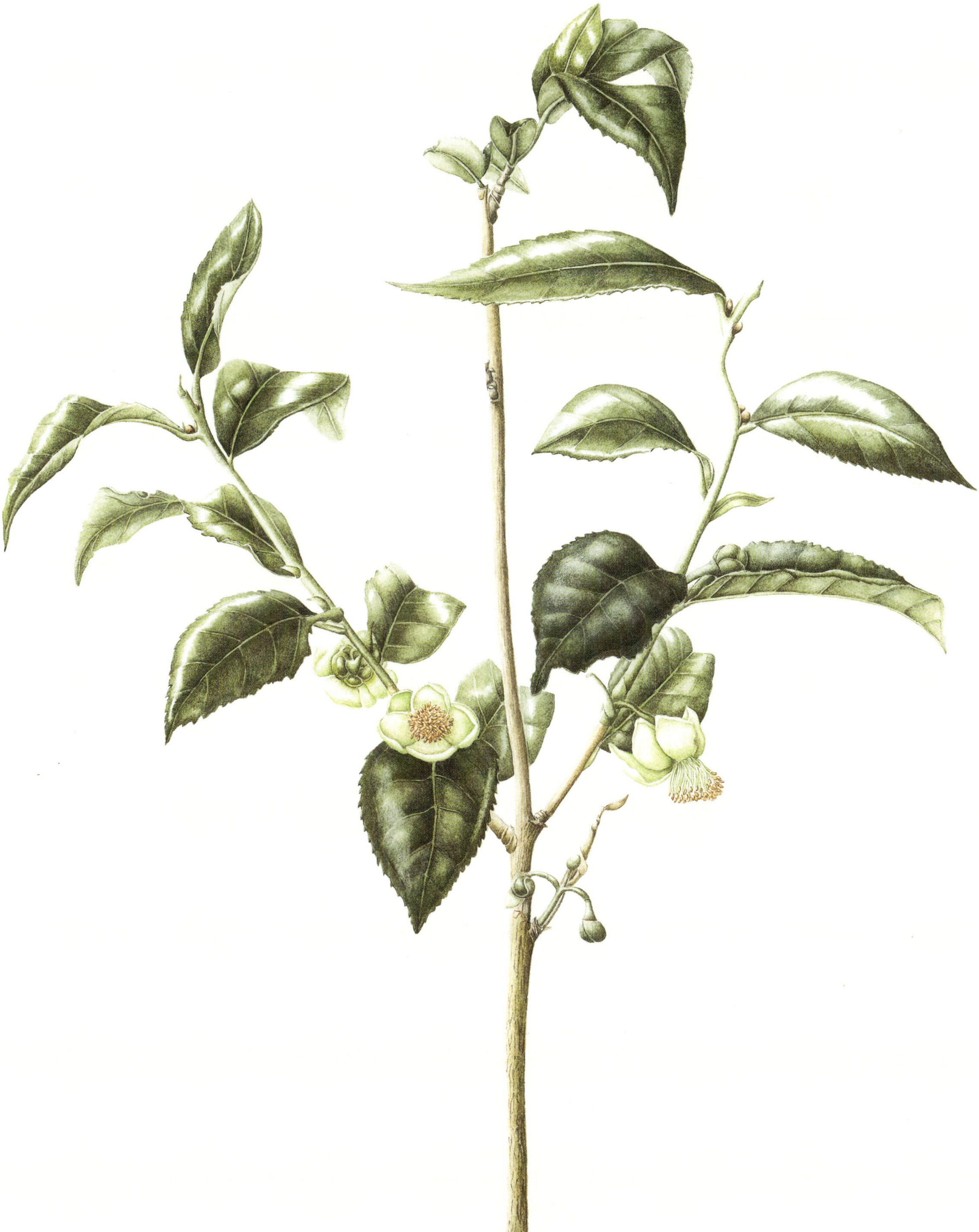
MF.

Capsicum annuum L. 'Nardello'
Family – Solanaceae

Alison Forbes Brown

Capsicum annuum is unknown in the wild, but probably has its origin in tropical America. The variety *Capsicum annuum* var. *longum* is the source of the spice paprika. It is milder than other varieties. Fruits of capsicums, rich in vitamin C, are known as peppers and they are grown in many parts of the world. The capsicum used in medicine is usually from *C. minimum* but different species are permitted in some pharmacopoeias. The active ingredient is capsaicin; internally it is used to dispel flatulence, externally it is used as a counter-irritant. The cayenne pepper of commerce is normally a blend of varieties of capsicum. Capsicum oleo-resin is in pepper spray used for law enforcement and self-defence.

'Nardello', supplied by the Henry Doubleday Research Association in 2000, is described by them as 'an Italian heirloom grown by the Nardello family, which produces a large number of slender and twisty fruits'.

About the artist

Alison Forbes Brown was born in Scotland, educated in Kenya and Zimbabwe and is world-travelled. After a full-time career in business, she turned her many capabilities to horticulture and botanical art, gaining a distinction the City and Guilds Amenity Horticulture course in 1993 followed by the Royal Horticultural Society Certificate (Credit) in 1994.

Alison gained a Diploma in botanical illustration at the English Gardening School at Chelsea Physic Garden in 1996 and followed this by studying Natural History Illustration at Brighton University from 1997 to 1999.

A founder member, now Fellow, of the Chelsea Physic Garden Florilegium Society, she was their Programme Secretary for three years (1996–9) and continues to play an active part by keeping databases for the Society.

Watercolour, pencil and pen and ink are Alison's favoured media and her work has been acquired for the archives of the Hunt Institute and Chelsea Physic Garden. A number of her pen and ink works have been used in publications for the Chelsea Physic Garden booklets and Annual Reports.

She is a member of the American Society of Botanical Artists and is a painting member of the Society of Floral Painters.

She has shared many exhibitions in London and in Sussex, also in the Florilegium Society exhibition at the Hunt Institute in the summer of 2000, and shared in the group Gold medal awarded to the Florilegium Society by the RHS in January 1999 and in the RHS Silver Gilt medal awarded to the Botanical Art Group at Bromley College in 1997.

Alison's work is held in many private collections both at home and abroad, and she is herself a collector.

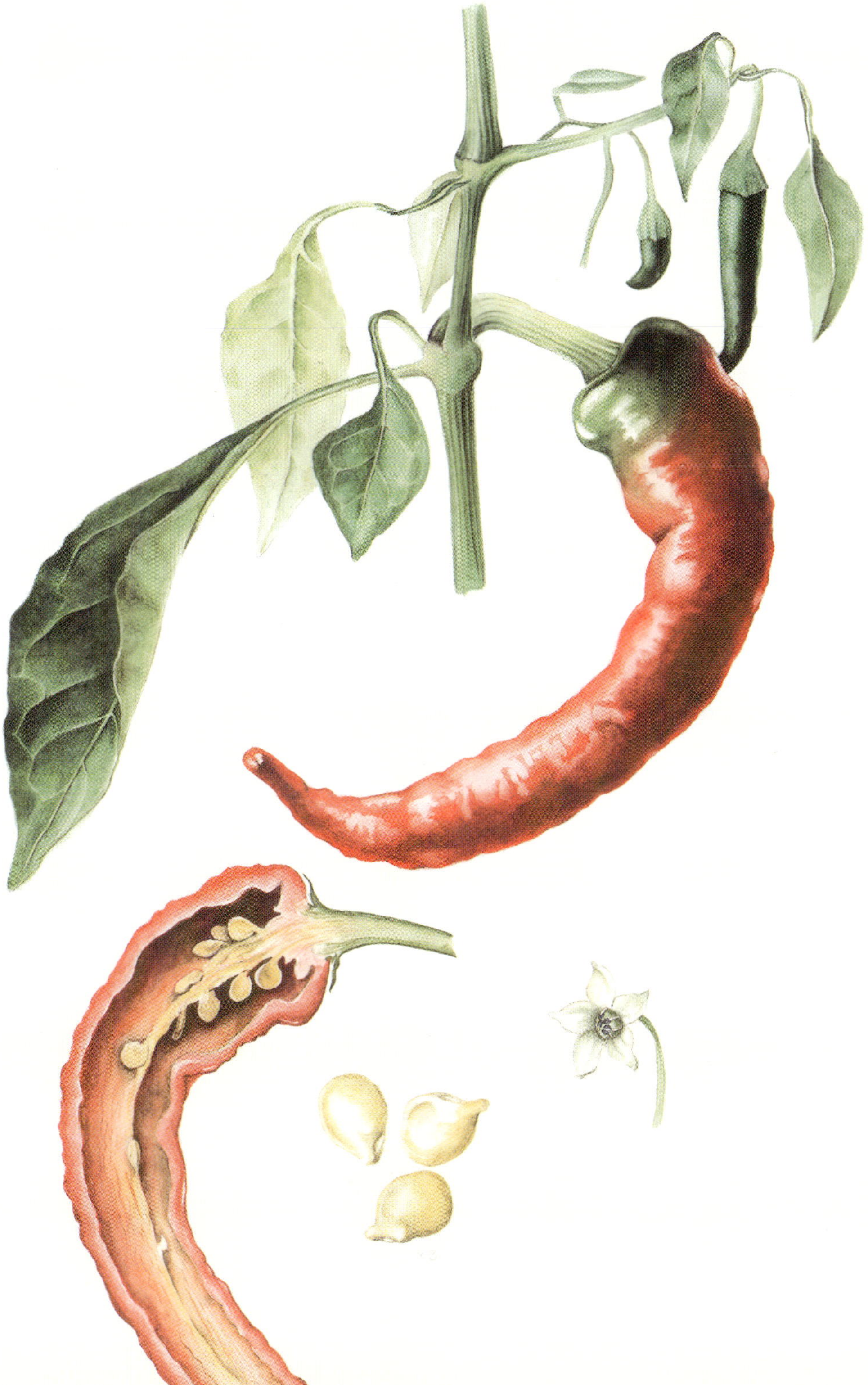

Alison F. Brown

Centaurea montana L.
Family – Compositae

Chrissie Lightfoot

Known as perennial cornflower, it flowers from June to September. It is a popular garden plant in the UK and is found wild in the mountains of Europe. It prefers chalky soil and can grow to over two metres in height.

About the artist

Chrissie was born and raised in London and originally trained and worked as a scenic designer with BBC TV. She took a career break while her children were young and returned to work freelancing for TV, film and exhibition companies.

In 1997 Chrissie enrolled to study botanical illustration at the English Gardening School. Since graduating with a Distinction she has been painting full-time, exhibiting in several group exhibitions both in London and America, and painting to commission.

Her work is held in the Hunt Institute as well as at Chelsea Physic Garden. Chrissie's work has also been selected for inclusion in the Highgrove Florilegium which is being created under the umbrella of the Prince of Wales's Charitable Foundation and which will celebrate and record in a permanent way the flora in the garden at Highgrove.

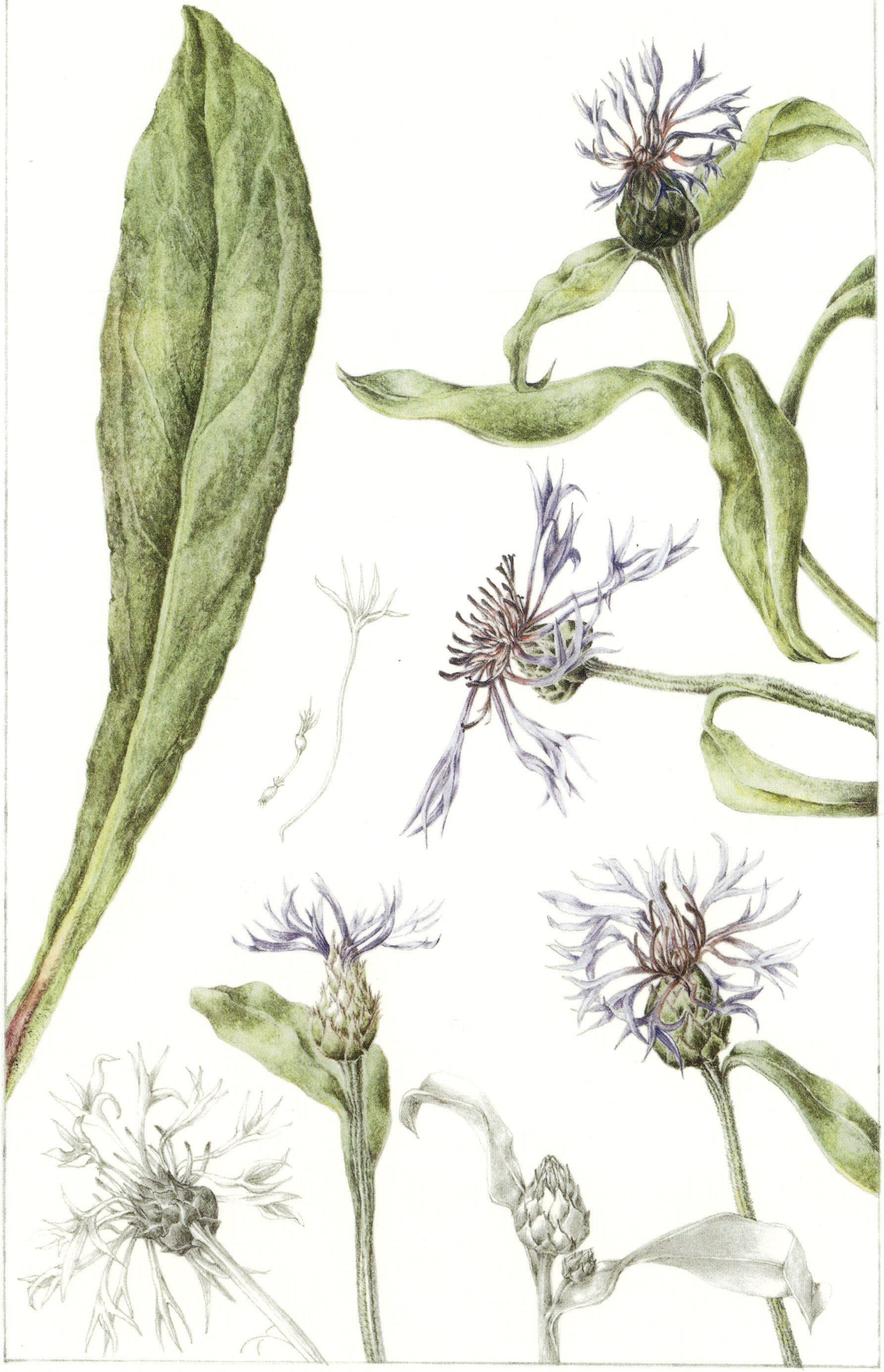

Centaurea montana x1 CM '99

Cercis siliquastrum L.
Family – Leguminosae

Penny Stenning

The generic name *Cercis* is derived from the Greek work for a weaver's shuttle (because the mature fruits have a similar shape). Known as the Judas tree, this is reputed to be the tree on which Judas Iscariot hanged himself. It is indigenous to the eastern Mediterranean area. It flowers in early spring often before the leaves open. The pea-like flowers are born on mature twigs, branches and the main trunk. In the USA the redbud, *Cercis canadensis* grows wild and is a striking feature of the countryside in the spring. A purple leaf form of *C. canadensis*, known as 'Forest Pansy' is grown in the UK by garden enthusiasts. There is no recorded medicinal or economic use of these plants.

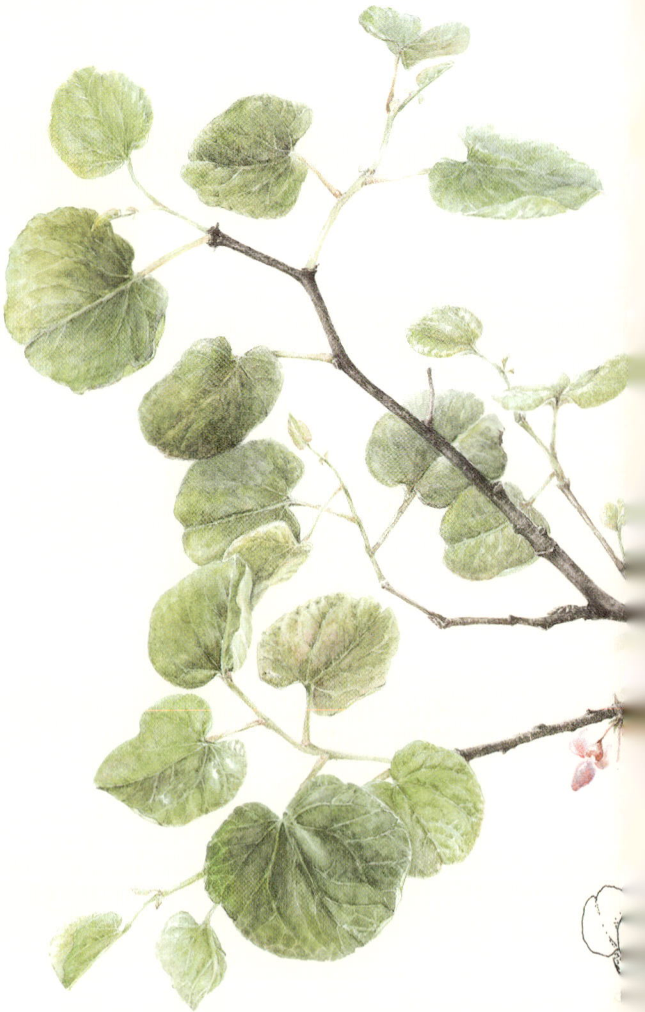

About the artist

Penny was born in 1940 into an army family. Her early years were spent in two to three year postings around the world. It was this experience of different climates and geography that stimulated Penny's love of the variety of plant life and growth form.

Painting was always a hobby for Penny until more time in later life allowed a more serious study of the techniques. A course of botanical illustration with Elizabeth Jane Lloyd at Chelsea Physic Garden led to membership of the Chelsea Physic Garden Florilegium Society, first as a painting member, now as a Fellow. Penny is also a founder member of the Eden Project Florilegium Society in Cornwall.

Penny's work is in several collections, both private and museum, and she is also a member of the Society of Botanical Artists and regularly exhibits at their annual show in London. In 1999 she was awarded their Certificate of Botanical Merit.

A pen and ink illustration of *Scabiosa cretica* by Penny was used to decorate the cover of the 2004 *Index Seminum*. This is the seed catalogue which Chelsea Physic Garden issues annually, offering seed from its plants to other botanic gardens around the world.

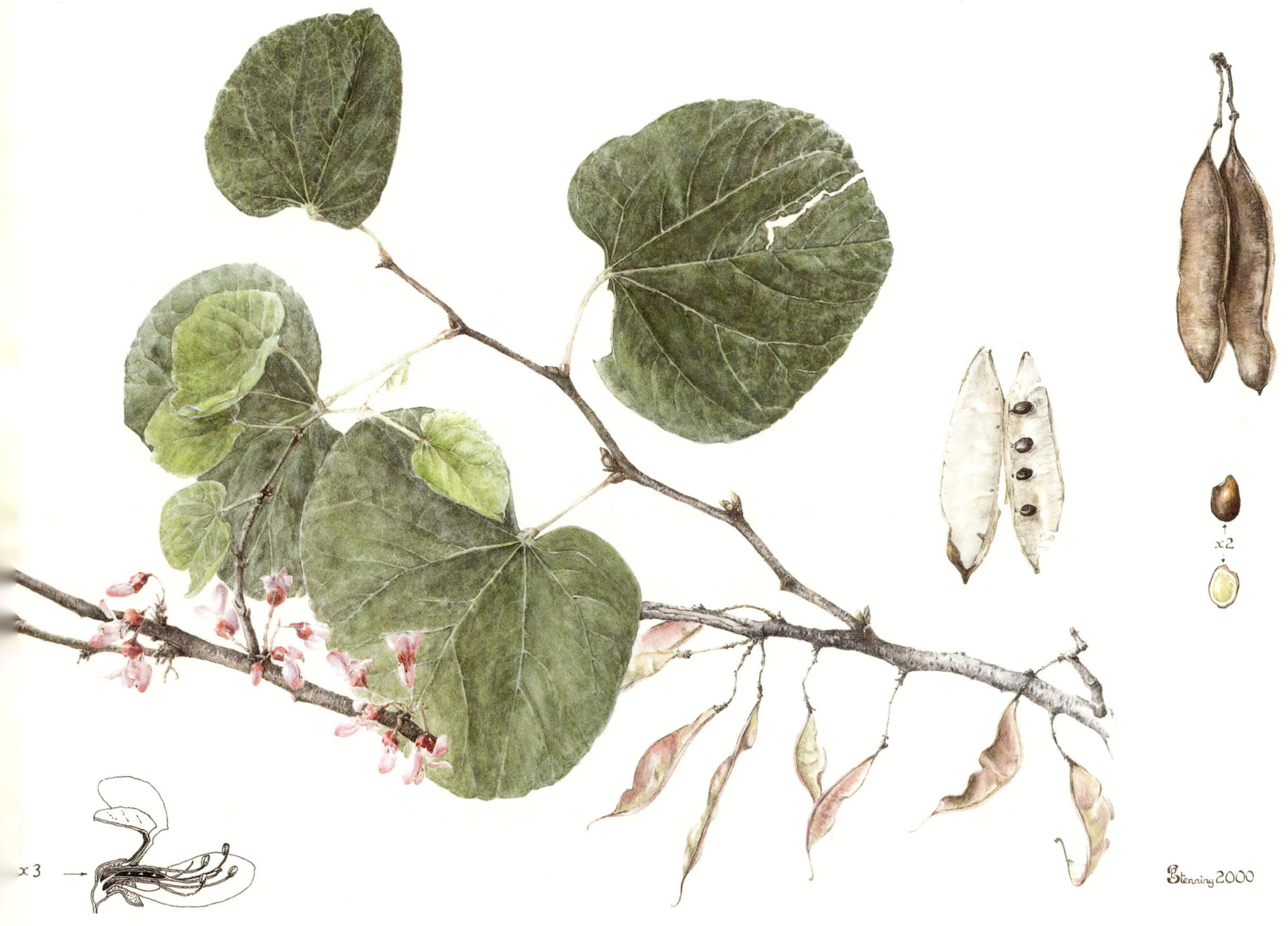
x 3
x2
Stenning 2000

Colutea orientalis Miller
Family – Leguminosae

June Hyde

The authority for naming this plant is Philip Miller. This species comes from the southern part of the Russian Federation and northern Iran. The species generally grown in gardens is C. *arborescens*, (also known as bladder senna). It has yellow pea-like flowers and large papery bladder-like seed pods which delight children with a loud bang when squashed. The leaves of C. *arborescens* are said to have a purgative action similar to the true senna (*Senna italica*) for which they have been used as an adulterant.

About the artist

June Hyde was born in 1936 and for twenty years worked as a photographic stylist for magazines, the advertising industry and photographic studios. She then spent three years at a Teacher Training College and became a primary school class teacher for fourteen years, completing her career as an individual support teacher in a special educational needs unit.

June has exhibited in south London, including with the Friends of Horniman Art Exhibitions.

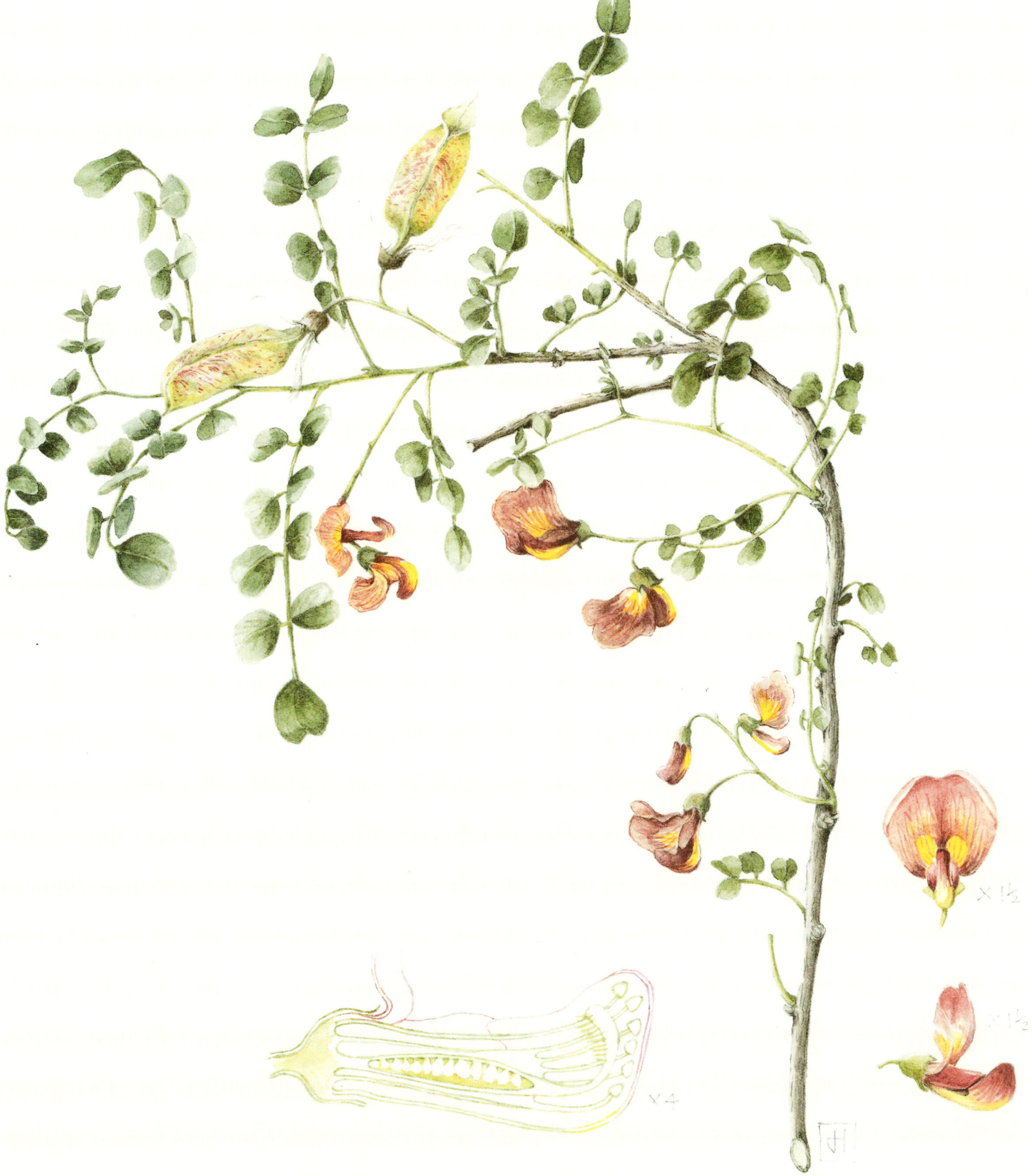

× 1½
× 1½
× 4

Cornus amomum Miller
Family – Cornaceae

Ianthe King

Cornus amomum was the first dogwood to arrive in Britain, coming from eastern North America in 1683. It has similar medicinal properties to the American dogwood, *C. florida*. The bark was used by the native Americans to treat fevers such as malaria but was displaced when the Europeans introduced Peruvian bark (the source of quinine). Other uses include treating anthrax, erysipelas and as an antiseptic and stimulant.

About the artist

Ianthe King was born in 1930 in Lincolnshire and spent her school days in Leamington Spa. Her father was an accomplished watercolour artist and encouraged Ianthe's keen interest in nature and conservation. After her family grew up Ianthe pursued her interests in printing and etching. She also studied photography for some years, culminating in an award from the Royal Photographic Society.

Ianthe says that the trigger for her entry into the world of portraying plants was a course given by Anne-Marie Evans at West Dean College. She continues to hone her skills at her local Adult Education College.

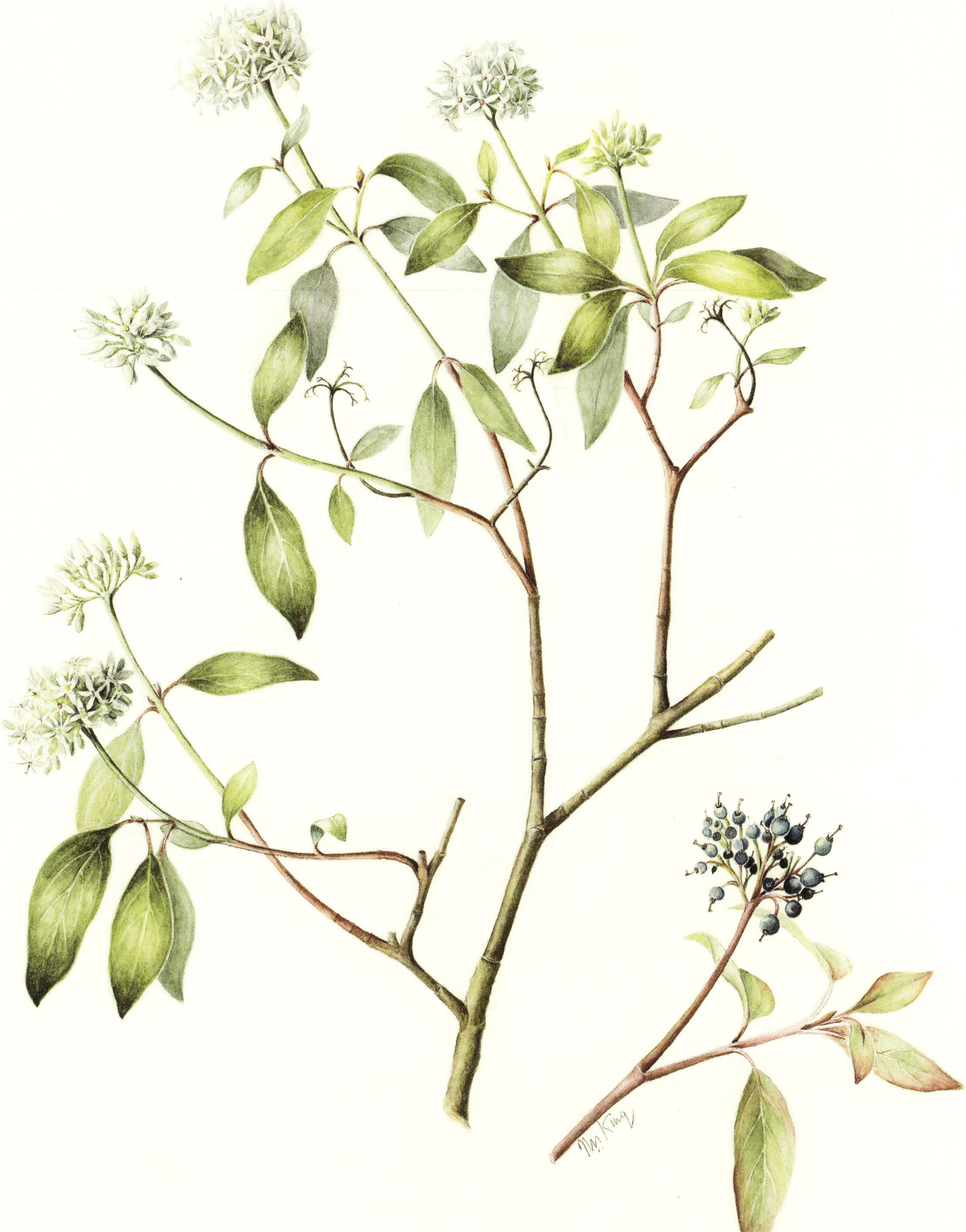

Crataegus monogyna Jacq. ssp. *azarella* (Griseb.) Franco
Family – Rosaceae

Charmian White

Crataegus monogyna is a common tree or hedge shrub in the British countryside, known as hawthorn or may. It is the only British plant to have its name associated with the month in which it blooms. In spite of its connection to the month of May, records of its first blooming range from mid-April to the beginning of July. The subspecies painted here is distributed from Spain to the Balkans, the southern part of the Russian Federation and the Mediterranean. The tree in the Physic Garden was planted in 1981.

The plant appears in a number of foreign pharmacopoeias. It acts on the heart in a similar manner to digoxin (derived from the woolly foxglove, *Digitalis lanata*). In the UK it is used in herbal medicine as a heart remedy and also for treating variations in blood pressure.

About the artist

Before Charmian was two she was drawing on whatever came to hand. Both her father and grandfather were artists. As she grew up her main interest became music and she achieved success as a concert singer, a career which she combined with bringing up two children.

After a period of illness and a divorce, Charmian remarried and rediscovered her artistic skills. She took courses at Putney Art School, Kew Gardens and with Clair and Kery Dalby. Charmian then started exhibiting at RHS London shows. She later took the opportunity to study botanical illustration with Anne-Marie Evans from 1996 to 1998 before finally becoming a painting member of Chelsea Physic Garden Florilegium Society.

RHS medals: Silver Gilt 2000, Silver 1995, 1996, Bronze 1998

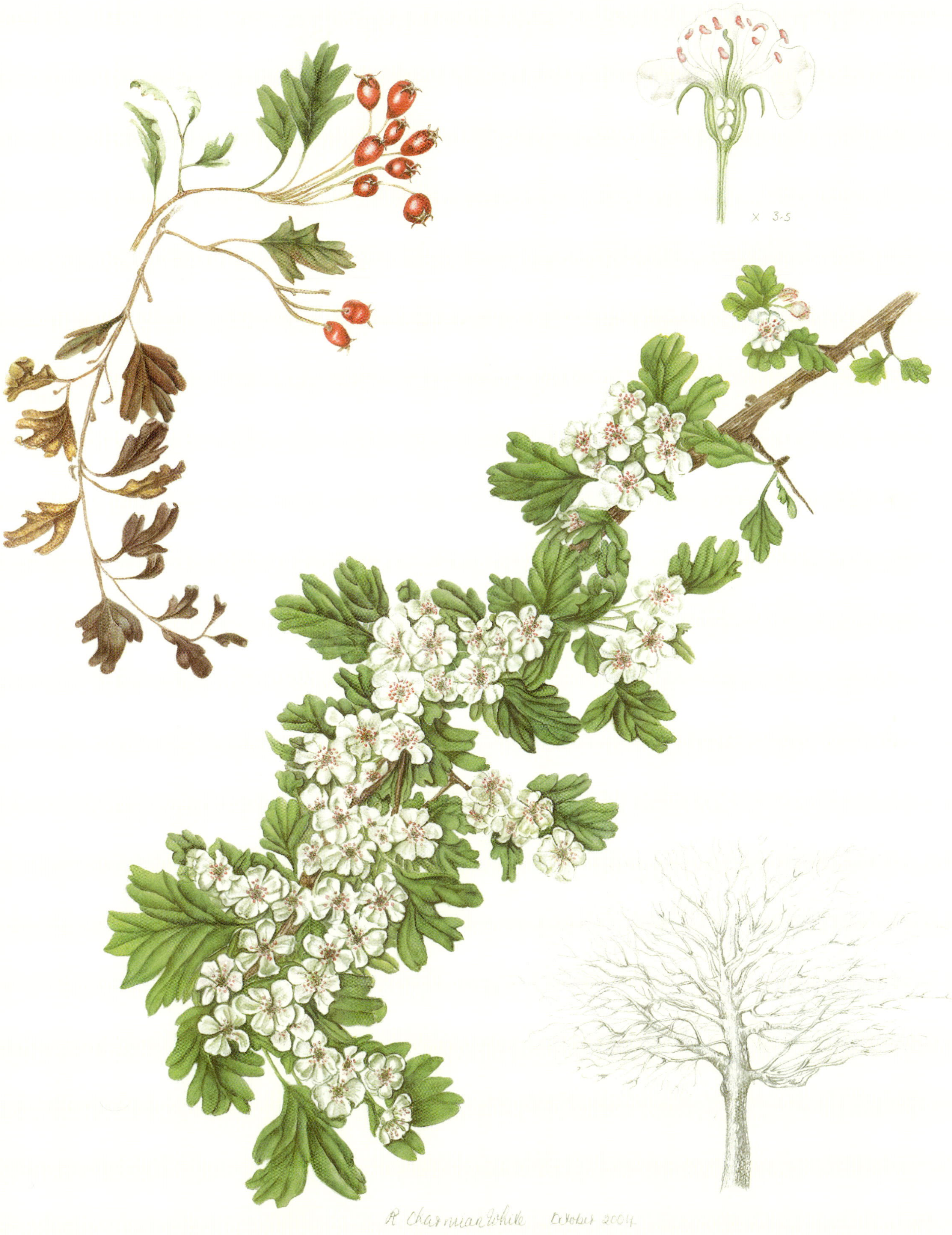
X 3.5
R Charman White October 2004

Cydonia oblonga Miller
Family – Rosaceae

Margaret King

The generic name of the true quince, *Cydonia*, is the same as that of the old capital of Crete, now called Chania. The name is derived from Kydon, the grandson of King Minos. The place-name *Kydonia* appears in Minoan linear B tablets. The mythological Golden Apples of the Hesperides were probably quinces. The true quince is not to be confused with plants of the genus *Chaenomeles* which are known as the japanese quince. *Cydonia oblonga* was introduced into England in the thirteenth century. The Portuguese name for quince is *marmelo* and the confection prepared from the fruit is known as *marmelada* – the origin of the English word 'marmalade'.

Culpeper, the seventeenth century herbalist, says that the 'cotton or down of Quinces... laid as a plaister, made up with wax, it brings hair to them that are bald, and keeps it from falling, if it be ready to shed.'

The seeds have been used to make setting lotions and other toiletries. The mucilage from the seeds has been used as a suspending agent.

About the artist

Margaret King was born in Zimbabwe and for much of her working life was the director of a Public Company in London. She holds the Order of the British Empire, which was awarded for services to the retail industry. Margaret has also served as a magistrate in London.

Margaret was the founder Chairman of the Chelsea Physic Garden Florilegium Society and her role in setting up the Society is detailed in the brief history to be found earlier in this volume.

Most of her painting is done to commission. Her work is in the collections at Chelsea Physic Garden, the Hunt Institute, the Malilangwe Conservation Trust in Zimbabwe and private collections in Britain, the USA, South Africa and Germany. Her work has been published in many Chelsea Physic Garden publications, including the *Index Seminum*.

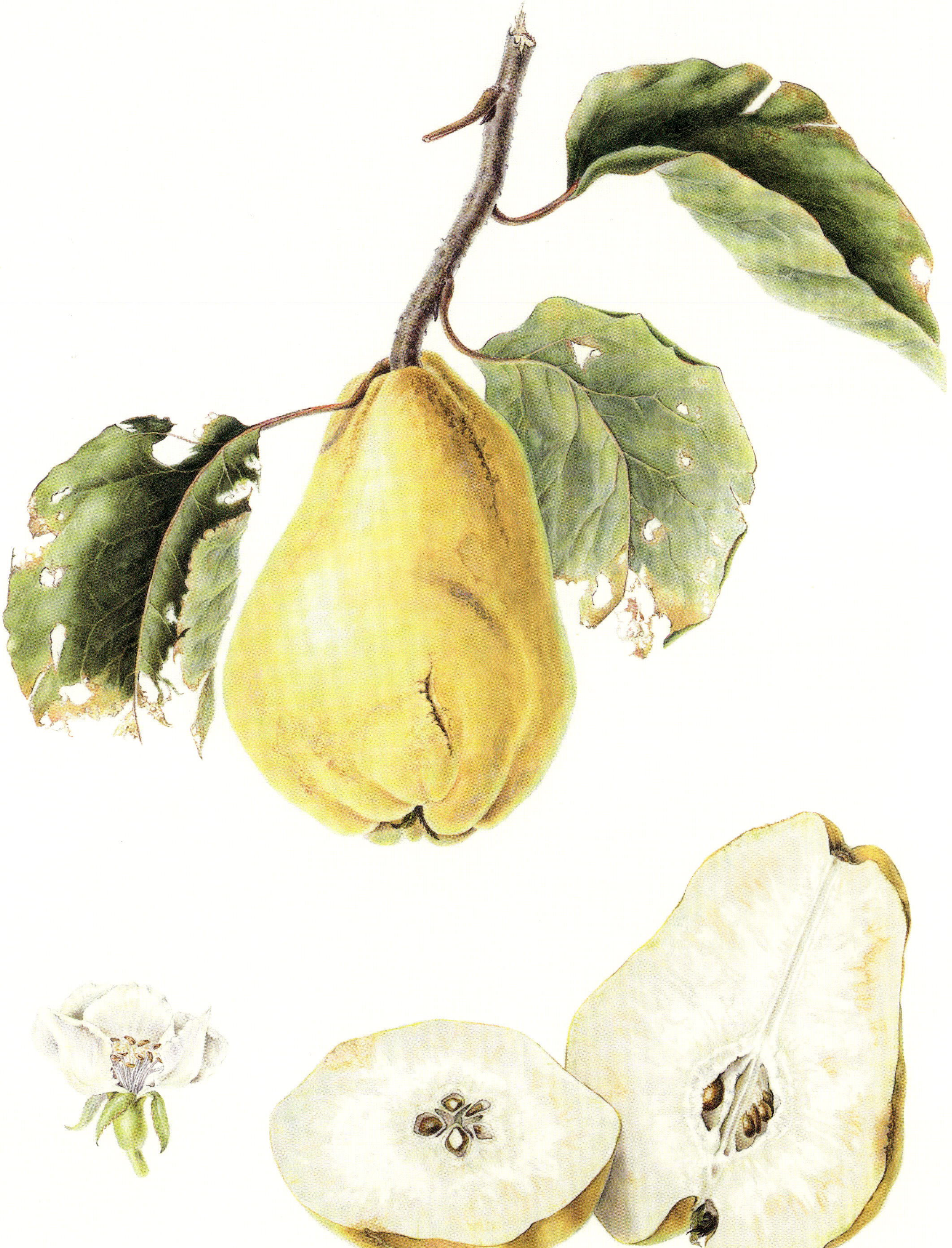

Datura stramonium L.
Family – Solanaceae

Ruth Hall

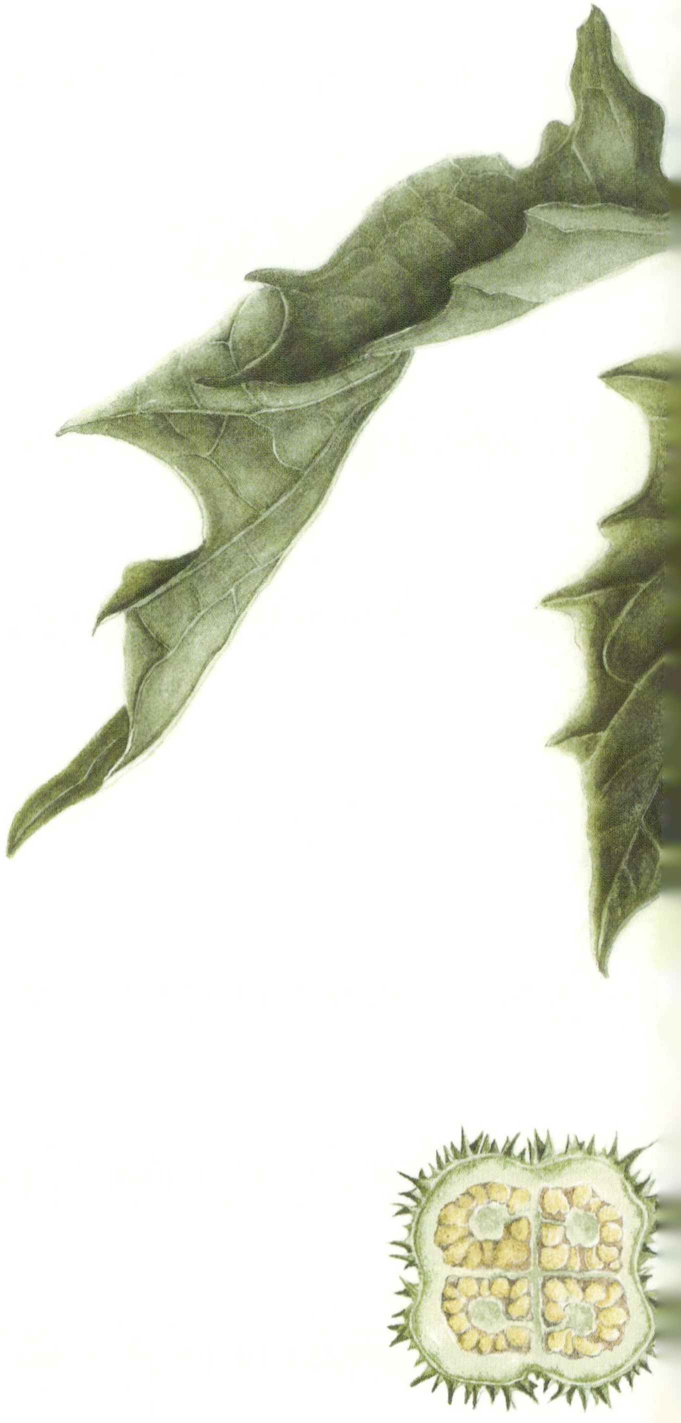

Commonly known as thorn apple, this American species is also known as Jimson weed (a corruption of Jamestown, the settlement in Virginia, where it was probably first observed in the USA). Many species of *Datura* have been grown for their attractive trumpet-like flowers, often under the name of angels' trumpets. In recent years woody perennial daturas with pendant flowers have been placed in the genus *Brugmansia*.

The first *British Pharmacopoeia* (1864) had monographs for both the leaf (*stramonii folia*) and the seed (*stramonii semina*). The seed was used to prepare a tincture (an alcoholic extract), no specific use was assigned at that time to the leaf. By the 1950s the leaf was the only part of *stramonium* appearing in monographs. The active constituents of *stramonium* are hyoscyamine and hyoscine. Preparations of stramonium were used to treat spasmodic asthma, the tincture being used as an ingredient in a liquid medicine. Similar preparations were administered by the Algonquin in northeastern America to adolescent males during initiation rites. The substance was known as *wysoccan*.

About the artist

Ruth is a fine artist with a passion for flowers. Since her first exhibition in London in 1990 her career has been through many stages. She originally trained in ceramics. After travelling in South America and the USA Ruth resettled in England in 1986. With the arrival of her first child she began to focus her creative talents into botanical painting.

Her work has been published in natural history books and as card designs. Ruth has exhibited at the RHS with paintings of flowers from D.H.Lawrence's *Sons and Lovers* and a set of paintings of plants from Derbyshire hay meadows. Ruth has exhibited also at Pashley Manor, The Sorbonne, the Ingleby Gallery in Derbyshire and Naples.

Ruth teaches botanical painting in both London and Kent. She believes that the rising popularity of the painstaking pursuit of botanical illustration reflects a need for order and the contemplation of beauty in an uncertain and unstable age.

RHS medals: Silver Gilt 1993, 1994

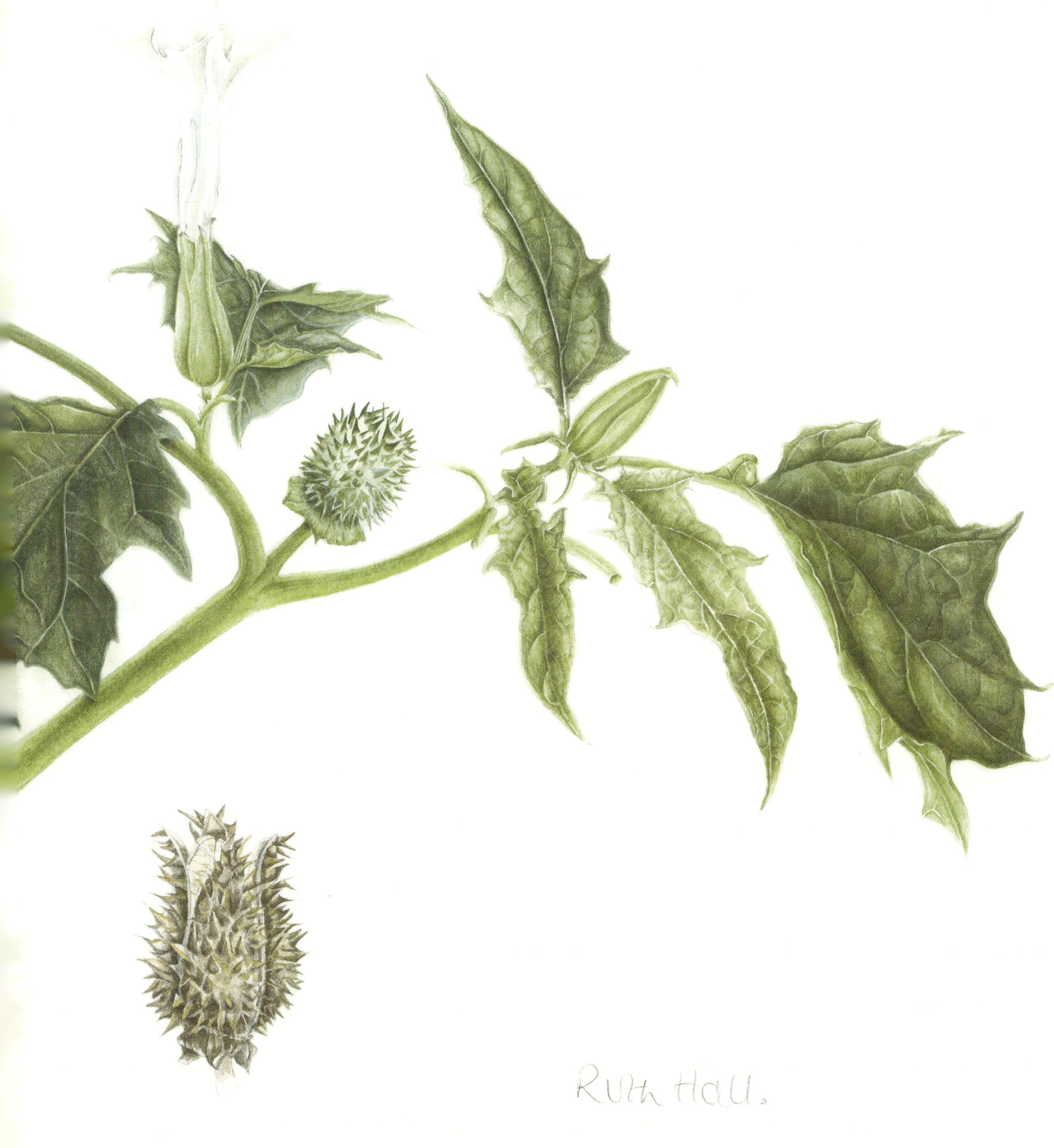
Ruth Hall.

Dianthus glacialis Haenke.
Family – Caryophyllaceae

Angelique de Folin

Dianthus glacialis, a delicate species, comes from the eastern Alps and Carpathian mountains.

In the seventeenth century, over 300 varieties of Dianthus were recorded. The old name of gillyflowers was applied generally to plants of this genus. Culpeper (1653), writing about 'clove gilliflowers' says 'It is vain to describe an herb so well known'. He then commends them as 'great strengtheners both of the brain and heart, and will therefore serve either for cordials or cephalics, as your occasion will serve.'

The species *Dianthus superbus* is grown in China and Japan and is known as *qu mai*. It is said to clear 'damp heat'. It used to treat conditions of the kidneys and urinary tract. It has also been used to treat eczema.

About the artist

Angelique was born in Paris. In the early 1980s she studied painting at the Académie Roederer school of Art and jewellery design at the Chambre Syndicale de Joaillerie de Paris. She then studied for a diploma in social science before, in 1987, starting as a porcelain painter in her own studio in Paris. In 1992 she married and moved her studio to London. She sold to a large number of collectors in France, USA, Britain, Italy and Switzerland. In 1996 she was chosen by the Grands Ateliers de France to be the sole representative of the art of porcelain painting at their exhibition of the work of the leading French craftsmen.

In 1997 she studied botanical painting under Anne-Marie Evans at the Chelsea Physic Garden, London. Angelique then started exhibiting her botanical paintings in London, including a solo show at Hortus Gallery, Milan and New York. Her work was included in the Hunt Institute's 10th International Exhibition in 2001.

In 2004 one of Angelique's paintings was selected for inclusion in the Highgrove Florilegium. This is presently being created under the umbrella of The Prince of Wales's Charitable Foundation and will celebrate and record in a permanent way the flora in the garden at Highgrove.

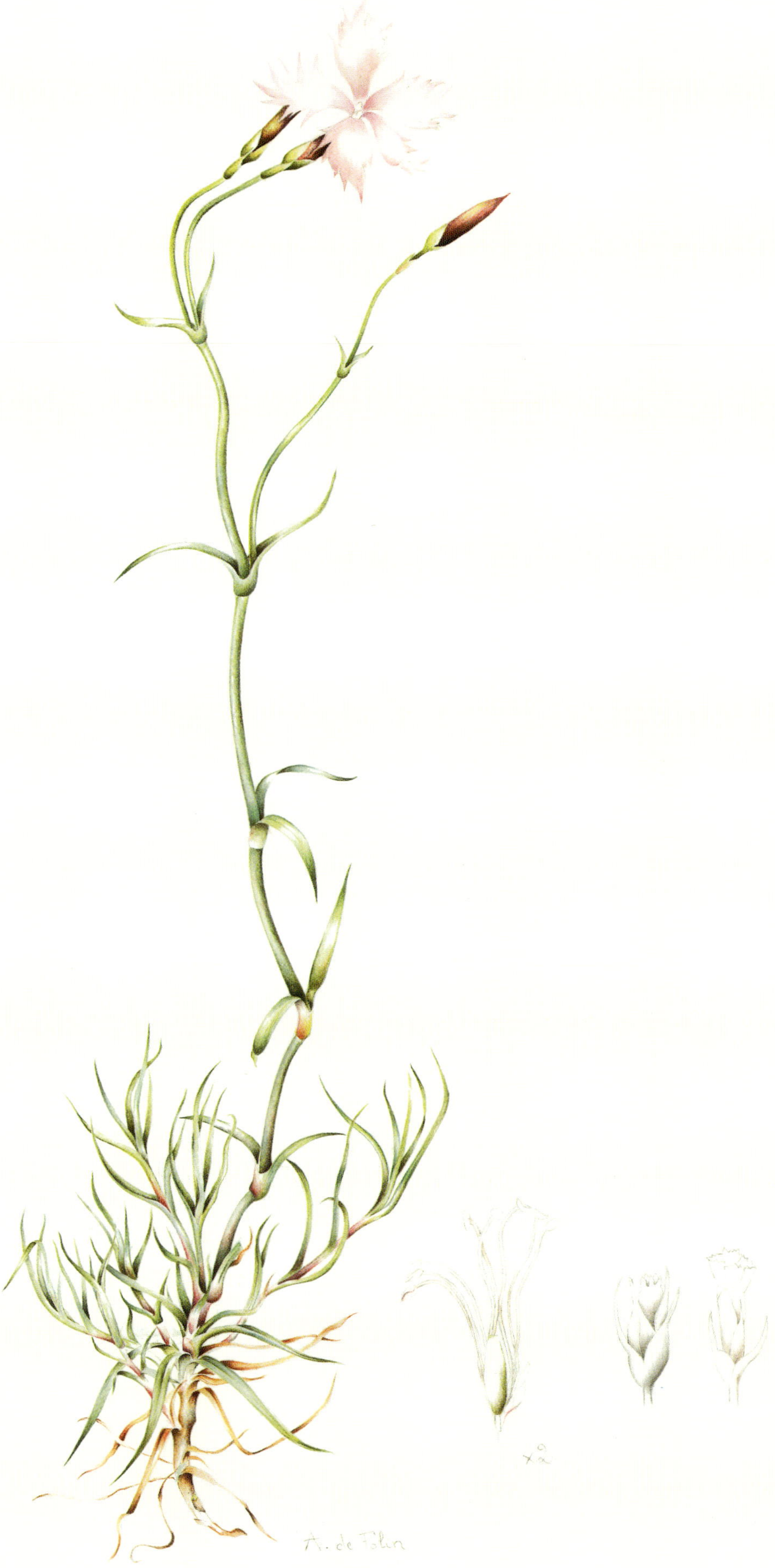
x2

Dianthus juniperinus Sm. ssp. *bauhinorum* (Greuter) Turland
Family – Caryophyllaceae

Yvonne Glenister Hammond

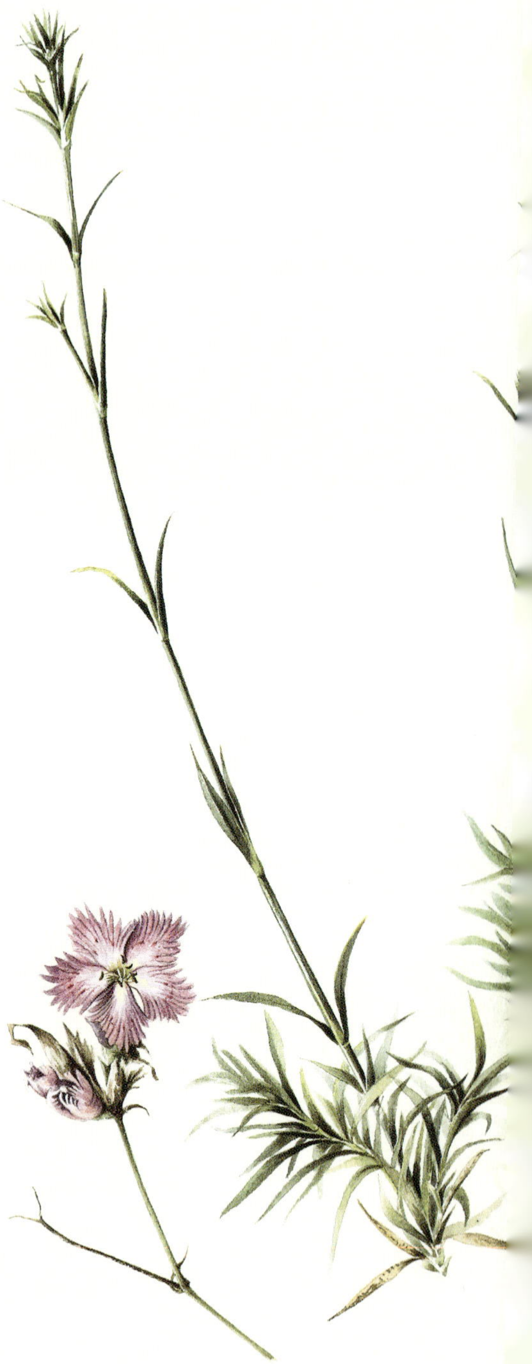

This species is a plant endemic to Crete, growing on limestone cliffs. The material at Chelsea was collected from a west-facing calcareous cliff at an altitude of 810 metres. It is one of many endemic Cretan plants in the collections at the Physic Garden.

The common names of pinks, carnations and gillyflowers are used freely in relation to this genus. Gerard (1597) writes of 'clove gilloflowers' and of 'pinks or wilde gilloflowers'. He says of a conserve prepared from the first 'is exceedingly cordial, and wonderfully above measure doth comfort the heart, being eaten now and then'. For the pinks he writes 'These are not used in physicke, but esteemed for their use in garlands and nosegaies'. Gerard's reference to the clove and the family name for this genus both allude to the similarity of the scent of dianthus to that of the clove used as a culinary spice. The spice consists of the dried flower buds of the tree *Eugenia caryophyllus*, a native of the Molucca Islands.

About the artist

Yvonne is inspired by the play of light on flowers, fruit and vegetables. She likes to create tactile images bathed in glowing colour and arranged carefully on the paper in bold, confident compositions. Her work has a startling realism and strong wall-appeal. She paints in watercolour on paper and on vellum and applies as many as a dozen layers of fine translucent pigment to achieve the vibrant colours she observes in the plant world.

She has always drawn and painted for pleasure but took up botanical painting seriously in 1995 when she joined Anne-Marie Evans' classes at Chelsea Physic Garden.

Since then her work has been acquired in private collections world-wide including that of Dr Shirley Sherwood. She has three paintings in the Hunt Institute. She sketches wild flowers when travelling and also teaches botanical art. Her work has been selected for inclusion in the Highgrove Florilegium which is being created under the umbrella of the Prince of Wales's Charitable Foundation and which will celebrate and record in a permanent way the flora in the garden at Highgrove.

She is an enthusiastic supporter of the Artists for Nature Foundation, an international organisation run from the Netherlands which aims to draw attention to important but threatened wild areas of the world through art and artists.

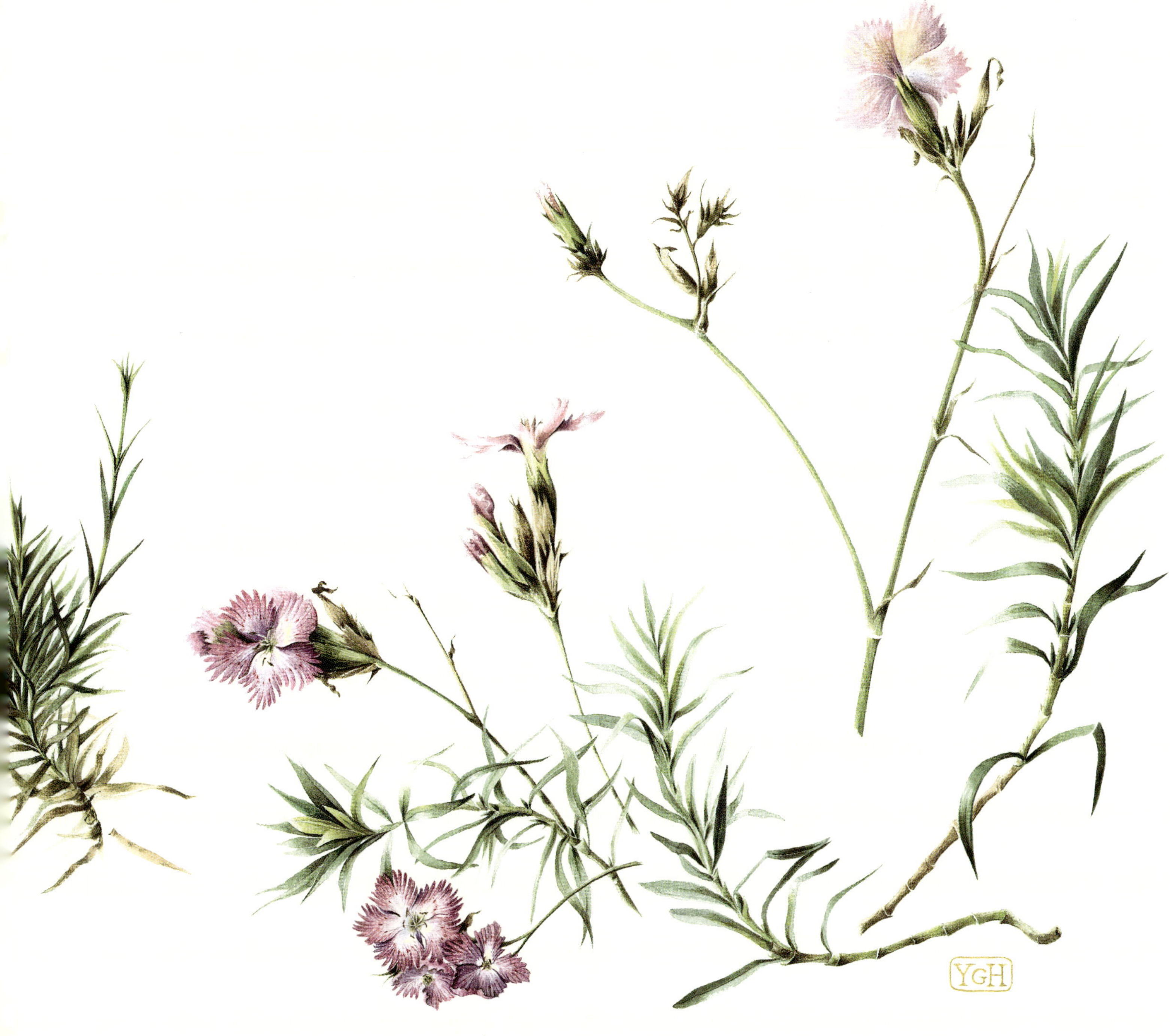

She is a founder member of the Chelsea Physic Garden Florilegium Society and took part in the Royal Horticultural Society's exhibition when the Florilegium Society was awarded a group Gold Medal for paintings of plants associated with Philip Miller. She has also shown paintings of tulips and Fuchsia at RHS London Shows.

Yvonne grew up in London and now lives in the Bedfordshire countryside with her husband, the naturalist, writer and wildlife art expert, Nicholas Hammond

RHS medals: Gold 1999, 2000, Silver Gilt 2001, 2005

Digitalis grandiflora Miller
Family – Scrophulariaceae

Judy Wilson

Digitalis grandiflora has previously been known both as *D. ambigua* and as *D. orientalis*. It received an Award of Garden Merit from The Royal Horticultural Society in 1993. It was introduced into England in the sixteenth century and is indigenous to central and southern Europe.

Whereas the active ingredient digitoxin, used as a cardiac stimulant since 1735, is found in many species of the genus, today it is extracted from cultivated *D. lanata*.

About the artist

Judy Wilson was born in Cambridge in 1943 and started painting late in life when she joined an Adult Education course on botanical illustration run by Jane Leycester Paige in Northamptonshire. This opened up a wholly new and exciting world and gave Judy great encouragement. She exhibited locally and then started to show her work with the Society of Botanical Artists at Central Hall, Westminster.

Judy took part in the Chelsea Physic Garden Florilegium Society's 1999 display of paintings of plants associated with Philip Miller at the Royal Horticultural Society which was awarded a group Gold medal. She has also exhibited her work twice at the Hunt Institute.

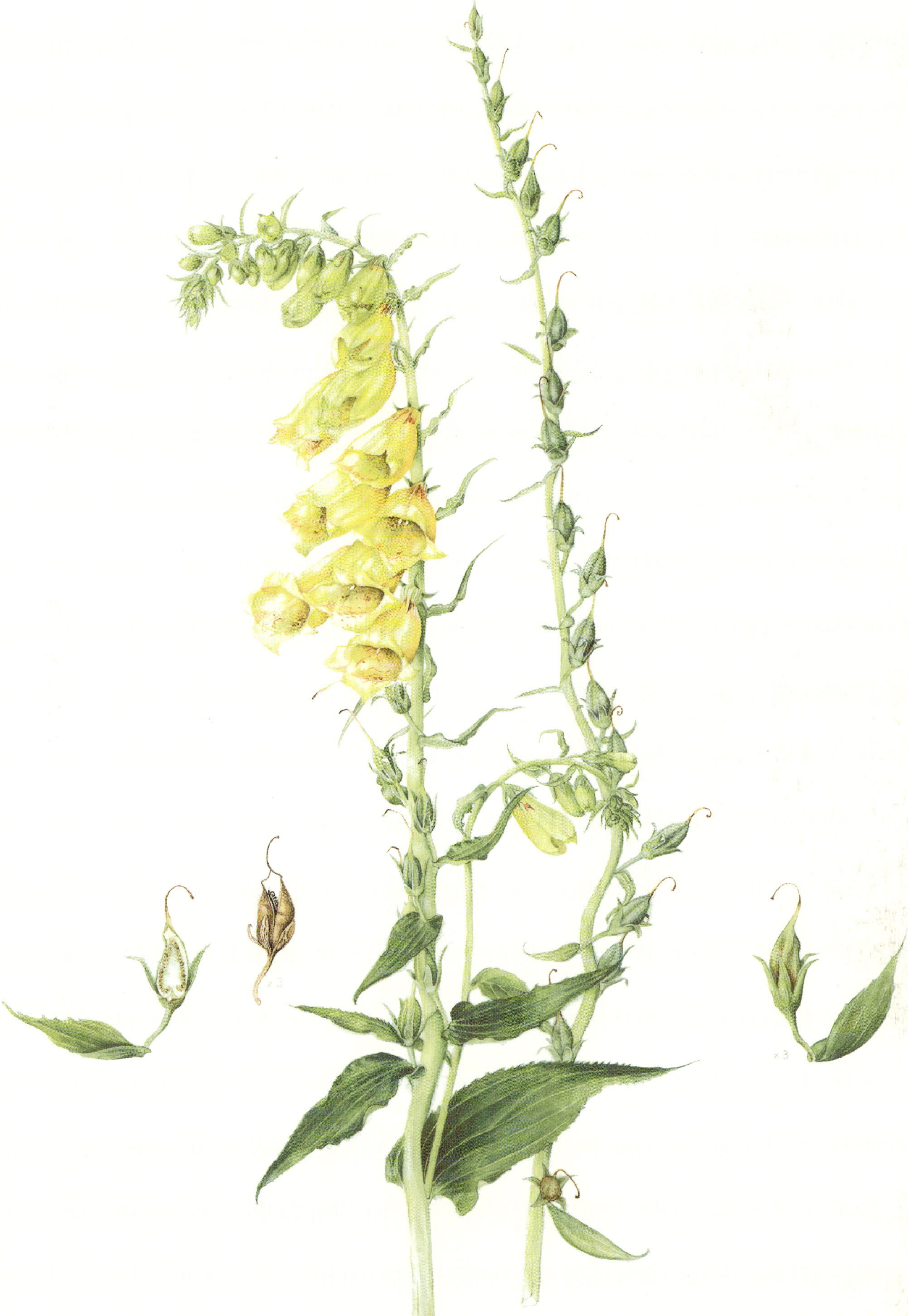
x3
x3

Ecballium elaterium (L.) A.Rich.
Family – Cucurbitaceae

Eiko Takano

Ecballium elaterium is best known by its common name, squirting cucumber. The generic name is derived from the Greek verb 'to throw out'. The fruit is picked before it matures and as it ripens the seeds and juice are ejected spontaneously, the result of very high fluid pressure inside the fruit wall. The juice is allowed to dry and the flakes are marketed as elaterium. The medicinal action is that of a strong purgative. There is a report of a French doctor 'suffering severely' after transporting some seeds of *E. elaterium* in his hat from the Jardins des Plantes across Paris to his home. He clearly did not know that the active ingredient is rapidly absorbed by contact through the skin! The plant is a common wasteland and roadside weed in the Mediterranean region.

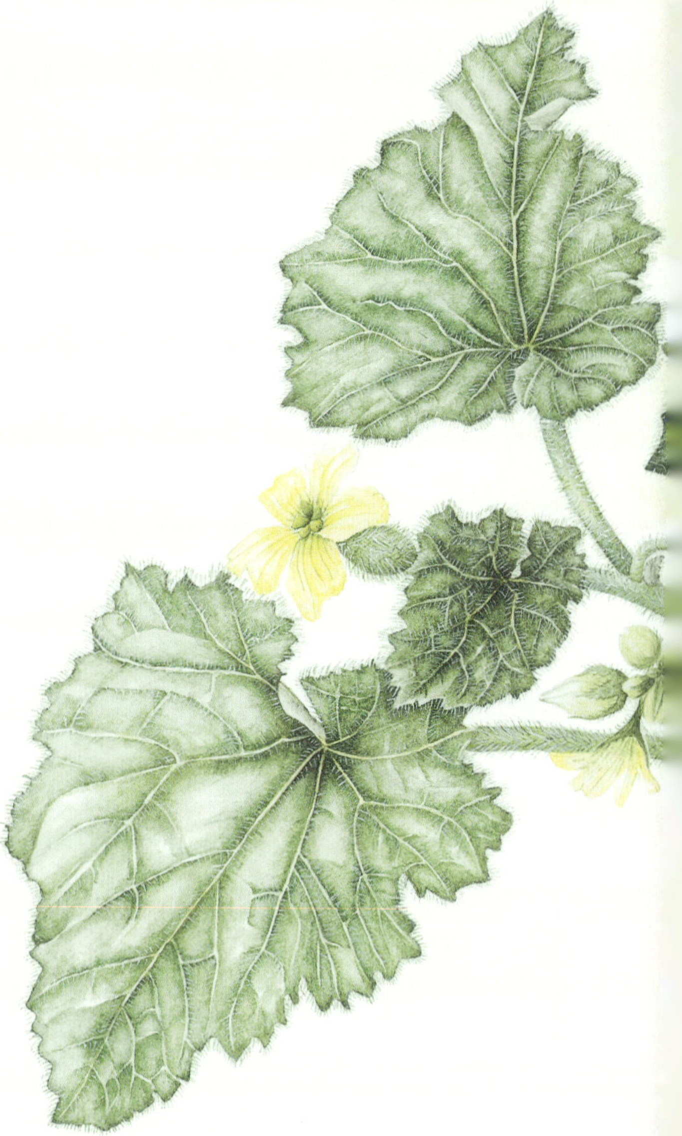

About the artist

Eiko Takano was born in Tokyo, Japan and has lived in England since 1988. She has studied botanical painting under several prominent teachers. She is a Member of The Society of Botanical Artists and was awarded Certificates of Botanical Merit at the SBA annual exhibitions in 1993 and 2000.

RHS medals: Silver Gilt 1999, 2000, Silver 2005

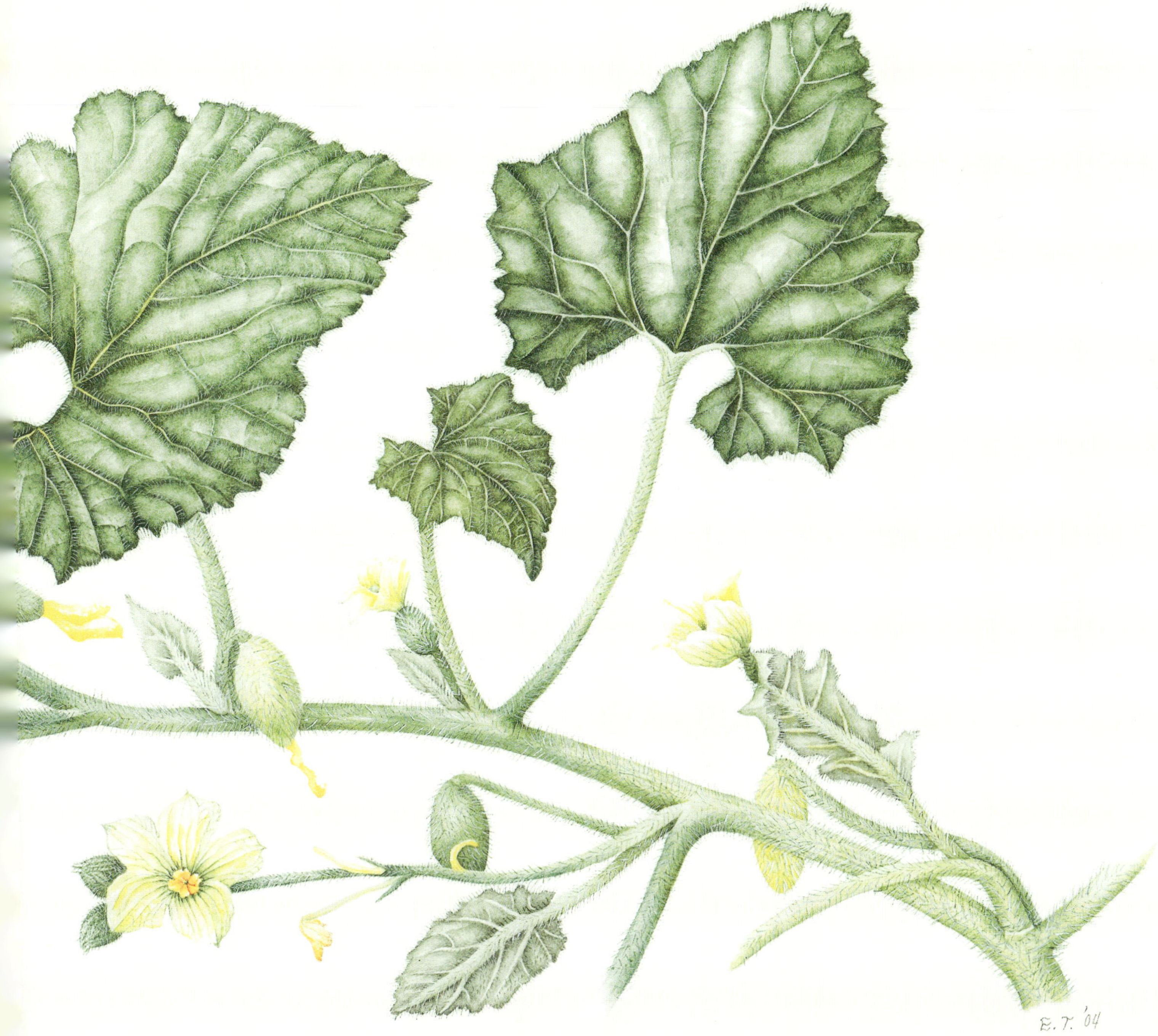
E.T. '04

Eruca vesicaria L. ssp. *sativa* (Miller) Thell.

Family – Cruciferae

Sally Hammerton

Commonly known as rocket, it is indigenous to the Mediterranean area and eastern Asia. It was particularly popular in Elizabethan times and is again now fashionable as a salad plant. It has been used medicinally as both a tonic and in cough medicines. It is also said to be anti-scorbutic (prevents scurvy). In strong doses it causes vomiting. It has also been recommended as an aid to digestion. This comes as no surprise as the generic name *Eruca* is derived from the latin for belch, *ructo*, as is the English word eructation. Linguistic evolution followed, *ructo* became *ruca* (Italian), then *rucetta, roquette* (French) and, finally *rocket*.

About the artist

Sally's interest in painting flowers and plants is rooted in her early years as a daughter of a knowledgeable and enthusiastic plantsman. The large garden was full of colour with interesting and unusual plants, shrubs and trees alongside many more familiar species. Although she enjoyed art at school she did not start painting seriously until she had a growing family at which time she joined a local art group. After a time she focused on painting plants in watercolour.

Sally joined Jane Leycester Paige's classes in Botanical Art at King's Cliffe, studying and developing knowledge and techniques under her tutelage for at least sixteen years.

In addition to the precision and accuracy essential to botanical work Sally also enjoys painting in a looser style which, she feels, successfully reflects the natural beauty and character of the subjects. Even the most modest plants deserve to be recorded alongside other larger or grander specimens. Painting subjects other than plants also increases her skill with the brush. Sally runs painting groups and workshops.

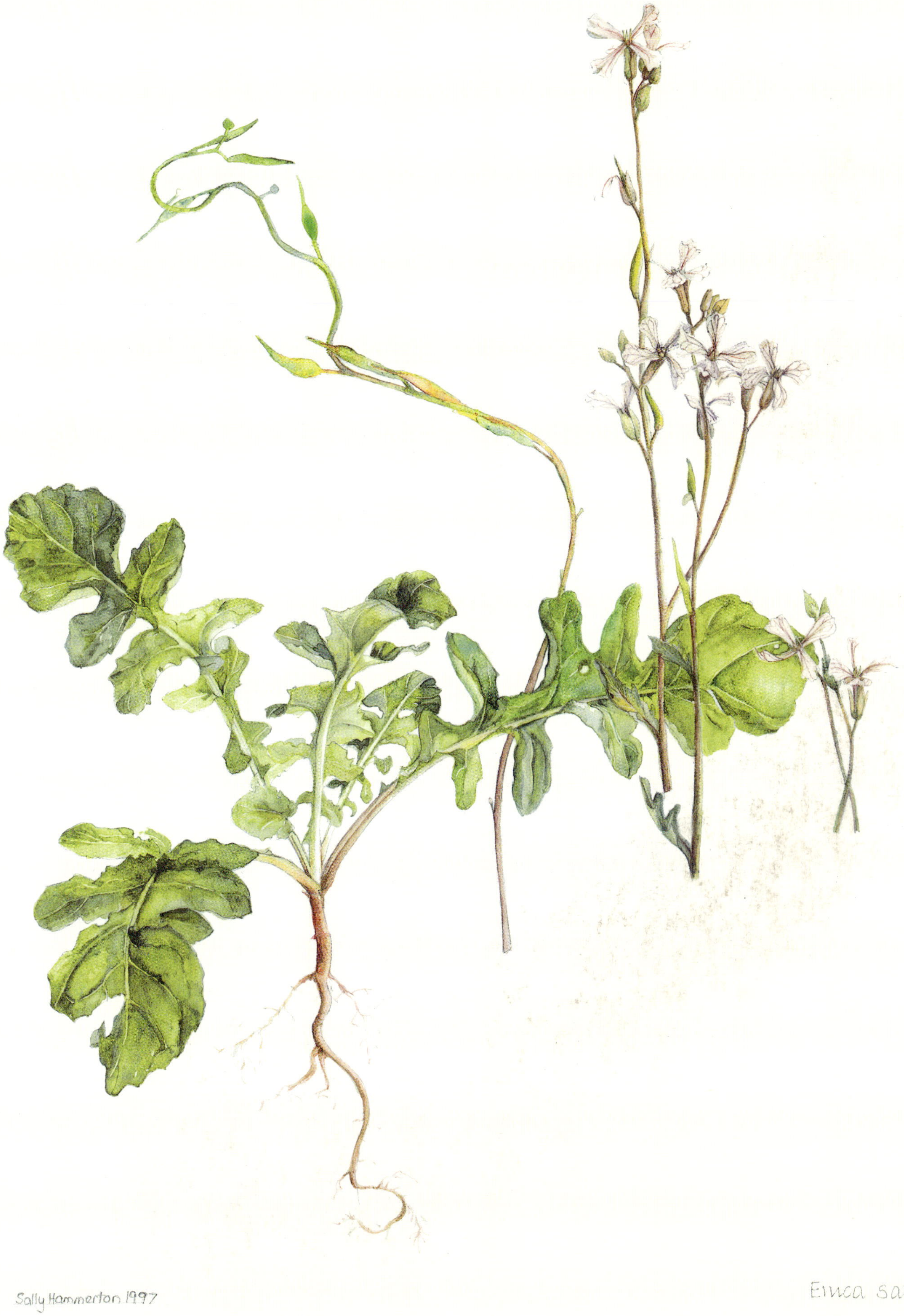

Sally Hammerton 1997

Eruca sativa

Eryngium caucasicum Fischer ex Steudel
Family – Umbelliferae

Rosemary Lindsay

As the name suggests, this plant like many other eryngiums, comes from the Caucasus. The material in the Physic Garden comes from St Petersburg Botanic Garden and was originally collected from a Russian experimental station at the same latitude. *E. maritimum*, commonly known as sea holly, is found on the coasts of southern England. *E. maritimum* has been used medicinally as an expectorant and for treating renal colic. The sweet, mucilaginous roots were candied and eaten as a sweetmeat.

About the artist

Rosemary Lindsay trained first in architecture at Kingston School of Art and worked in several architectural practices in London before moving into freelance botanical illustration. A fascination with the structure of plants led to this change of occupation. She is a painting member of the Society of Botanical Artists as well as of the Chelsea Physic Garden Florilegium Society

Rosemary's paintings have been included in the British Council Travelling Exhibition of British Illustrators, the Society of Botanical Artists' annual London exhibitions and several single artist shows. She has taken part in Art in Action at Waterperry, Oxfordshire, as an invited illustrator. Commissioned work includes drawings for the RHS Plant Registers and the *Plantsman* journal as well as for many private clients.

The growing of plants has been a lifelong interest and Rosemary's garden, frequently open to the public under the National Gardens Scheme, has been the subject of many articles in the national press. She regularly writes articles for the quarterly journal *Hortus*.

RHS medals: Silver 1980, 1981, Grenfell 1985, 1987

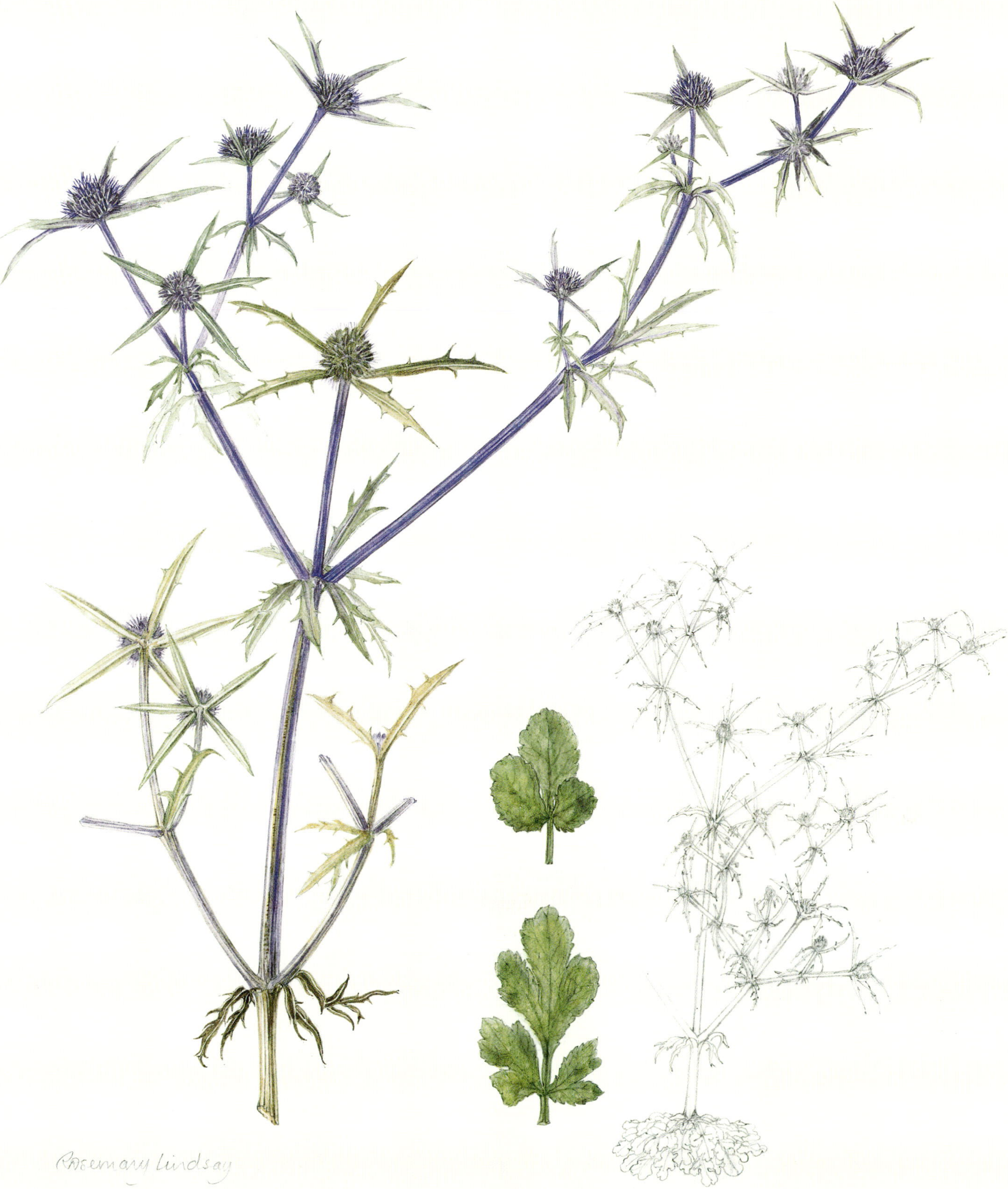

Eryngium caucasicum
2003

Eryngium giganteum M. Bieb.
Family – Umbelliferae

Jane Leycester Paige

This *Eryngium* has the nickname 'Miss Willmott's Ghost' after the eminent lady gardener from Warley Place in Essex. It was introduced into Great Britain in the nineteenth century from the Caucasus. *E.giganteum* usually dies after flowering but readily produces self-sown seedlings. Legend suggests that the plant would appear spontaneously in gardens that Miss Willmott had visited, the implication being that she had scattered some seeds during her visit.

The Physic Garden plant is derived from a collection by Martyn Rix near Trabzon, northern Turkey. Since its collection it has been redetermined as *E. giganteum* 'Silver Ghost'.

About the artist

After studying botany, zoology and geography at Advanced Level, Jane went to Westhill Training College in Birmingham to train as a Froebel teacher, taking art as her main subject.

From childhood she was encouraged by her mother to identify and paint wildflowers and by her father to study and develop an interest in early English watercolours. These two interests continue to influence much of her work.

Jane was elected a Founder Member of the Society of Botanical Artists in 1982 and is a Fellow of the Chelsea Physic Garden Florilegium Society. She regularly illustrated gardening magazines as well as books for BBC Publications and the RSPB. Her work is featured in *The Watercolour Artist's Flower Sketchbook* (2005).

Her work has been exhibited with the Royal Institute of Painters in Watercolour, the Royal Watercolour Society and regularly with the Society of Botanical Artists.

Jane and her husband, John Paige SWLA, together run a studio in rural Northamptonshire where they both teach various image-making techniques for recording the living world. They are both involved in Artists for Nature Foundation projects and for many years they have led painting, bird watching and botanising holidays for a wildlife travel company.

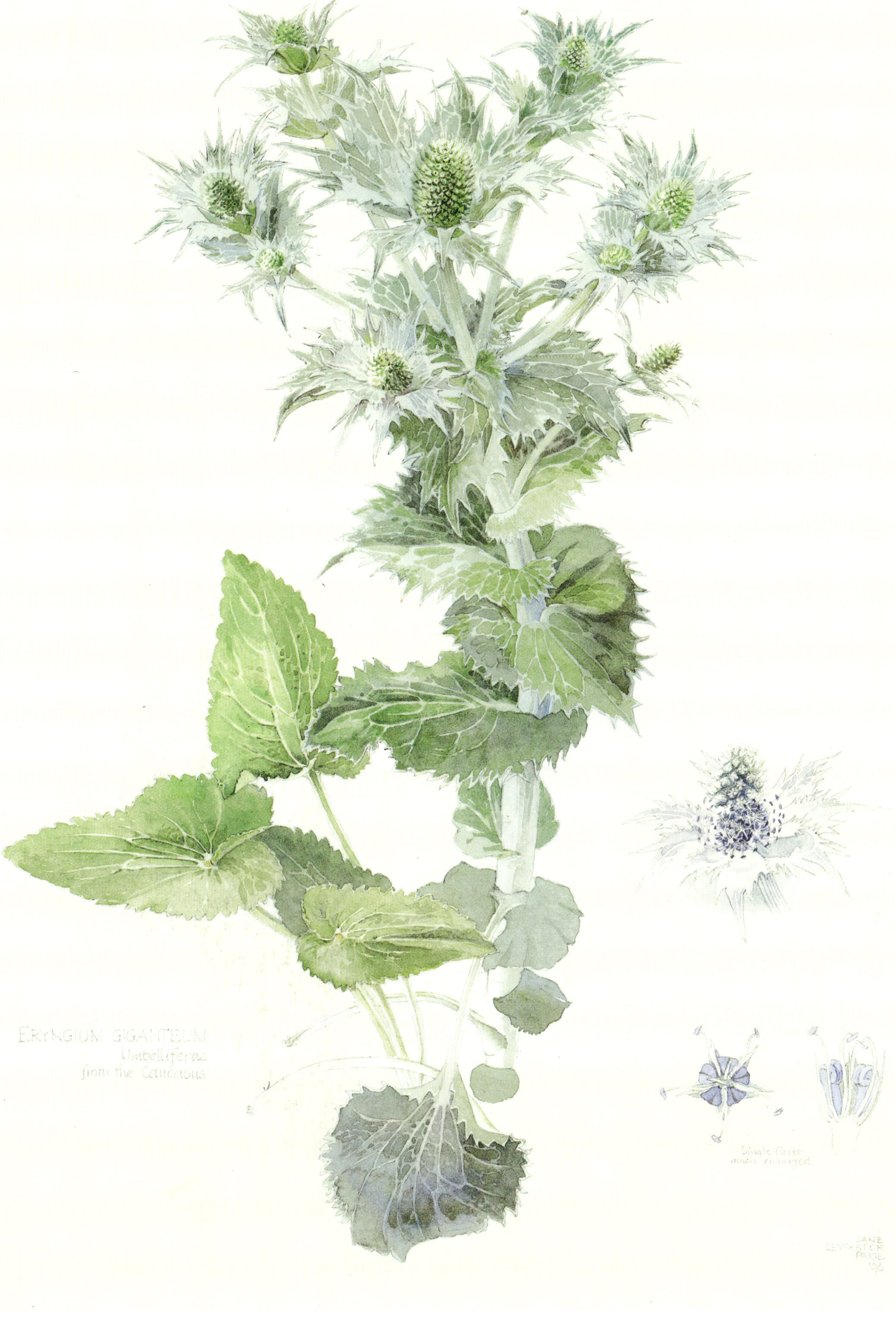
ERYNGIUM GIGANTEUM
Umbelliferae
from the Caucasus
Single flower
much enlarged
JANE
PAIGE
'96

Gaultheria procumbens L.
Family – Ericaceae

Valerie Bolas

This is a low-growing plant indigenous to eastern North America. For gardeners it provides good ground-cover particularly in shaded areas. One of its common names, wintergreen, will immediately remind sports players of the traditional smell of liniments and embrocations. Oil of wintergreen is obtained from the leaves of *G. procumbens* and is produced as a result of fermentation of the leaves in water. The oil is closely related to aspirin and is active when applied to the skin to relieve joint and muscle strains. Oil of wintergreen contains a very high proportion of methyl salicylate but the natural product also contains other substances that can cause skin eruptions. The *British Pharmacopoeia* has for many years directed that 'when oil of wintergreen, wintergreen, or wintergreen oil is prescribed or demanded, synthetically prepared methyl salicylate shall be dispensed or supplied'. Cases of death have been recorded where the oil has been swallowed. Pharmacopoeias in some countries allow the oil from *G. procumbens* or oil from the bark of *Betula lenta* (a species of birch) to be used for methyl salicylate but direct that the source of the product must be declared on the label.

About the artist

Valerie Bolas was a self-employed horticultural professional for twelve years, having previously been employed in a local commercial nursery. She decided in 1989 to learn to draw at Local Education Authority classes followed by a one year part-time Art and Design course. She had no formal botanical training but her deep interest in plants led to her specialising in botanical illustration and she enjoyed three short courses at the English Gardening School before undertaking the Diploma course in Botanical Illustration with Anne-Marie Evans in 1995 when she was awarded the Diploma with Credit.

Valerie's illustrations have been published in the *Garden of World Medicine* guide at Chelsea Physic Garden, *The Kitchen Garden* April 2000, a Local Heritage Initiative Project and, in 2004, *The Medicinal uses of Cannabis and Cannabinoids.*

Valerie has exhibited twenty-five times during the past twelve years and is currently tutoring a group of painters at Brogdale Horticultural Trust. She is a founder member and now a Fellow of the Chelsea Physic Garden Florilegium Society.

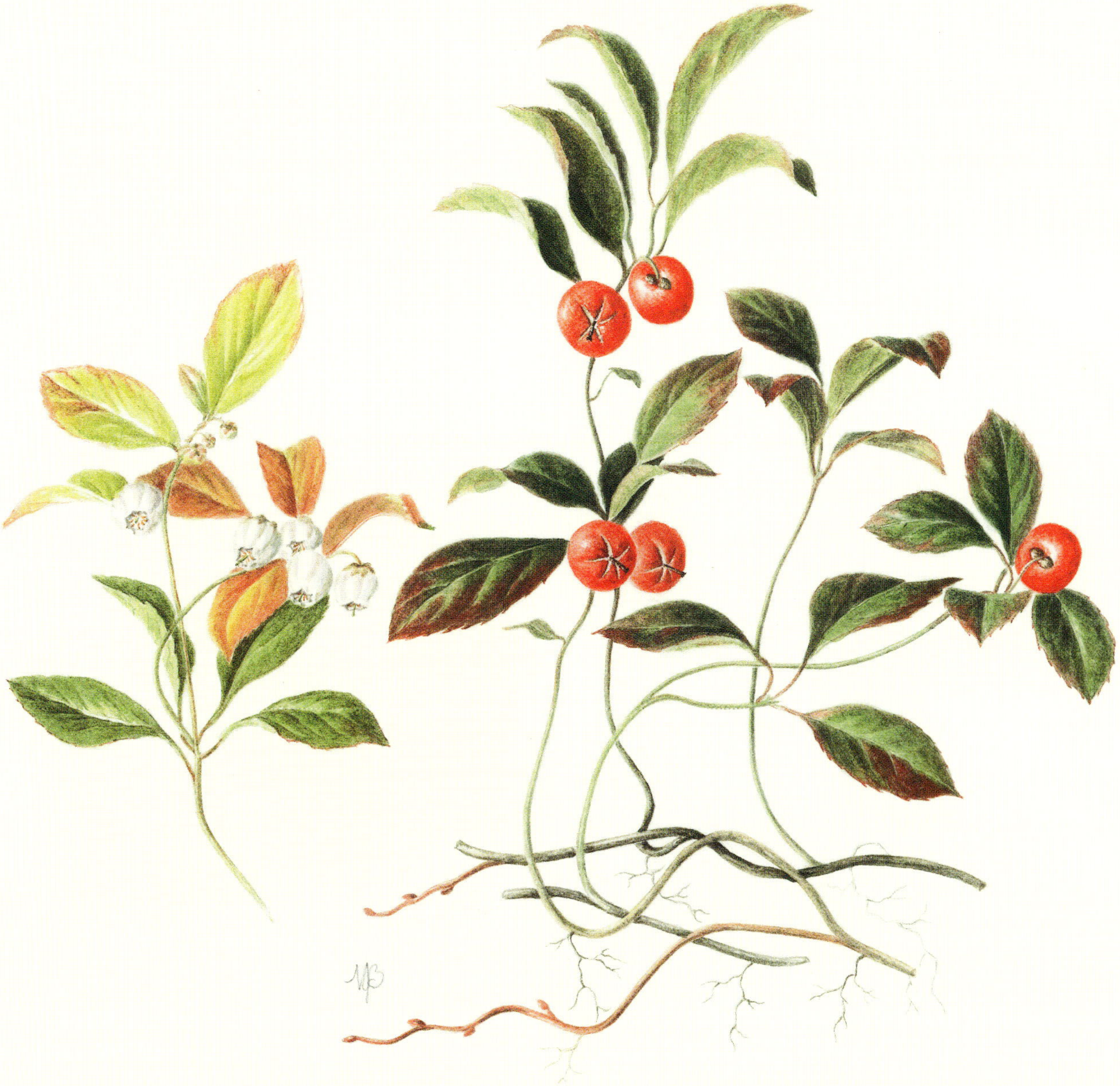

Geum pyrenaicum Miller
Family – Rosaceae

Kate Evans

Geums grow in many parts of the world from south America to the Himalayas. *G. pyrenaicum* is native to the Pyrenees. In the north of Britain the water avens, *G. rivale*, grows in damp woodlands, alongside watercourses and in ditches. One of the common names of *G. rivale* is cure-all. It is therefore surprising to find little reference to it in pharmacopoeias. Some of its properties are said to be astringent, antiseptic, febrifuge (reduces temperature) and tonic. Nicholas Culpeper (1653) says of avens, *G. urbanum*, (our only other native species) 'The decoction also being drank, comforts the heart and strengthens the stomach and a cold brain, and therefore is good in springtime to open the obstructions of the liver...'

About the artist

Kate Evans has had no formal art training, but has always had a lifelong love of flowers, gardening and art. On her return to Britain after living for many years in continental Europe, she attended short botanical painting courses at West Dean College and Chelsea Physic Garden under the tutelage of Elizabeth Jane Lloyd and later, Anne-Marie Evans.

Kate has exhibited widely in Britain and continental Europe and her paintings are held in private collections throughout the world.

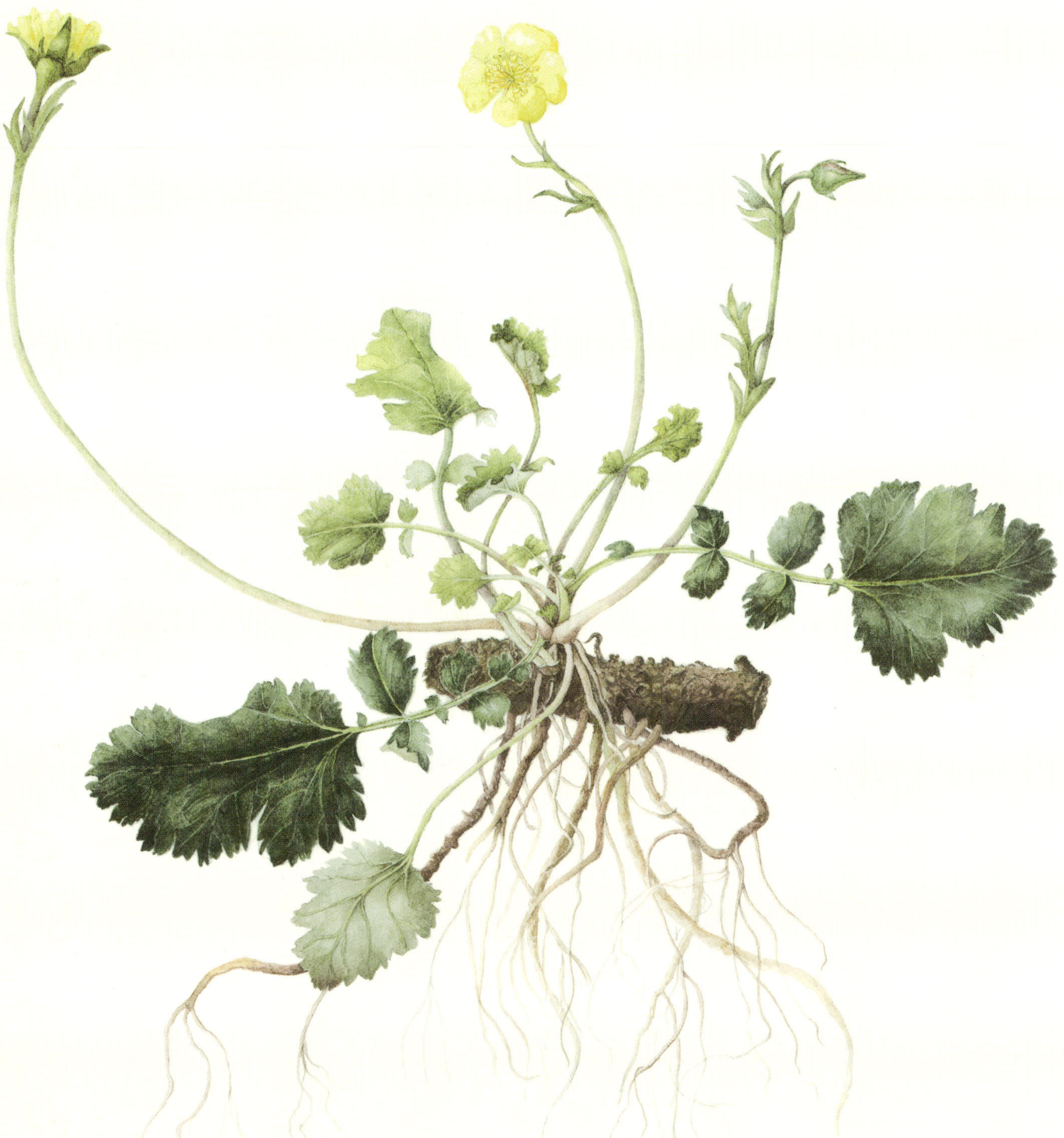

Glaucium flavum Crantz
Family – Papaveraceae

Jenevora Searight

Known as the yellow horned poppy it is to be found growing on sand dunes, shingle and waste ground, preferring well-drained chalky soils in Europe, north Africa and western Asia. The plant contains glaucine which has been used as an ingredient in cough mixtures, particularly in eastern Europe. The oil from the seeds was used in making soap and for burning in lamps.

About the artist

Jenevora studied Fine Arts at the Ecole National Supérieur des Beaux Arts in Paris. Afterwards, needing a niche, she studied picture restoration under the then consultant to the National Gallery in London. She then married and spent many years in Brazil. There she was asked to do some bird illustrations and so learnt how; and then had to learn botanical illustration as birds normally sit on something! She exhibited in Rio and was awarded several botanical prizes. Jenevora then became involved with the Margaret Mee Foundation which aims every year to send a Brazilian student of botanical art to Kew for several months for further training. The Foundation also supports other botanical students.

At present Jenevora is working on some illustrations for a large-format book on Macaws and is also preparing illustrations for a handbook for the birds of Brazil.

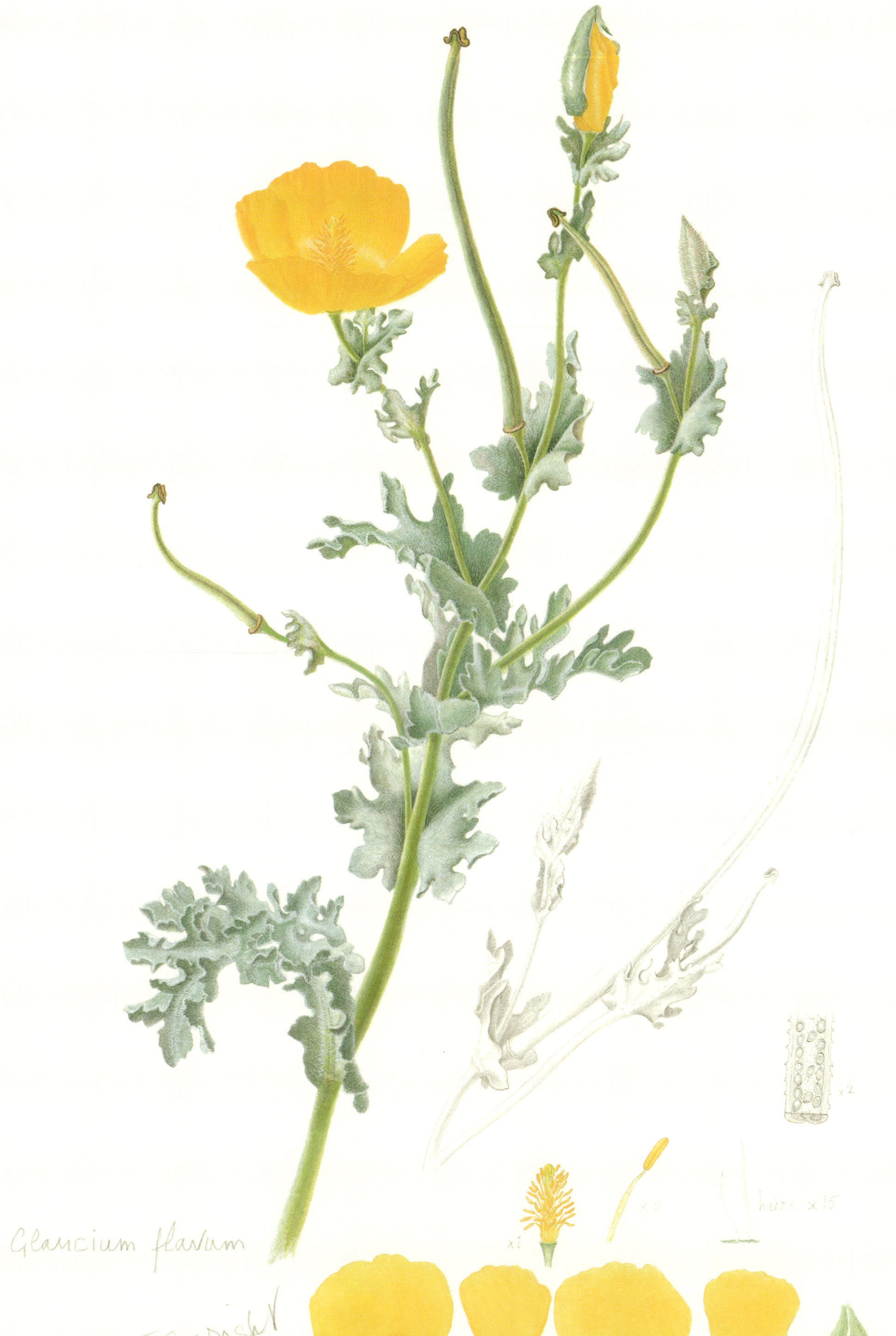
x 2
x1
hairs x 15
Glaucium flavum

Hoheria lyallii Hook. f.
Family – Malvaceae

Angie Girling

Hoheria lyallii, the lacebark, received an Award of Garden Merit from the RHS in 1993. It is a frost-hardy deciduous tree with white flowers produced in clusters during the summer, growing to five metres in height. *Hoheria* is in the same family as *Hibiscus* and is native to New Zealand. The name *Hoheria* comes from the Maori name, *houhere.*

About the artist

Angie started studying botanical painting at Sutton College of Liberal Arts in 1988. She has exhibited at the RHS London Shows on four occasions, most recently with paintings of *Ilex*. She has exhibited widely abroad and her work is reproduced on a wide range of stationery items produced by two companies. Her drawing of *Lavandula canariensis* adorns the cover of the 2005 *Index Seminum*.

Since 1995 Angie has taught botanical illustration in the Bath area and is the current President of the Bath Society of Botanical Artists.

RHS medals: Silver Gilt 2002, Silver 1993, Bronze 1994, 1997

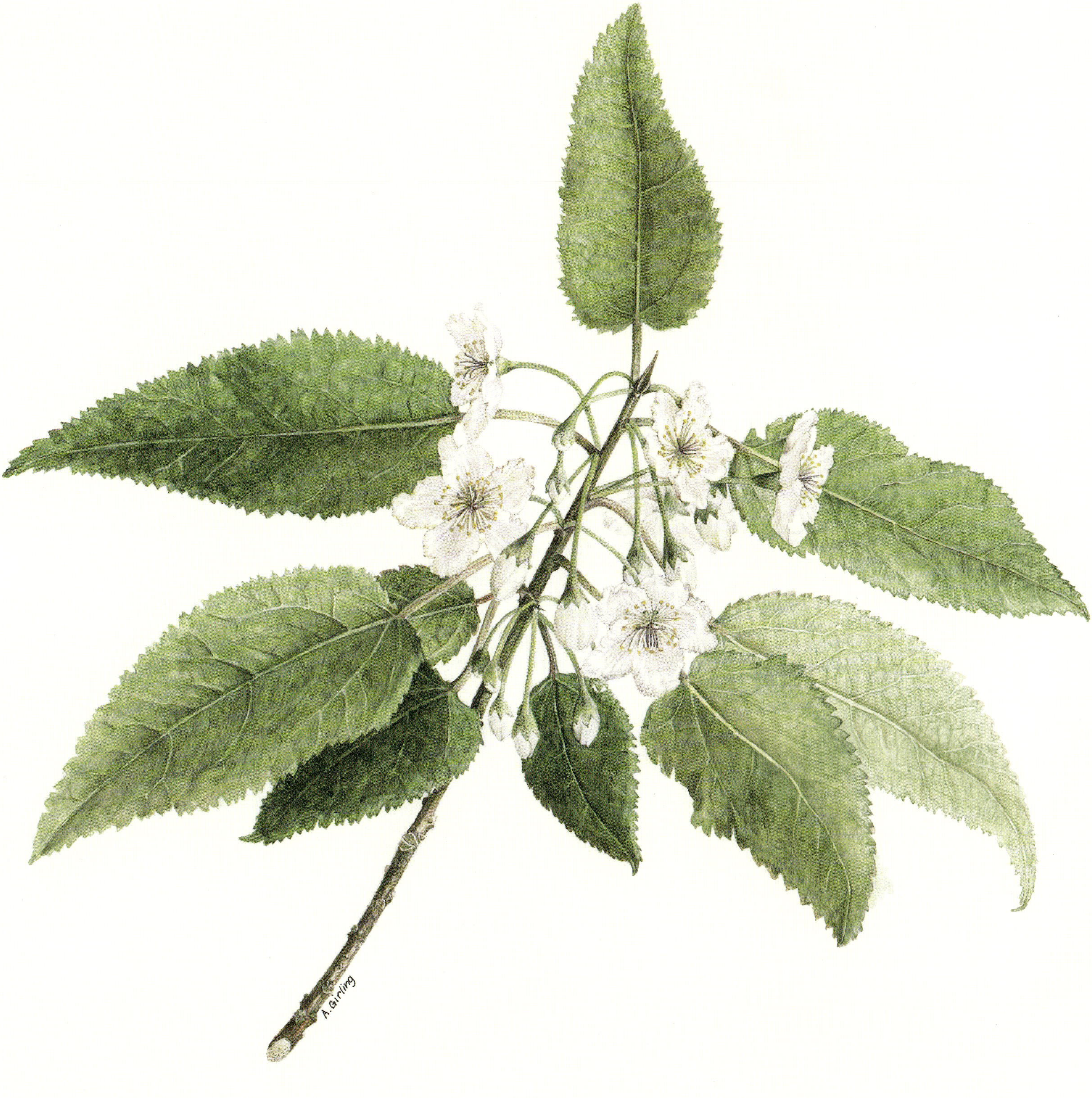
A. Girling

Ipomoea lobata Thell.
Family – Convulvulaceae

Barbara McLean

Ipomoea lobata is known as Spanish flag and is pollinated by birds. At least eight species of *Ipomoea* have been documented as having medicinal properties. Generally they are a source of resin known as jalap or scammony (formally used as a purgative). The best known British native member of this family is bindweed. Morning glory, another *Ipomoea,* is a popular garden annual. In the 1960s considerable concern was expressed that commercially available seeds of morning glory had hallucinogenic properties. Investigation by the Pharmaceutical Society showed only one species possessed the potential for this action.

About the artist

Barbara McLean has degrees in botany from the universities of Sydney and Strathclyde and is a Fellow of the Linnean Society of London. She has held research posts mostly in electron microscopy within departments of the University of Sydney; the Medical Research Council Laboratory of Molecular Biology, Cambridge; King's College London; Imperial College London and latterly at the University of Oxford. She has had research work ranging from the fine structure of muscle to structure and motility of plant cell membranes published in scientific journals.

Approaching retirement and having had a lifelong interest in art, Barbara obtained a Distinction in the Diploma in Botanical Illustration from the English Gardening School. This course revived an earlier interest in floral morphology and she is at present studying and recording *Tacca* species at Kew. Barbara is a Founder Member and Fellow of the Chelsea Physic Garden Florilegium Society and is also their Scientific Adviser.

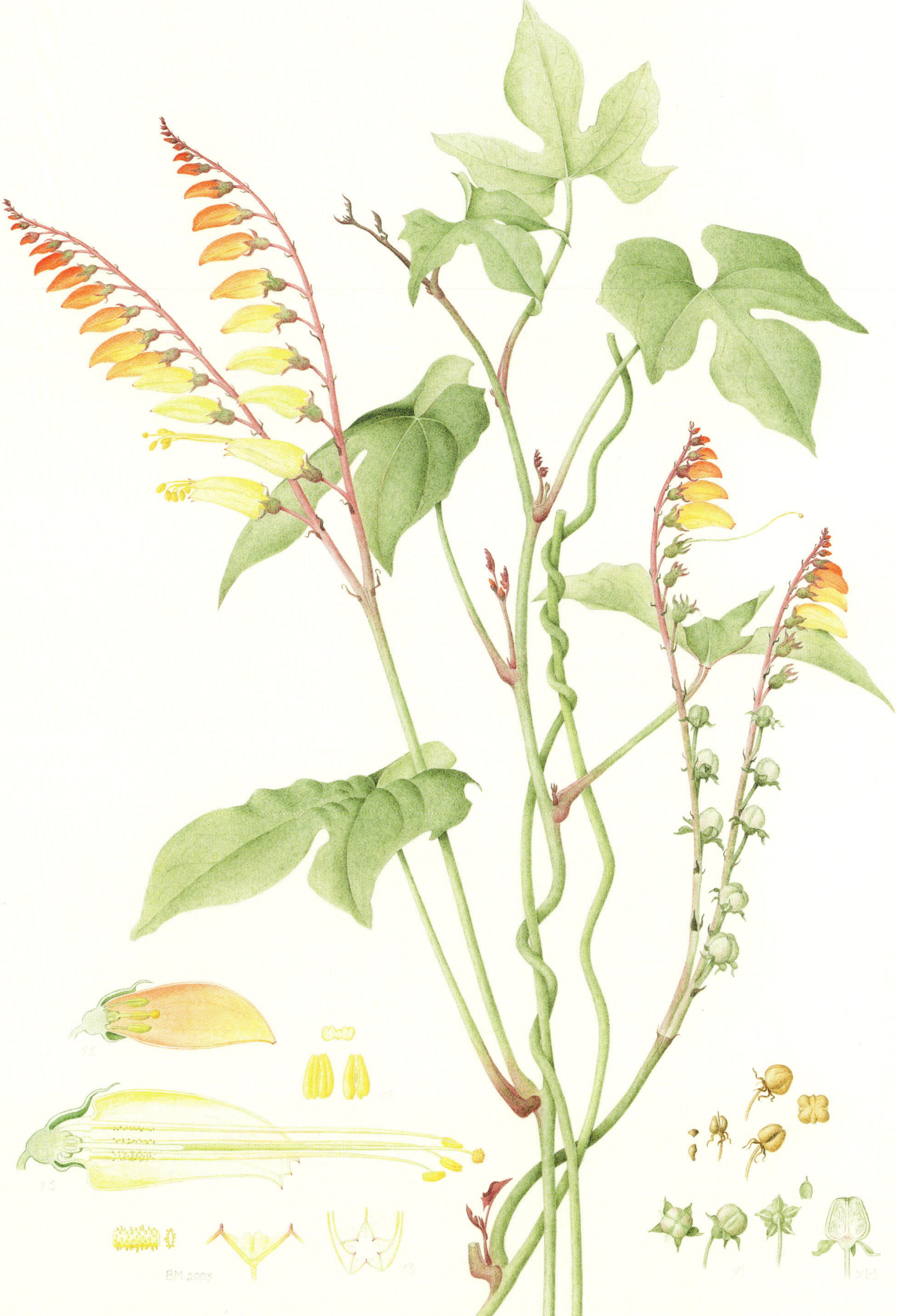
x6
x3
BM 2003
x3
x1
x1
x1.5

Jasminum nudiflorum Lindl.
Family – Oleaceae

Monica McAllen

Known as winter jasmine, *Jasminum nudiflorum* (from northern China) is widely grown in gardens. The flowers appear on the leafless branches between November and March. The plant is rambling in character and if the stems are supported they can grow to a height of three to six metres. It received an Award of Garden Merit from the RHS in 1993.

J. nudiflorum is one of many species. Jasmines are of doubtful use medicinally and a fatality from ingestion of the fruit of jasmine was recorded in the USA in 1861. Scented jasmines, including *J. officinalis*, are a source of an oil used in aromatherapy and are much valued in the perfumery industry.

About the artist

Monica McAllen MD FRCP spent her working life as consultant physician at University College Hospital, London. She specialised in asthma and allergy and published many research papers. She is a past President of the British Society for Allergy and Clinical Immunology. She retired from medicine in 1987.

She had been a painter all her life when time permitted and after retirement she took up botanical illustration. She studied under Anne-Marie Evans, both at the English Gardening School and in Rutland. She also studied miniature painting under Joan Joyce.

Monica quickly gained recognition as an artist of distinction, winning a Silver Gilt medal at her first RHS London Show in 1994. She has since exhibited regularly with the RHS. She has twice won the Certificate of Botanical Merit at the Society of Botanical Artists show. Her work is held by the RHS and by Chelsea Physic Garden.

Apart from exhibiting in London, Monica has had solo exhibitions at the Little Missenden Arts Festival and the Chalfont St Giles Festival in 1998. Her paintings have sold widely in both England and the USA. Monica's principal achievement in the field of botanical illustration is to have illustrated a wide range of Clematis species and cultivars. The resulting book, *Clematis – Plant Portraits of Species and Selected Cultivars* (2001) with a text by Robin Saville, was published to excellent reviews.

RHS medals: Silver Gilt 1994, 1996, Silver 1995, 1999

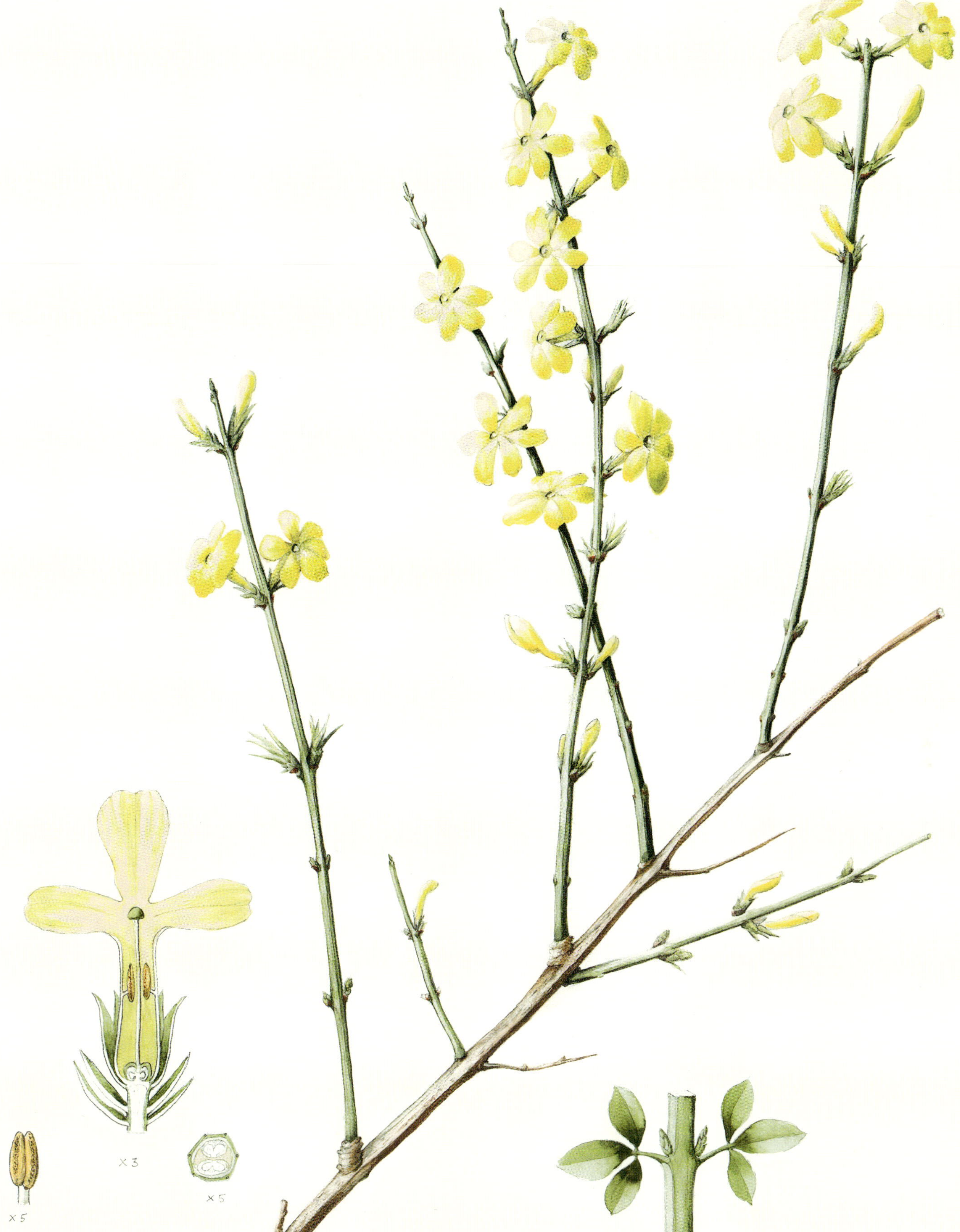
x 3
x 5
x 5
1·0 cm
MKM

Liquidambar orientalis Miller
Family – Hamamelidaceae

Lesley Catchpole

The authority for naming this plant, the oriental sweet gum, is Philip Miller, Gardener at Chelsea Physic Garden from 1722 to 1770. Miller is reported to have obtained his plant from France, the seed having come originally from the Levant where it is native. The medicinal product storax (the biblical balm of Gilead) is obtained by incising or beating the bark of the tree in spring, this causes the storax to be formed. The wounded bark is removed in the autumn and the liquid balsam obtained by pressing and the use of boiling water. Storax consists of a resin mixed with an oily liquid. In the 1900s it was stated to be seldom used. However it is listed as an ingredient of Friar's Balsam and benzoin inhalation in the *British Pharmacopoeia* in 2003.

About the artist

Lesley has studied botanical illustration at RHS Wisley, the English Gardening School and privately with Jill Coombs. She works with watercolour, pencil and pen and ink. She has exhibited with Sussex Artists, the Society of Botanical Artists and at the RHS in London. Her work is held in private collections in America, Canada, France and Brazil as well as at the Hunt Institute.

Apart from her painting, Lesley has had other careers with the Virology Department of the Wellcome Foundation and with a family business.

RHS medal: Silver 1993

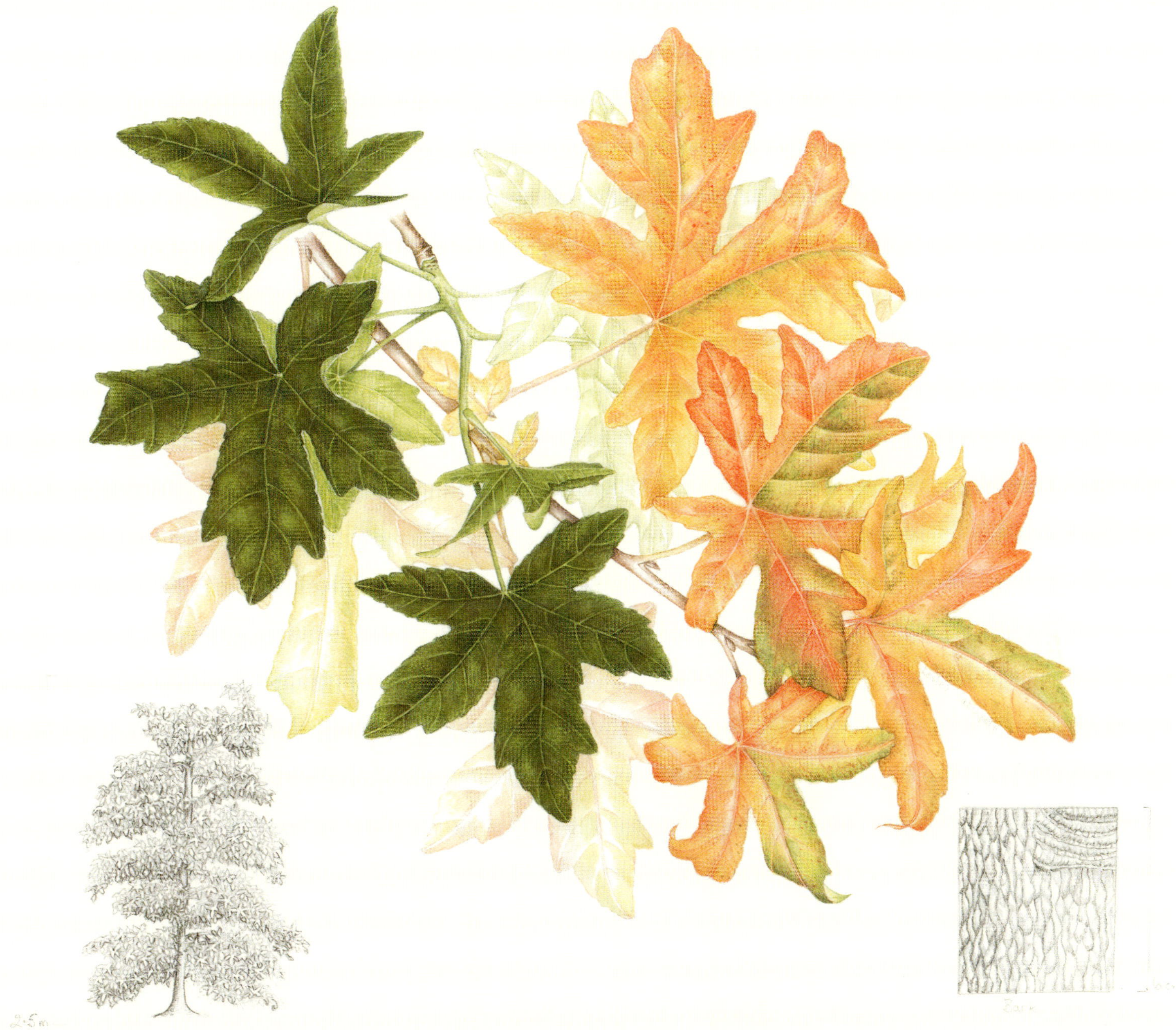
2.5m
Bark

Magnolia grandiflora L.
Family – Magnoliaceae

Margaret Stones

The discovery of this magnolia, the bull bay, is attributed to John Bartram (1699–1777). It is native to the southeastern United States. Bartram collected plants in America and was a regular contact of Philip Miller at Chelsea. Bartram's Garden in the suburbs of Philadelphia, the first botanic garden in the USA, is still open to the public. The name *Magnolia* commemorates Pierre Magnol, Professor of Botany at Montpellier Botanic Garden. Magnol taught Hans Sloane, the Physic Garden's benefactor, in Montpellier. The plant was introduced in 1734 and Chelsea Physic Garden was active in its establishment on many large estates in Britain.

In China, *M. officinalis*, known locally as *hou po*, was being used in the first century for relief of griping and flatulence.

About the artist

Margaret Stones has, for half a century, been one of the world's most productive and influential botanical illustrators. When asked to contribute an account of her career for this book the editor decided to quote Margaret verbatim because, otherwise, it would not be possible to convey with integrity the contribution of an artist with such a prodigious output of work. Margaret writes:

'Having been to art schools in Melbourne in the thirties, which at that time never taught botanical art, I left in 1951 for London where I knew I could see the work of the masters of that subject.

'The Royal Botanic Gardens, Kew and the Natural History Museum are great repositories and for me it was wonderful to see original work by Ehret, Sowerby, Redouté, the Bauers, Fitch and many others of the 18th and early 19th centuries, all working in their own particular way.

'What impressed me was the speed with which they must have worked, leaving behind a great volume of drawings, now mainly in museums and libraries. Some engraved and lithographed their own work.

'I have always worked independently for institutions. This gave me the freedom to practise in a general way.

'My first work was drawing in pen and ink from dried material on herbarium sheets. Working with botanists was, for me, the best introduction to botanical art.

'In 1956 I was invited to draw for *Curtis's Botanical Magazine* and I remained its principal contributing artist for twenty-five years.

'The RHS commissioned many lily drawings now held in the Lindley Library.

'*The Endemic Flora of Tasmania*, begun in 1962, went on for fourteen years and was published in six volumes. This was succeeded by a commission from Louisiana State University for two hundred works over ten years, also published; and a commission from the University of Virginia at Charlottesville for six Virginian wild flowers, published as part of Thomas Jefferson's 250th anniversary.

'My recent work since I returned to Australia in 2002 was to design a pair of tapestries for Government House, Melbourne, where they now hang.'

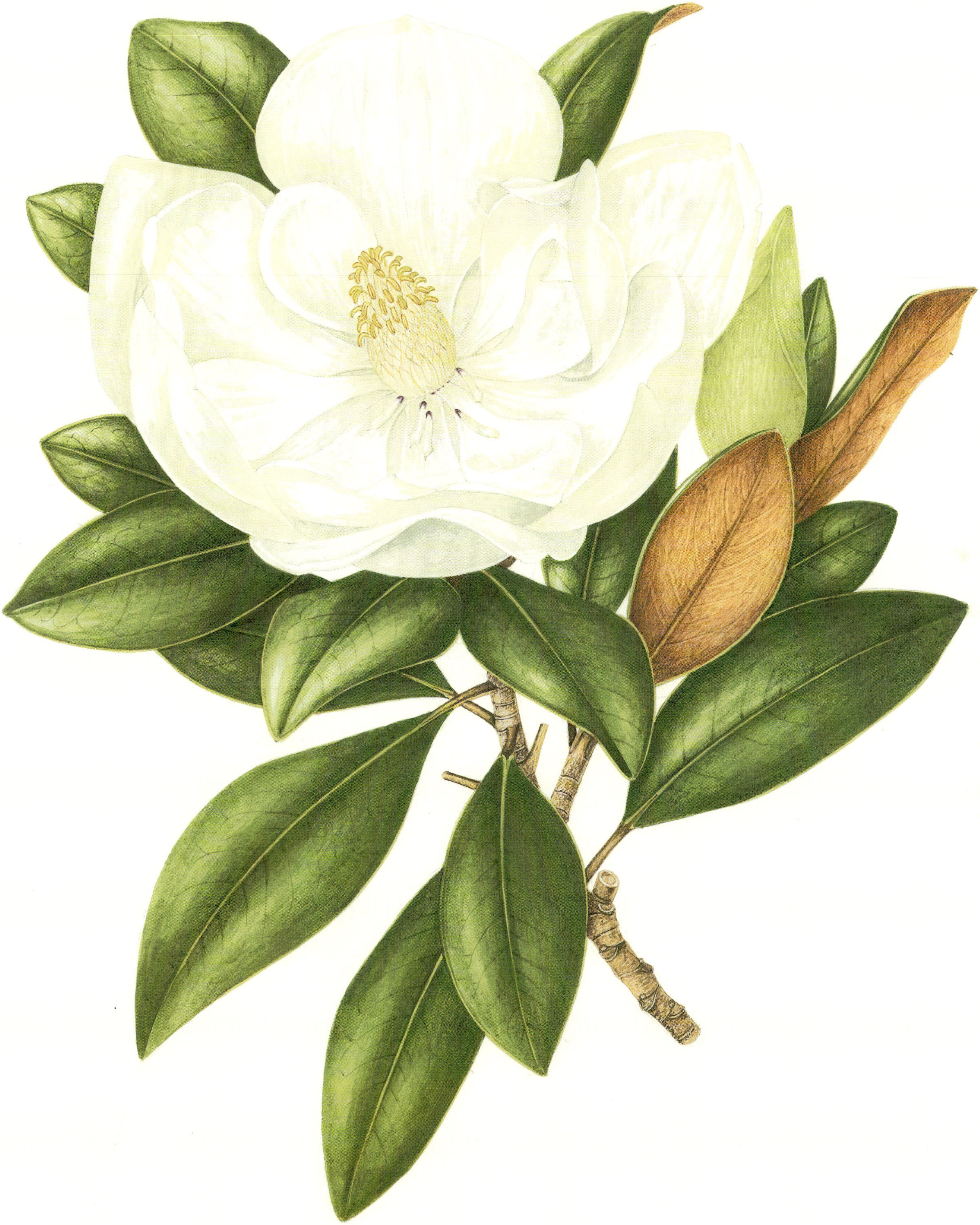

Morus alba L.
Family – Moraceae

Sarah Gould

Known as white mulberry, this species should not be confused with the more common black mulberry (*M. niger*). The white mulberry is a native of China and its leaves, which are vary variable in shape, are the traditional food for silkworms. The milky sap forms a sticky rubber-like latex, which is thought to give strength to the filaments of the silkworm. The white mulberry does not grow well in Britain. The fruit is insipid if eaten raw.

The attempt by King James I to set up a silkworm farm in the grounds of Buckingham Palace was frustrated because he had chosen the black mulberry. The fruit of the black mulberry has been used widely in a variety of confections.

This painting is on vellum.

About the artist

Sarah Gould qualified in 1978 as a landscape architect with a post-graduate Diploma in Urban Design from the Oxford School of Architecture. The Landscape Diploma course at the Gloucestershire College of Art and Design in Cheltenham included three terms of study at Pershore College of Horticulture which instilled a broad working knowledge and lifetime appreciation of plants.

In 1989, after several years in private practice and then at home with two young children, she studied botanical illustration with Anne-Marie Evans. In 1990 she joined the Leicestershire Society of Botanical Illustrators with whom she still paints. In 1996 she joined the Chelsea Physic Garden Florilegium Society. She became a Fellow in 2002.

In 1991 Sarah began to work on calfskin vellum and now paints almost exclusively on this medium, holding day workshops in vellum painting throughout the country. She has exhibited with the Royal Horticultural Society, the Hunt Institute, in New York, at the Natural History Museum in London and at the Hortus Gallery in Chelsea. Her work is held by the RHS Lindley Library and in numerous private collections in Europe and America.

RHS medals: Silver Gilt 2000, 2002

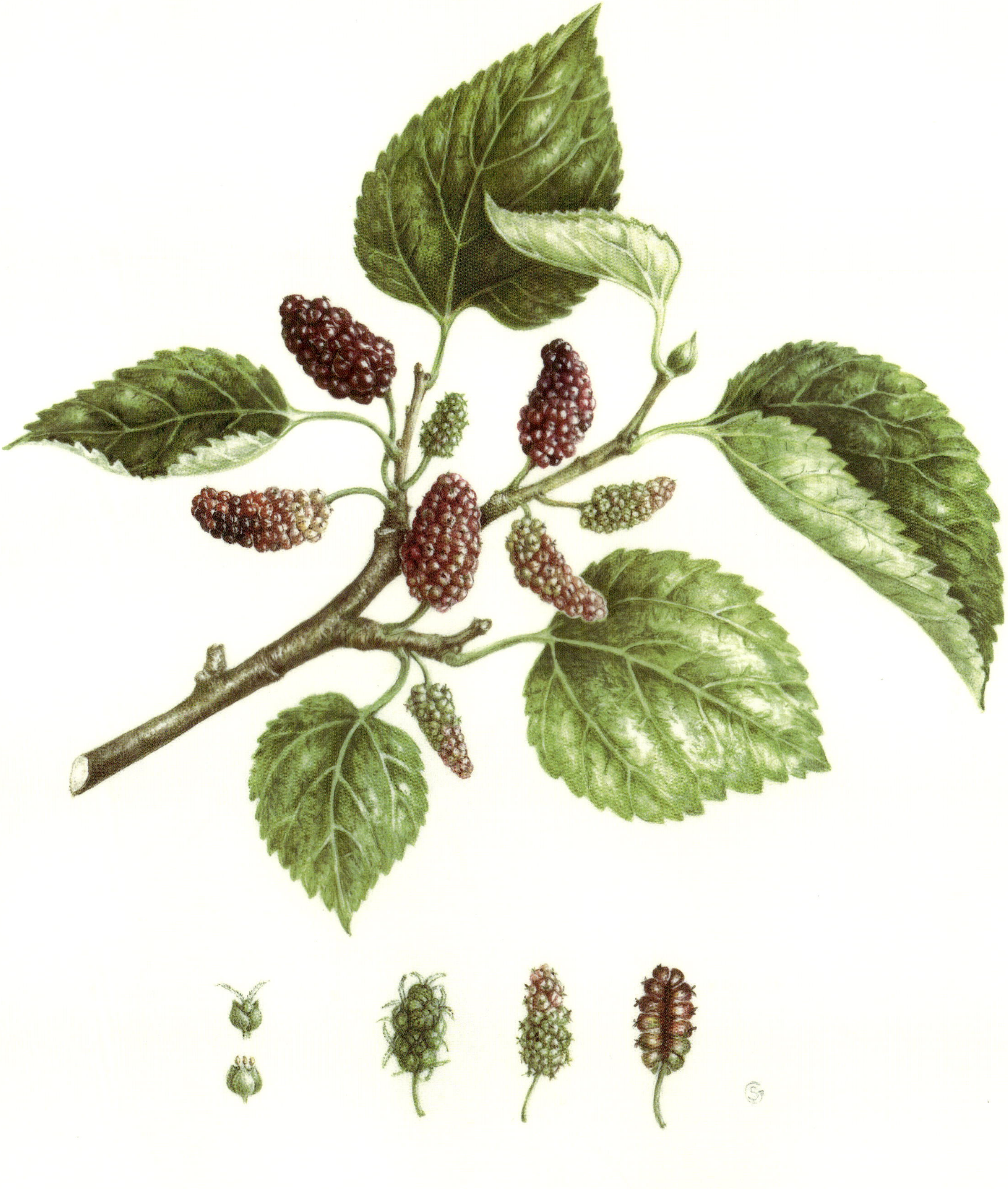

Olea europaea L.
Family – Oleaceae

Mariella Baldwin

The dove sent out by Noah from the ark brought back a leaf of the olive. Records mentioning the olive tree go back to some 3000 years BC and some evidence suggests that it was domesticated in the eastern Mediterranean area about 10,000 years ago. Olive oil is obtained from the ripe fruits, virgin oil being produced by cold pressing the fruit, which contains up to about 40 per cent oil in the fleshy part. Oil of a lower quality is made by using boiling water to aid further extraction. Olive oil is nutritious and mildly laxative. Apart from that of sunflower seeds and walnuts, it has the lowest saturated fat content of any common food source. At least four scientific reports show that olive oil is better than polyunsaturated oils in preventing heart disease. It has been used in the preparation of soaps and as an ingredient of liniments and ointments. Its main use in the twenty-first century is in the preparation of foods. The leaves were traditionally used to crown the victor in the Olympic games, a tradition that was revived at the 2004 games in Athens.

The Chelsea tree is the largest olive grown outside in Britain. It has been regularly pruned and is therefore difficult to age, but it is likely to have been planted in the late nineteenth century. In hot years it produces well. In the great drought of 1976 it produced about three kilos of fruit. In the hot summer of 2003 the olives were harvested, brined and consumed by the gardeners!

About the artist

Mariella was born in 1958 and took her Diploma in Botanical Illustration at the English Gardening School in 1988. She works in watercolour, pencil and pen and ink. During the past five years she has displayed her paintings at thirteen group exhibitions both in England and the USA. Apart from at Chelsea Physic Garden, her work is held by the Hunt Institute. Mariella is now herself involved with teaching at the English Gardening School, West Dean College and the London Sketch Club.

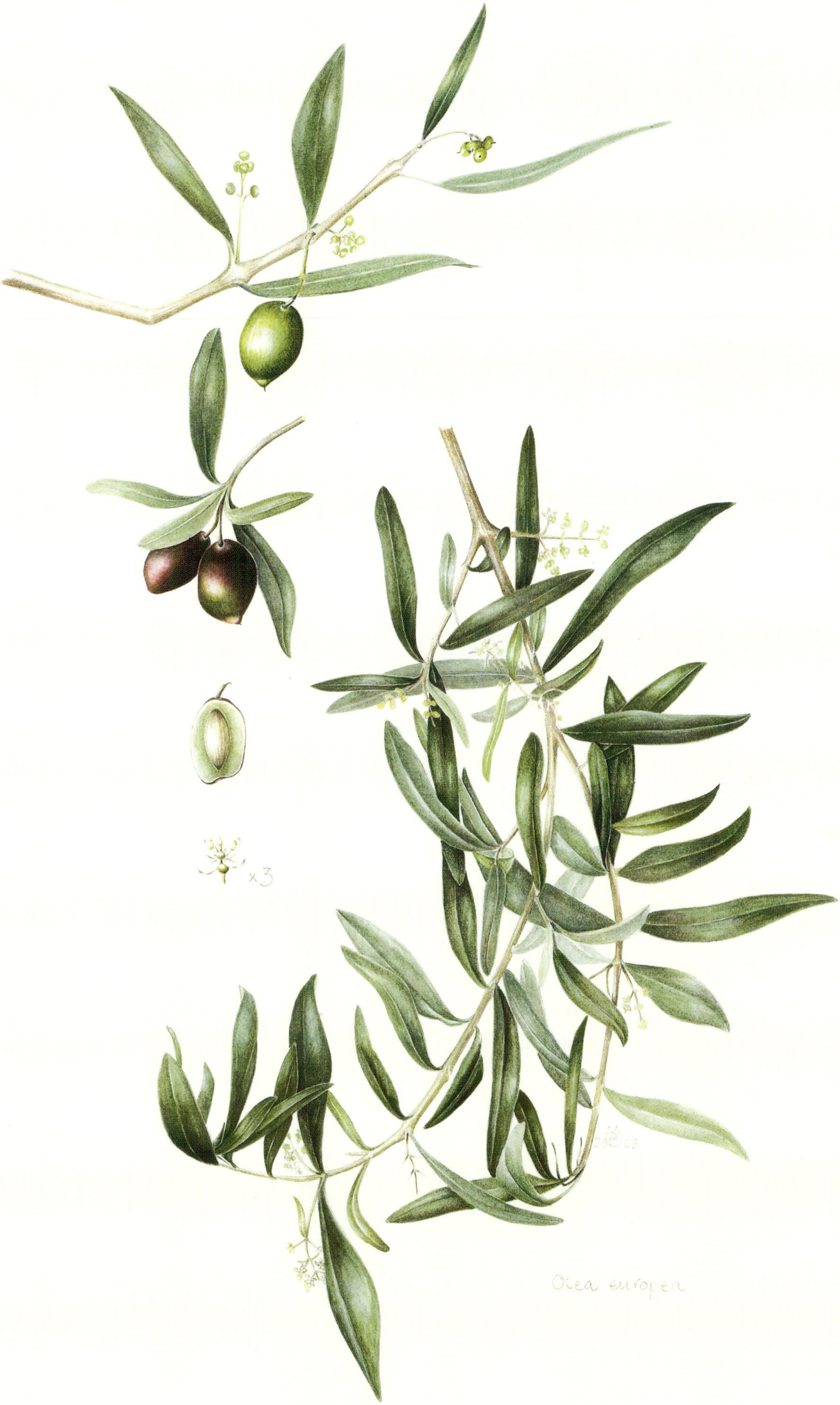
x3
Olea europea

Paulownia tomentosa (Thunb.) Steudel
Family – Scrophulariaceae

Janet Callender

Several species of *Paulownia* are available in cultivation. *P. tomentosa* is the best known and it can reach fifteen metres in height. The tree is native to central and west China, but was introduced to France from Japan in 1834. The genus is named after the daughter of Czar Paul I of Russia, Anna Paulowna.

The flowers are violet-blue and similar in shape to those of the purple foxglove in the same family. The flower buds are formed in autumn and are susceptible to early spring frosts. *Paulownia* is either grown as a tree or as a stooled specimen. The tree flowers in early spring before the leaves emerge. Stooled specimens do not produce flowers and are grown solely for the architectural value of their exceptionally large lobed leaves. The wood, when available, is used by wood turners to produce bowls and other domestic articles. It is particularly noted for its very low density. The wood has also been used in the manufacture of gunpowder.

About the artist

Janet Callender began serious botanical painting after retiring from teaching the violin and viola, and studied with various teachers at West Dean College, Chichester. She has been exhibited at three London Shows of the RHS, and has exhibited in Bath and with the Society of Botanical Artists at the Central Hall, Westminster. Over the past five years she has opened her studio for the Oxford Artweek.

Janet is a Fellow of the Chelsea Physic Garden Florilegium Society and has exhibited with the Society at the RHS in London, the Hunt Institute, the EU Patent Office in Munich and at the Footstool Gallery, St John's, Smith Square.

Her passion since the age of two has been gardening and she draws her inspiration from the plants she grows in her garden.

RHS medals: Silver for paintings – 1998, 1999, Silver for photographs – 1997, 1998, 2000, Bronze 2004

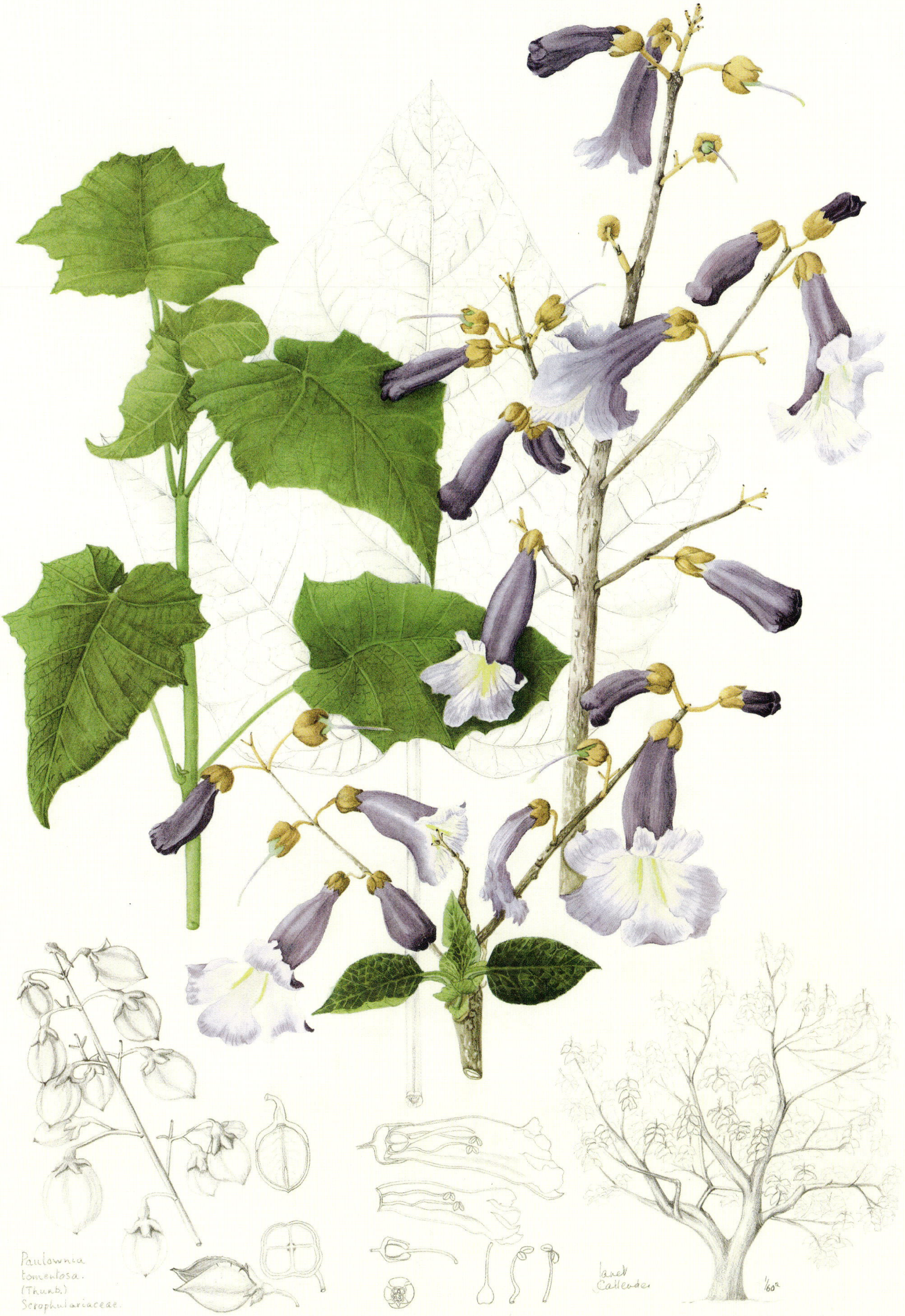
Paulownia
tomentosa.
(Thunb.)
Scrophulariaceae.

Penstemon heterophyllus Lindl.
Family – Scrophulariaceae

Peggy Dawe

The generic name of this plant refers to the prominent fifth stamen which has become a sterile staminode. There are over 200 species of *Penstemon* grown as garden bedding plants. They are native to the western United States. *P. heterophyllus,* the foothill penstemon from California, is considered to be one of the most beautiful of penstemons. The plants can be grown from seed or over-wintered as rooted cuttings in a frost-free environment.

About the artist

Peggy Dawe has lived all her life in Surrey and is a keen gardener, specialising in cottage-style gardening. She finds her garden a rich source of inspiration for painting in both watercolour and oils. She has specialised in botanical illustration since 1983 when she attended two courses on the subject tutored by Claire Dalby at Juniper Hall Field Centre near Dorking. She particularly enjoys the challenge of small flowers and intricate leaves.

Peggy is a member of the Society of Botanical Artists and the Society of Floral Painters as well as being a Fellow of the Chelsea Physic Garden Florilegium Society. She has exhibited widely in Europe and at RHS London Shows. Two of her illustrations of *Clematis* were acquired for the RHS Lindley Library collection. Peggy's paintings have been published as greetings cards and she has illustrated *The Gardener's Guide to Growing Hardy Geraniums* (Bath and Jones, 1994) and *Hardy Geraniums for the Garden* (Jones, 1992 and 2001).

Latterly, Peggy has travelled widely in Europe seeking out the mountain flora. She is a member of the Alpine Garden Society. Some of her paintings have been used to illustrate the *Alpine Garden Society Journal*. She has been awarded their Silver Artistic Medal for winning twenty-five first prizes at Alpine Garden Society shows.

RHS medals: Silver Gilt 2003, Silver 1989 (twice), 1991, 1993, 1995, 1996, 1998 (twice), 1999, 2000, Bronze 1987, 1988, 1991, 1993, 2005

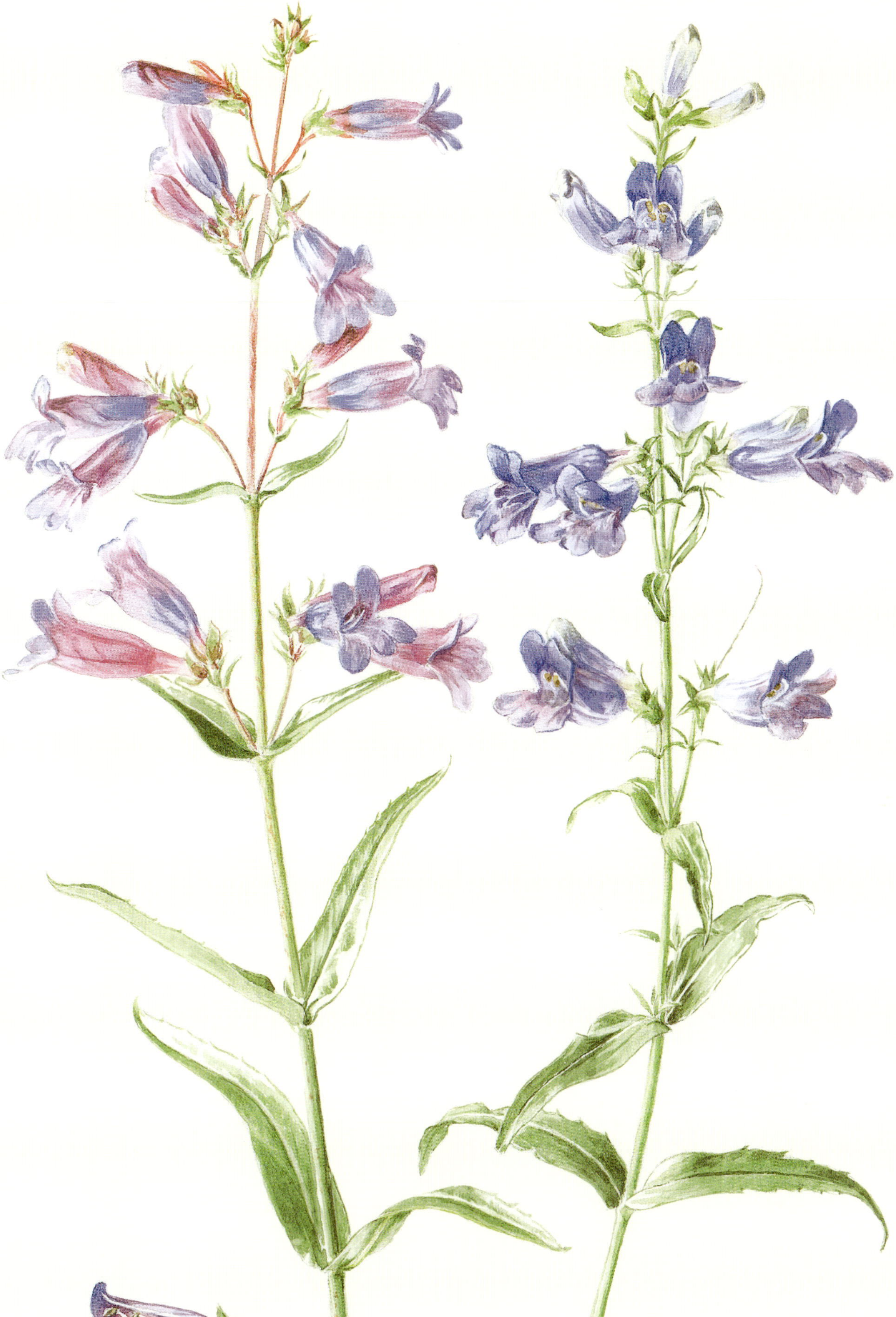
PD

Phlomis tuberosa L.
Family – Labiatae

Valerie Bradburn

Phillip Miller, who first cultivated this plant in 1759, is recorded as saying 'The leaves of Phlomis are greatly recommended by some persons to be used as Tea for Sore Throats'. This species is widely distributed from central and southeast Europe to central Asia.

About the artist

Valerie was born and grew up in southeast London. At grammar school she regretfully had to stop art classes at the age of eleven but at home was encouraged to be creative by her mother, who had studied at Chelsea Art College. Valerie obtained Advanced Level Botany as part of her sixth form studies and then qualified as a doctor at London University. Part of that training was the importance of careful observation and attention to detail. Service in the Royal Navy as a Surgeon Lieutenant followed until she married another Naval Officer and had two children. The family, after several moves around the UK and Canada, finally settled in Somerset where Valerie worked full time in Community Health Services for women and children.

Shortly before retiring from medicine Valerie attended classes with renowned teacher of botanical illustration Anne-Marie Evans. Since joining the Chelsea Physic Garden Florilegium Society Valerie has additionally exhibited at the Society of Botanical Artists, as well as at shows in her home West Country.

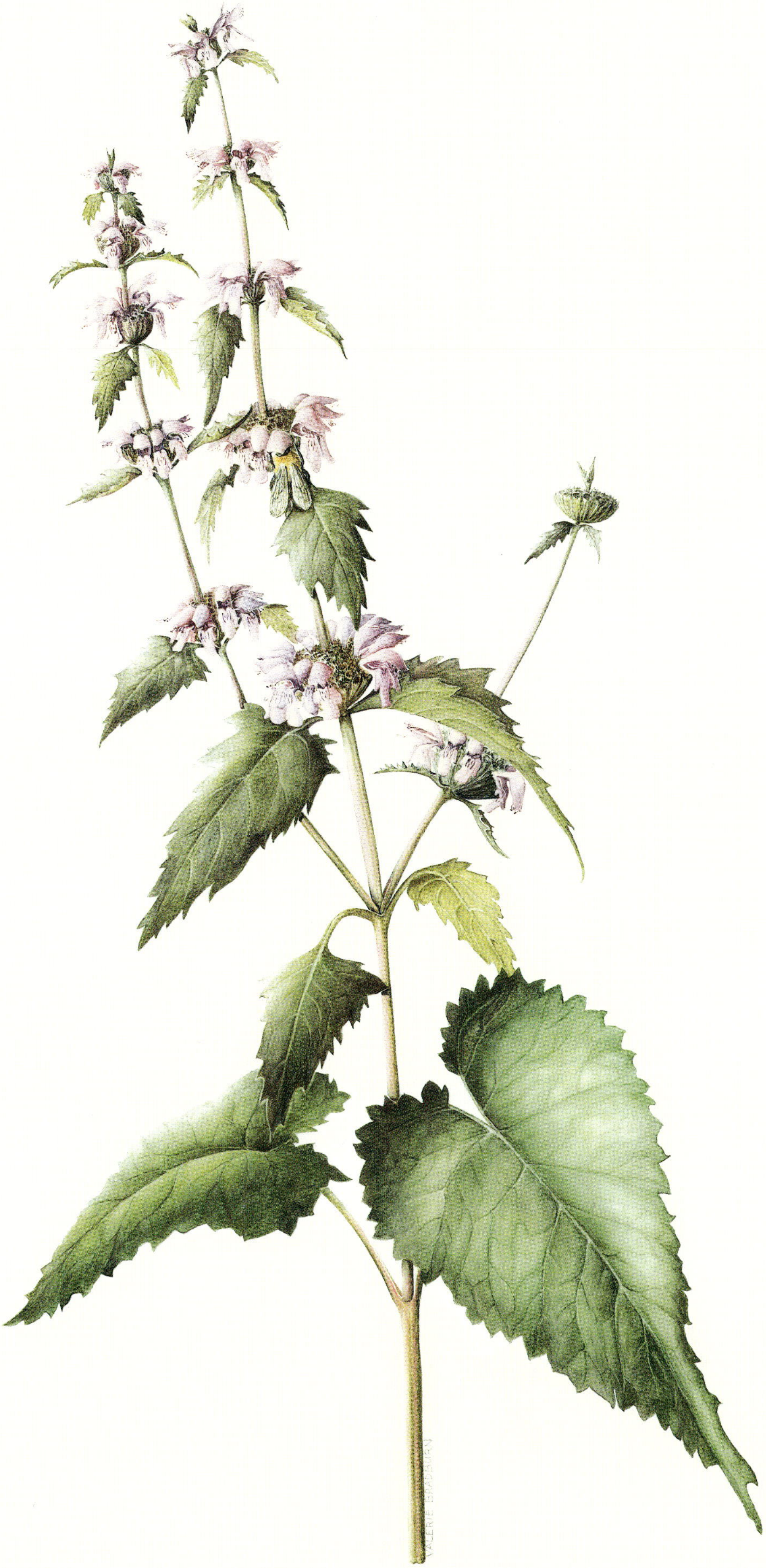
VALERIE BRADBURN

Platycodon grandiflorus (Jacq.) A. DC
Family – Campanulaceae

Masako Sasaki

This species, found in China, Manchuria and Japan, is known as the balloon flower on account of the shape of its inflated buds. The plant comes from northeast Asia and grows to about sixty centimetres in height. White, pink and double-flowered forms of *Platycodon* are also available from nurseries. *P. grandiflorus* is used in traditional Chinese medicine for the treatment of bronchitis, pneumonia, laryngitis and lung abscesses. In Japan it is used as an expectorant.

About the artist

Masako Sasaki was born in 1939 and trained for more than ten years in Japan in the fields of metal carving and enamelling. She is an enamel jewelling artist and woodblock printmaker.

After moving to England in 1988 she started botanical painting, studying at Sutton College of Liberal Arts and with Annie Farrer at Kew. Masako has also studied botany in the wild with the Field Studies Council.

She has twice been awarded the Certificate of Botanical Merit at the annual Society of Botanical Artists exhibition (1994, 1998).

Masako is an active member of several societies including the Society of Botanical Artists, the American Society of Botanical Artists and the Japanese Association of Botanical Illustration. She has exhibited widely and, since her recent return to live in Japan, has had a solo exhibition in Tokyo and has participated in a group show of wildlife and botanical art, again in Tokyo. Apart from the Chelsea Physic Garden archive, her work is held by the Hunt Institute and in the Shirley Sherwood collection.

RHS medals: Gold 1994, 2001, Silver Gilt 1998, Silver 1996

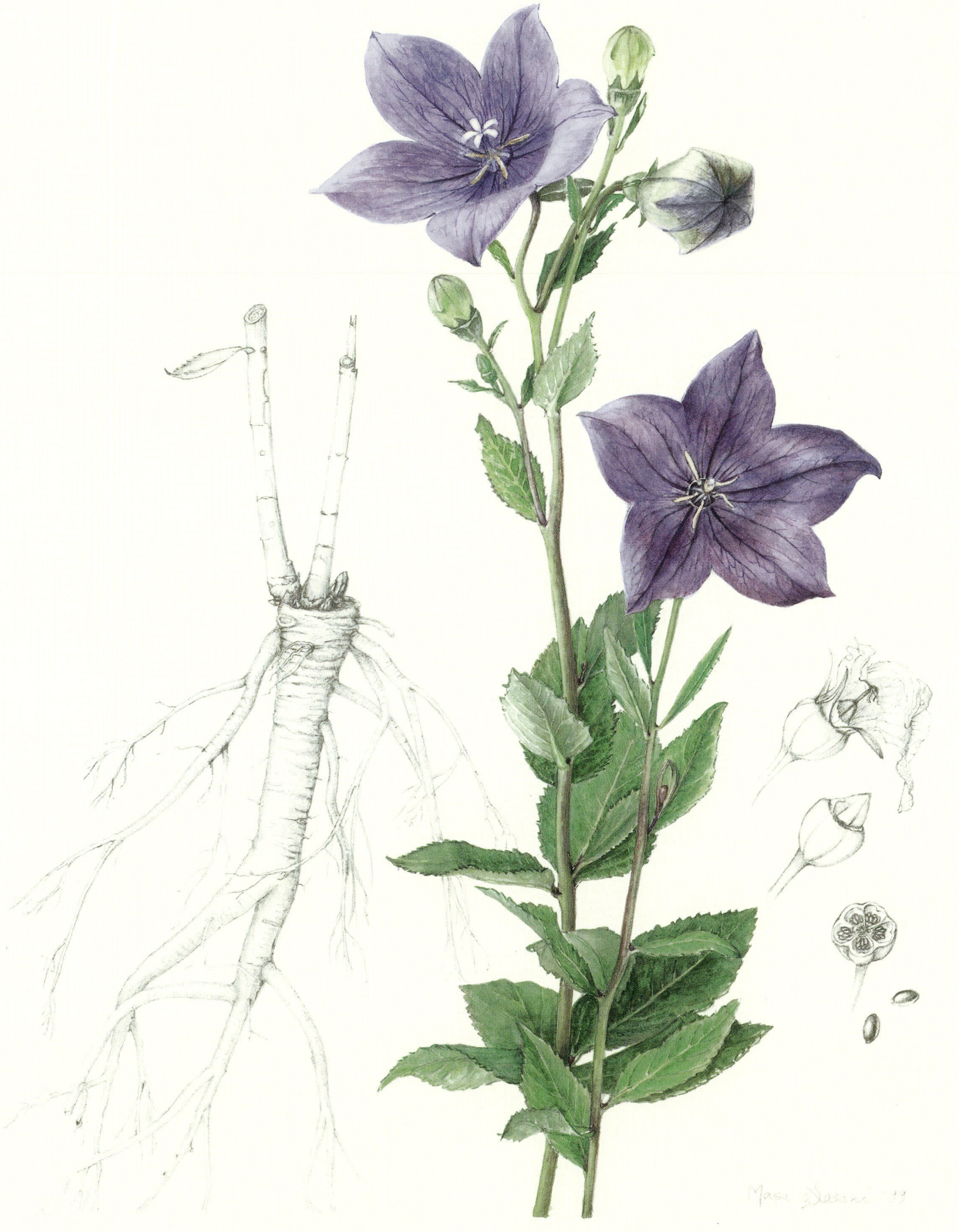

Pulsatilla vernalis Miller
Family – Ranunculaceae

Martin Allen

The authority for naming this plant from the European mountains and Siberia is the Chelsea Gardener, Philip Miller. Its common name is spring pasque flower. There are several pasque flowers in garden cultivation and all should be regarded as poisonous.

The common pasque flower, *P. vulgaris*, was used in medicine against nervous exhaustion, catarrh and as a sedative. Four monographs containing pulsatilla appeared in the 1934 *British Pharmaceutical Codex.*

About the artist

Martin Allen graduated in 1991 from Nottingham University with a BSc in Horticulture. He began painting in 1992 as therapy for a long-term illness (ME), at a course taught by Colin Swinton. He works as a Consultant in Horticulture and Botanical Conservation in the northeast of England and is painting modern botanical art for an exhibition.

Martin was awarded the Society of Botanical Artists Certificate of Botanical Merit in 1996 and 1998.

He was commissioned to design plates for the Royal Horticultural Society's Collectors' series (1995–1998) and has exhibited at Addendum, Henley-on-Thames 1997 (solo) and Hortus, London 2001 (group exhibition).

RHS medals: Gold 1995, 1997

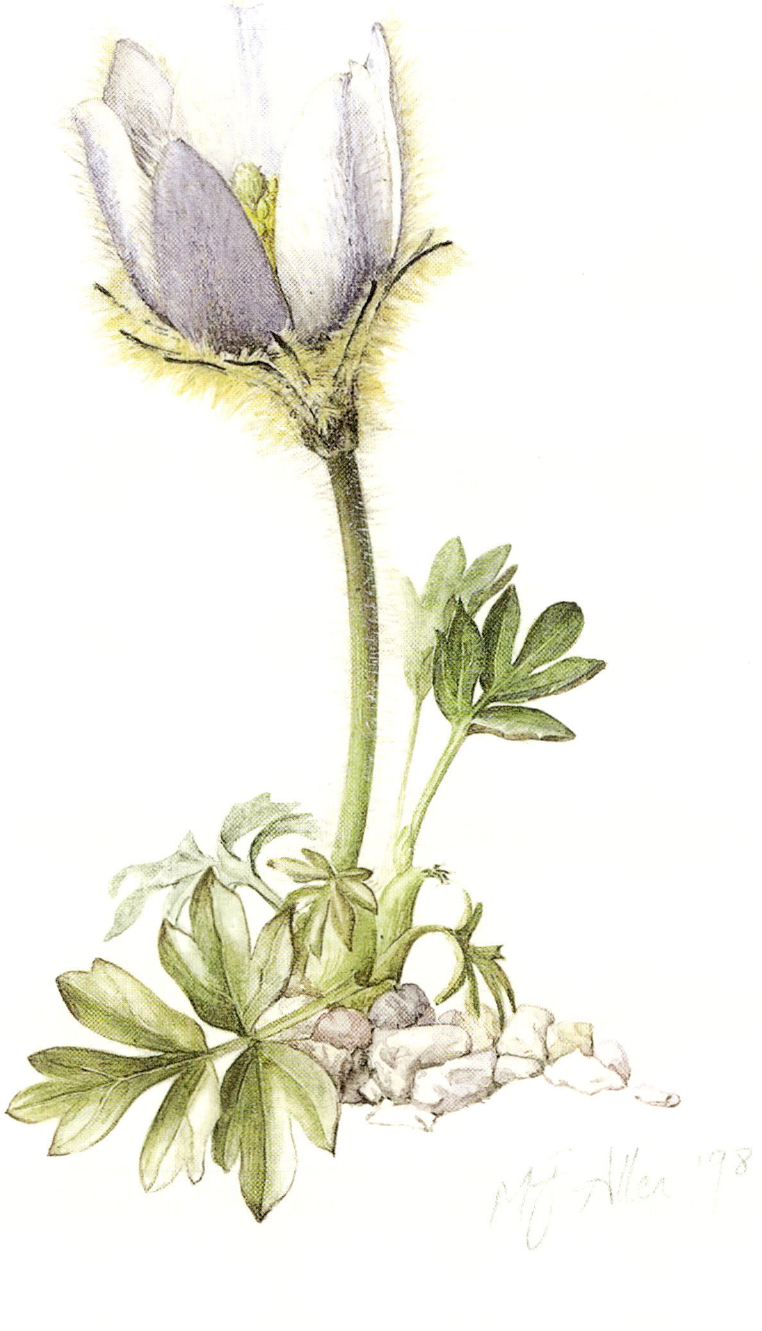

Punica granatum L. (1)
Family – Punicaceae

Joanna Craig-McFeely

Although the pomegranate arrived in Britain in the fourteenth century, it is one of the earliest recorded plants, being specifically mentioned in the Old Testament book of Exodus, dated about 1500 BC. It is also mentioned in the books of Numbers and Deuteronomy where it was growing in 'a land of wheat, and barley, and vines and fig trees'. Some 400 years later it appears in the Song of Solomon. A fine specimen of pomegranate will be familiar to visitors to Chelsea Physic Garden, growing on the wall adjacent to the Swan Walk entrance.

The pomegranate is native to the eastern Mediterranean area through to the Himalayas and is widely grown through Europe. It is also known as the Carthaginian apple, a reference to the ancient city of Carthage in Tunisia. It is listed in Joseph Miller's *Index Horti Chelseiani* of 1772 as one of the many plants growing in Chelsea Physic Garden at that time.

The rind (outer coat of the fruit), the fruit pulp and the bark have all been used in medicine. The uses range from expelling tapeworms, treating conjunctivitis and a cure for dysentery to use as a contraceptive. An extract of the dried fruit has been shown experimentally to inhibit the growth of many bacteria.

This painting is on vellum.

About the artist

Joanna is married with four grown-up children. On leaving school she would have liked to attend art college but instead qualified as a physiotherapist and later set up in private practice. Despite the demands of married life and a full-time career she also ran part of the British Ski Federation for several years and became a silversmith.

In 1997 with no previous art training, after buying a small botanical painting of a chestnut, she was so intrigued by it that she decided to study the art of botanical illustration. A year later she gave up her physiotherapy practice and since then has been painting and exhibiting regularly in London, the provinces and abroad. She paints in watercolour on paper and vellum.

Joanna has exhibited at the RHS London Shows regularly and in 2003 she showed eighteen paintings of *Magnolia* on vellum. In 2004 Joanna was awarded the Joyce Cummings Presentation Award for best botanical watercolour at the Society of Botanical Artists annual exhibition. Her lily portrait appears in *The Art of Botanical Painting* (2004). Her work has been selected for inclusion in the Highgrove Florilegium which is being created under the umbrella of the Prince of Wales's Charitable Foundation and which will celebrate and record in a permanent way the flora in the garden at Highgrove.

Joanna is currently a member of the Chelsea Physic Garden Florilegium Society, the Society of Botanical Artists, the Society of Floral Painters and the American Society of Botanical Artists.

RHS medals: Silver Gilt 1999, 2002, 2003, Silver 2001, Bronze 1999

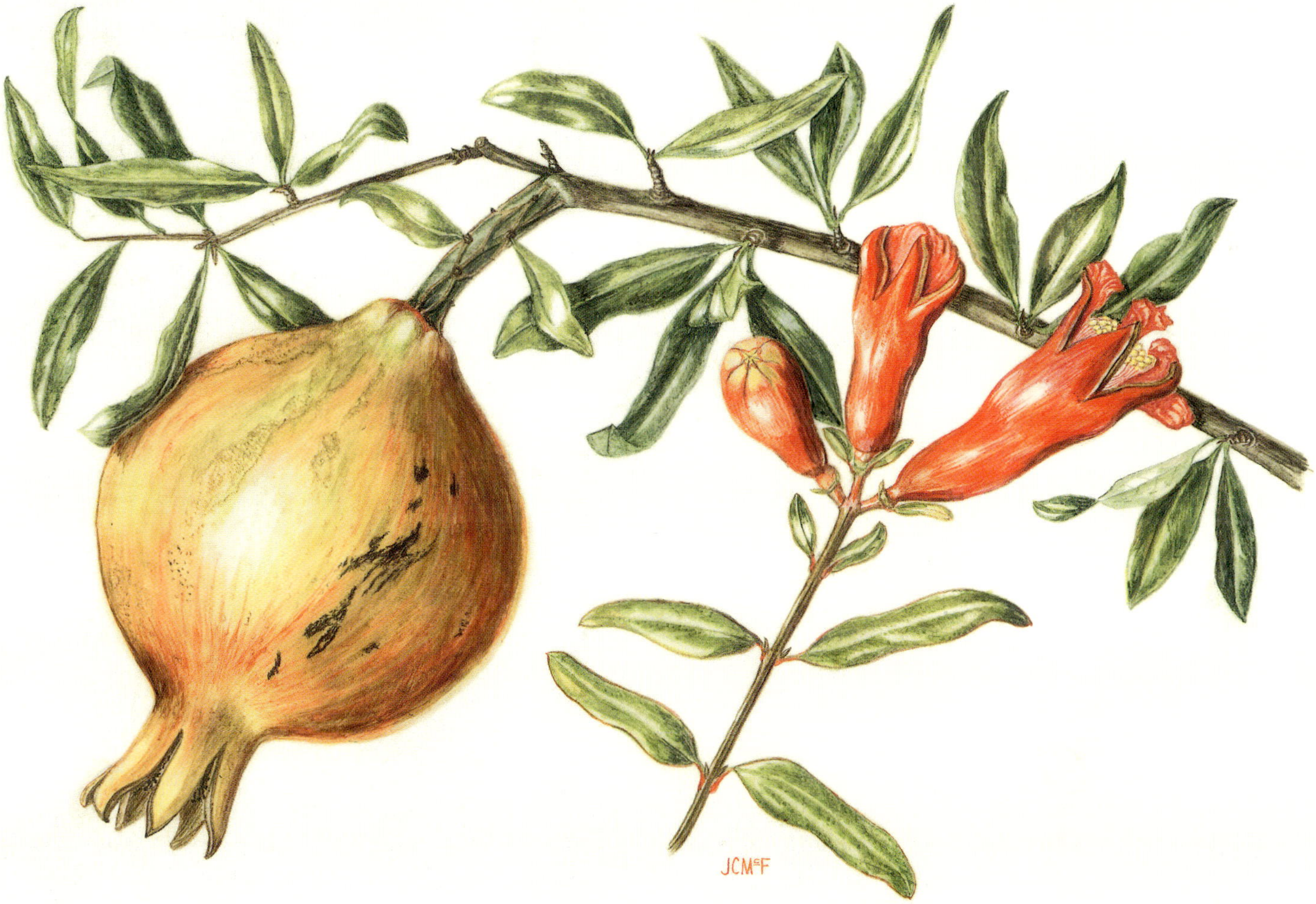
JCMcF

Punica granatum L. (2)
Family – Punicaceae

Caroline Hervey-Bathurst

For information about this plant, see the previous plate.

About the artist

Caroline studied painting at St Martin's School of Art with Jehan Daly, at Sir John Cass College with Vivian Pitchforth RA, and at the English Gardening School with Anne-Marie Evans.

She has exhibited at the Royal Society of Portrait Painters for fifteen years, the Royal Academy of Arts Summer Exhibitions for eleven years and, latterly, at the Woodhay Gallery, the Ursus Gallery, New York and botanical art exhibitions in Mayfair galleries. Caroline has had three solo exhibitions at Piers Feetham Gallery, London (1997, 2000 and 2004). She is often commissioned to paint portraits, family groups, houses, gardens, landscapes, interiors and horses and dogs.

Apart from at Chelsea Physic Garden her work is held in the British Museum (a portrait of John Gere, former Keeper of Prints and Drawings) and in the collection of the late Sir Brinsley Ford.

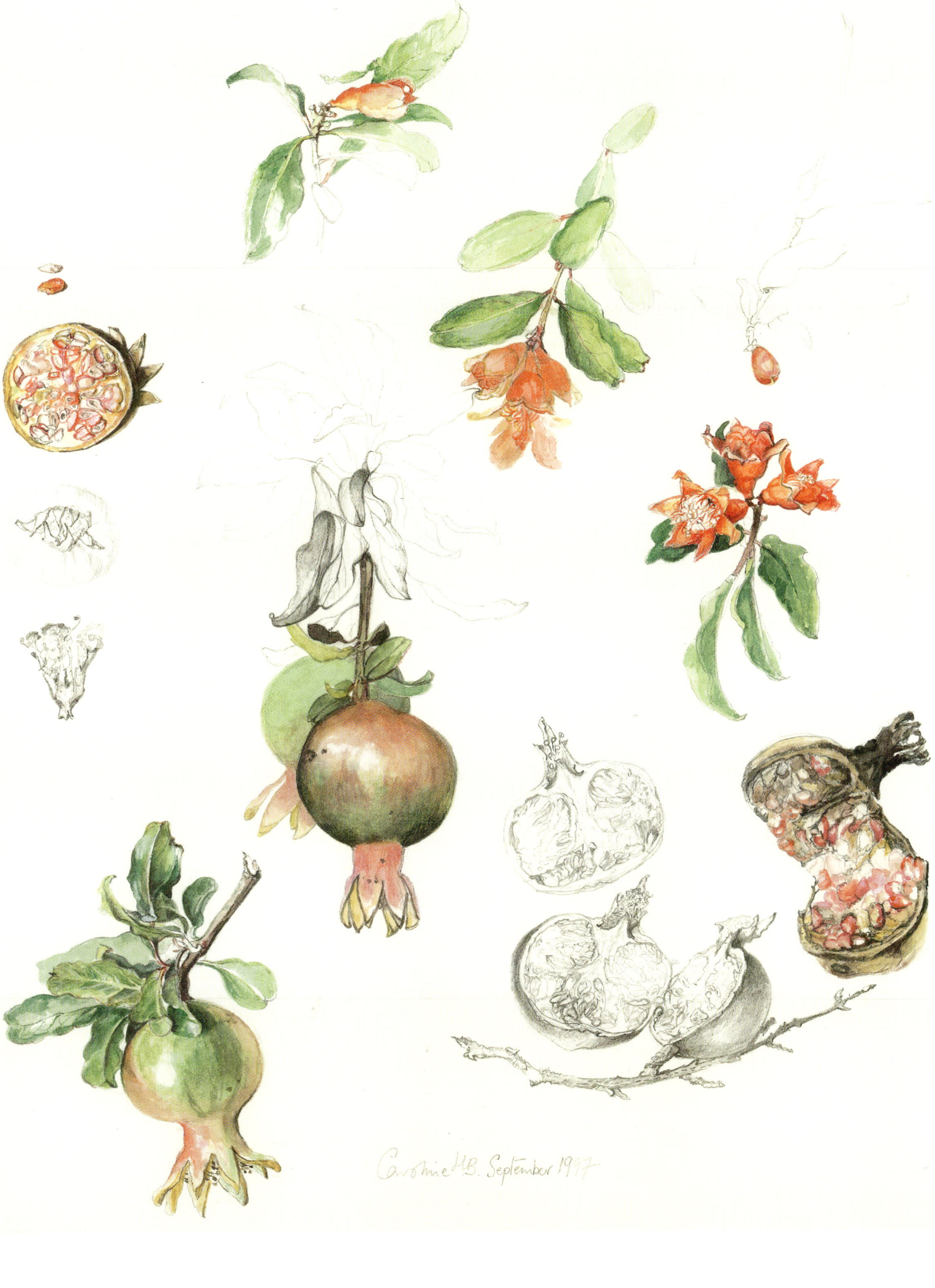
Caroline H.B. September 1997

Quercus coccifera L.
Family – Fagaceae

Kay Rees-Davies

The Biblical 'oak' in Genesis (35.8) refers to *Quercus coccifera*, an evergreen tree with prickly foliage, native to the western Mediterranean, southern Europe and northwest Africa. It is commonly called the kermes oak because it is often infested with a sap-feeding insect, *Coccus ilicis*, which can be collected to yield a scarlet dye similar to cochineal (which, itself, is manufactured from sap-feeding insects on *Opuntia* cactus plants). This oak-derived material is the scarlet of biblical references. The word kermes derives from the Turkish word for red. The Physic Garden tree was planted in about 1940.

In Britain only two species of oak occur, *Quercus robur* being the commoner, dramatically different in appearance from this Mediterranean species. *Q. robur* is interwoven into the history and legend of England. Oaks are slow growing trees that can reach a great circumference over the centuries. King Arthur's Round Table, which can be viewed in Winchester, is reputed to be a single slice cut from a tree of exceptional diameter.

The medicinal use of oak is derived from the astringent properties of its bark, preparations of which may be used as a gargle for sore throats or in lotions or ointments to treat haemorrhoids.

About the artist

Kay Rees-Davies, who lives on the North Wales coast, is a freelance artist who specialises in botanical illustration and flower portraiture.

Her work has been shown at many group exhibitions and galleries all over the UK including the Society of Botanical Artists and the Royal Horticultural Society. Kay was awarded Gold medals for her RHS exhibits of Ivies from the National *Hedera* Collection, Old Apple Varieties and for a collection of *Streptocarpus* species.

Her work is in several permanent collections including the Hunt Institute, the Lindley Library of the Royal Horticultural Society and the Shirley Sherwood Collection.

Kay Rees-Davies has had work published in *An Introduction to Drawing Flowers* (1994), in *Plantas Endemicas e Avores Indiginas de Cabo Verde* (1995), and in *Contemporary Botanical Artists* (1996). Illustrations have been published in the *Curtis's Botanical Magazine* (1997) and *Watsonia* (1999). Her work was included in *Fine Botanical Paintings* (2000) and in *Arte y Botanica* (2002). The most recent publication including some of Kay's work is *The Art of Botanical Painting* (2004).

Kay Rees-Davies is a member of the SBA, and was awarded the Society's Certificate of Botanical Merit in 1994 and again in 2003. She is a founder member and President of the North Wales Society of Fine Art and also a member of the Botanical Artists of Ness Botanic Garden, where she has been tutor for many years. She holds classes and workshops throughout the country.

RHS medals: Gold 1996, 1998, 2003, Silver Gilt 1994, Silver 1991, Bronze 1992

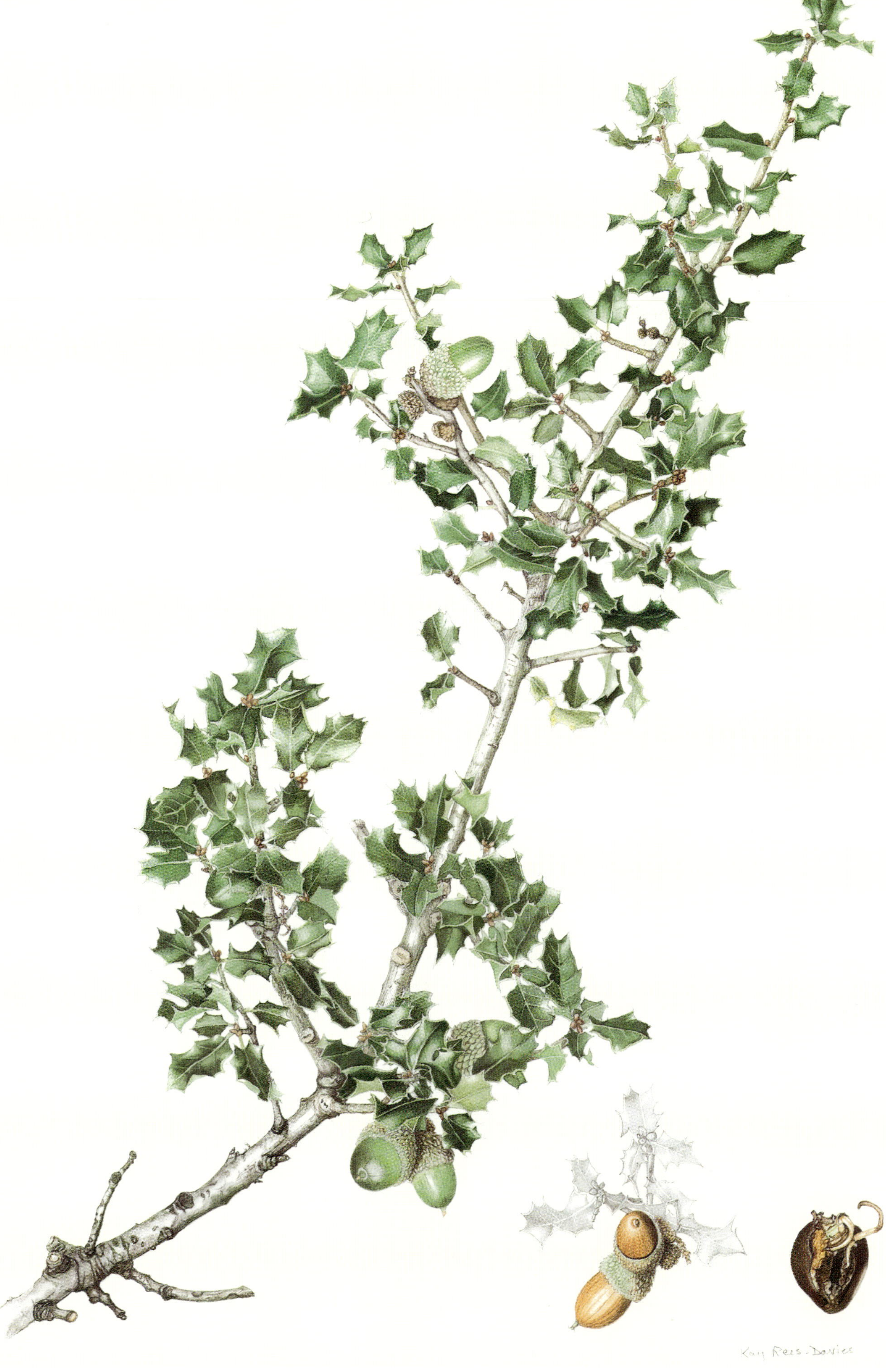
Kay Rees-Davies

Ribes americanum Miller
Family – Grossulariaceae

Shirley-Ann Nunn

This flowering currant, from the northern United States, is in the same genus as the black and red fruiting currants and the gooseberry. The Chelsea plant was obtained from Moscow Botanic Garden. The blackcurrant, *R. niger*, is used to prepare the well known blackcurrant juice which is a rich source of vitamin C. The leaves, fruit and bark have been used in herbal medicine for conditions such as sore throats, fevers and as a diuretic.

About the artist

Shirley was a Sister at the Royal Marsden Hospital until 1979, when she decided to pursue her interest in botanical painting. In 1986 she attended the English Gardening School's first course on botanical painting. She became a Member of the Society of Botanical Artists in 1988 and served for a year as a Member of their Council. Shirley became a Member of the Chelsea Physic Garden Florilegium Society in 1998 and rapidly achieved the status of Fellow.

In the early nineties she was commissioned to undertake a memorial painting to Harry Burlinson, an eminent Pharmacist and a world authority on the manufacture of medicinal tablets. This entailed considerable research into his life and work. The plants associated with him were identified and specimens found, or grown in Shirley's garden. The painting, which illustrates more than twenty plants, now hangs in Birdsgrove House in Derbyshire, the Convalescent Home of the Royal Pharmaceutical Society. The research associated with the painting and a photograph were recorded in the Christmas edition of *The Pharmaceutical Journal* in 1993 under the title of 'A Botanical Tablet'.

Following publication of 'A Botanical Tablet' Shirley was asked to paint fifteen portraits of medicinal plants for the 75th anniversary calendar of the National Pharmaceutical Association (NPA). Initially the commission was only for copyright but after publication the NPA Board decided to purchase all the paintings. The paintings were shown at the RHS in November 1995 and were awarded a Silver medal.

In 1996 Shirley was commissioned to paint a series of illustrations of *Alstroemeria* for a plant breeder who was introducing new varieties and naming them after members of the Royal Family. Shirley was required to produce two original paintings of each new hybrid. One painting was presented to the named Royal by the breeder, the other was for his private collection. Shirley painted 'Princess Alexandra', 'Princess Alice'and 'Queen Elizabeth the Queen Mother'.

This painting of *Ribes americanum* was included in the Florilegium Society's gold medal winning exhibit at the RHS Westminster Show in 1999. It was included together with her painting of *Helleborus niger* as part of the Society's exhibition at the Hunt Institute in April 2000.

As well as painting, Shirley's other interest was gardening. For many years her garden in Surrey was open under the National Gardens Scheme.

Shirley exhibited annually with the Society of Botanical Artists. She also exhibited at Hillier's Arboretum in Hampshire, the RHS and a number of other venues.

Shirley died in May 2001.

RHS medals: Silver 1986, 1995

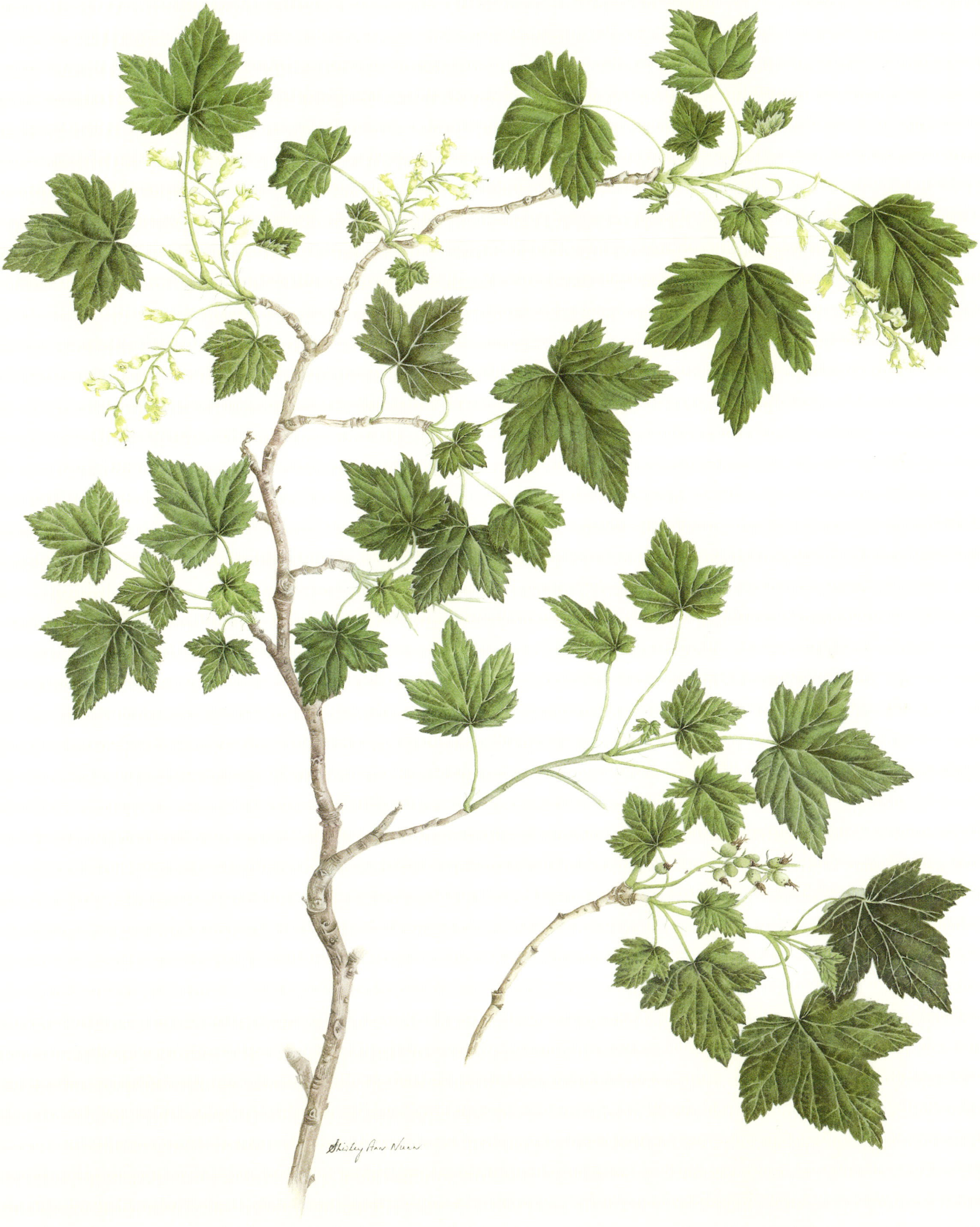
Shirley Ann Nunn

Romneya coulteri Harvey
Family – Papaveraceae

Elisabeth Sherras Clark

This plant, also known as the matilija poppy and California tree poppy, was discovered by Thomas Coulter (1793–1843). The generic name *Romneya* is after Coulter's friend T. Romney Robinson, an Irish astronomer. In California and Mexico it is found growing in the scrubland of the coasts and canyons. In gardens the plant can be difficult to establish but, once established, the plant develops invasive underground roots which will penetrate hard landscaping.

About the artist

Elisabeth received a traditional art training at the Ruskin School of Art, Oxford. For many years she taught art and design at Tiffin Girls' Grammar School and lastly was Head of Creative Textiles at Tolworth Girls' Comprehensive School. In addition to full-time teaching Elisabeth continued painting in oils, engraving glass and designing textiles. She recently came to watercolour painting (which was absent from the Ruskin curriculum) and it was a revelation when she discovered that she could bring life and vibrant colours to her painting of flowers. Elisabeth has concentrated on painting roses, paeonies and poppies.

Elisabeth has a passion for travel and began illustrating the subjects she saw in Kashmir, New Zealand and Guyana. In 1993 she accompanied an Oxford University plant collecting expedition to the Cameroon in Central Africa, the third wettest country in the world — during the wet season! She painted whatever plant was presented to her and this resulted in a solo exhibition at the Royal Geographical Society and a Silver medal at an exhibit at the RHS.

In recent years she has taught her skills at West Dean College, RHS Wisley and the USA, New Zealand and Australia where she spends the winter months.

RHS medal: Silver, 1990, 1992

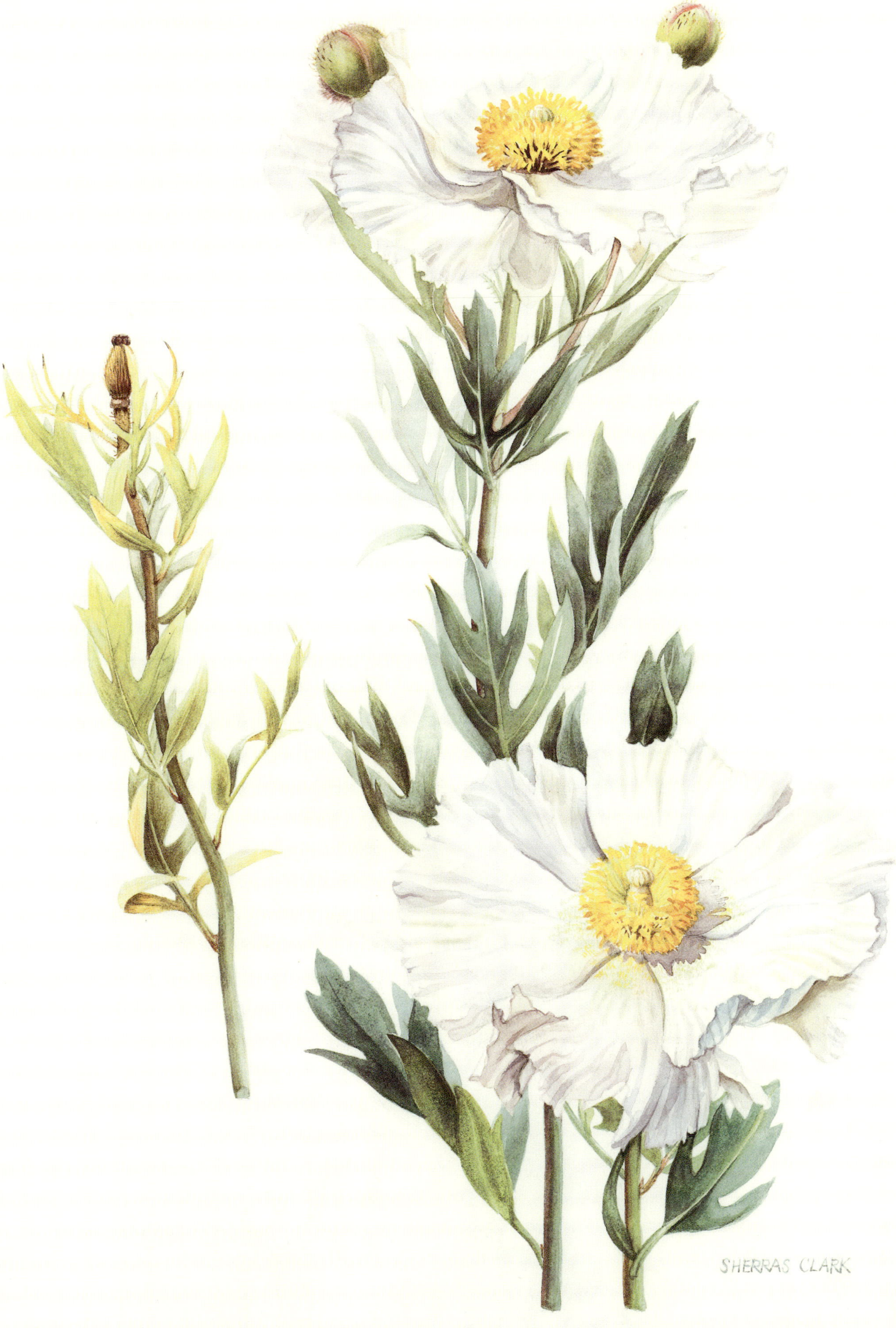
SHERRAS CLARK

Rosa 'Scabrosa'
Family – Rosaceae

Ruth Woakes

The genus *Rosa* has been subdivided into over twenty groups dependent upon growth form and flowering habit. *Rosa* 'Scabrosa' is a hybrid cultivar in the Rugosa group but its parentage is uncertain. It received an Award of Garden Merit in 1993. Roses are considered to have originated in the Middle East, and the Greek Island of Rhodes took its name from the flower. Indeed, coins of Rhodes from 400 BC bore an illustration of the rose, unmistakable because of the accurate way in which the variability of the sepals was recorded in the images. Fossil remains, which have only ever been found in the Northern Hemisphere, indicate that roses are possibly thirty-five million years old.

A variety of rose preparations has been made, including otto (attar) of roses (by steam distillation of the flowers), rose water, rose petal jam and even rose petal sandwiches. The *British Pharmacopoeia* of 1864 had three monographs relating to roses, two for rose petals and one for rose hips. The rose hips were obtained from the dog rose, *R. canina*. Rose hips have been recognised for many years as a rich source of vitamin C. Its concentration reaches 300 mg per 100 grams of tissue, surpassing that in guavas and blackcurrants. Wild rose hips were harvested during World War Two for the manufacture of rose hip syrup.

About the artist

Ruth was born in India in 1925. At the age of seven she was sent back to England and boarding school. She spent many holidays with her paternal grandparents. Her great grandfather was G.G.Kilburn, artist of the hunting scene. Her grandmother was one of the first woman students at the Slade School of Art. Ruth spent much time painting and drawing with her grandmother in those early years. Her parents moved to Australia in 1938 and Ruth went to school in Sydney where she was taught art by Signor Rubio.

In 1944 Ruth entered the Society of the Sacred Heart where education was the principal work. Later she returned to England and to Camberwell School of Art where she studied weaving with Peter Collingwood and Tadek Beutlich.

In latter years holidays in Greece have given Ruth the chance to study and draw the local flora and encouraged her to join botanical painting courses back in England, including with Anne-Marie Evans at the English Gardening School.

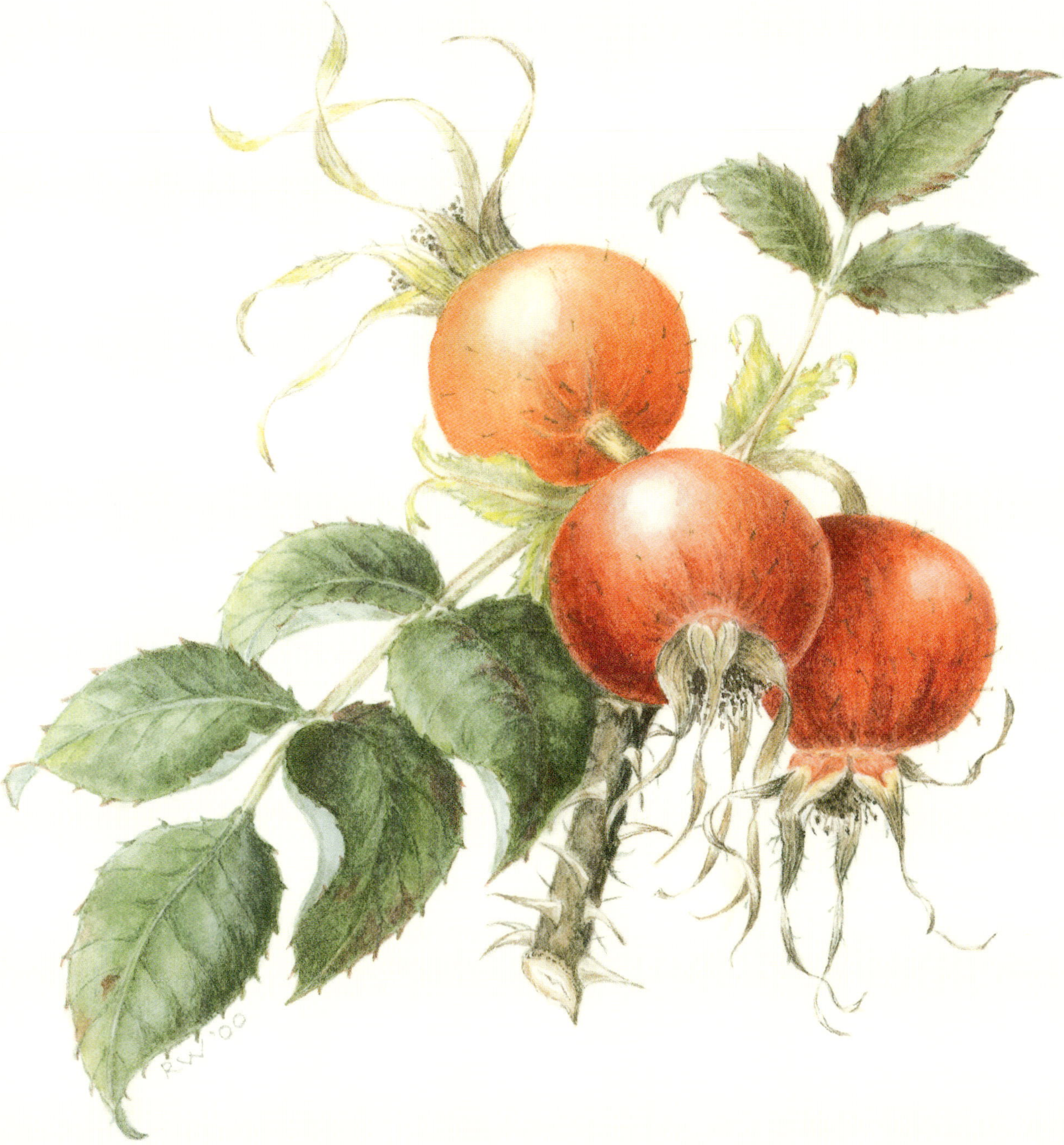

Salvia discolor Kunth
Family – Labiatae

Barbara Clemence

This species, known as Andean sage, is found wild in only a very small area of Peru. It is one of over one hundred and fifty species of *Salvia* available from UK nurseries. The name *Salvia* comes from the Latin *salvere*, to be well or to be in good health, and is a reference to its medicinal properties. Monographs for sage appear in a number of European Pharmacopoeias and a British Standard (2999/13:1965) was published for Oil of Spanish Sage (*Salvia lavandulifolia*). The common sage, *Salvia officinalis*, is best known for its culinary use, although it is also used in herbal medicine as an astringent, an antiseptic an aromatic a carminative and a tonic. Other species are used to flavour foods and alcoholic drinks as well as sources of hallucinogens.

About the artist

Barbara Clemence originally trained in graphic design in Nottingham but soon specialised in botanical illustration. Working principally in watercolour, she has a keen interest in traditional media such as egg tempera, vellum and silver-point, regularly using them in her work. Barbara also pursues projects outside of traditional botanical illustration, once providing illustrations for an environment film project on acid rain, as well as teaching regular painting and illustration classes in the Rutland area.

Her elegant and detailed designs have been commissioned by a major ceramics manufacturer, as well as being reproduced in ranges of prints and greetings cards. Working from her studio overlooking the Rutland countryside, her original designs have been sold to private collectors world-wide. She is a regular exhibitor around the UK and has been invited to show at the National Exhibition of Wildlife Art for the past four years. The Rutland Millennium award was presented to Barbara for her depiction of 'A moment in time' with a detailed watercolour of a dandelion seed head. Barbara joined the Chelsea Physic Garden Florilegium Society in 2003.

RHS medals: Silver 1993, 2002

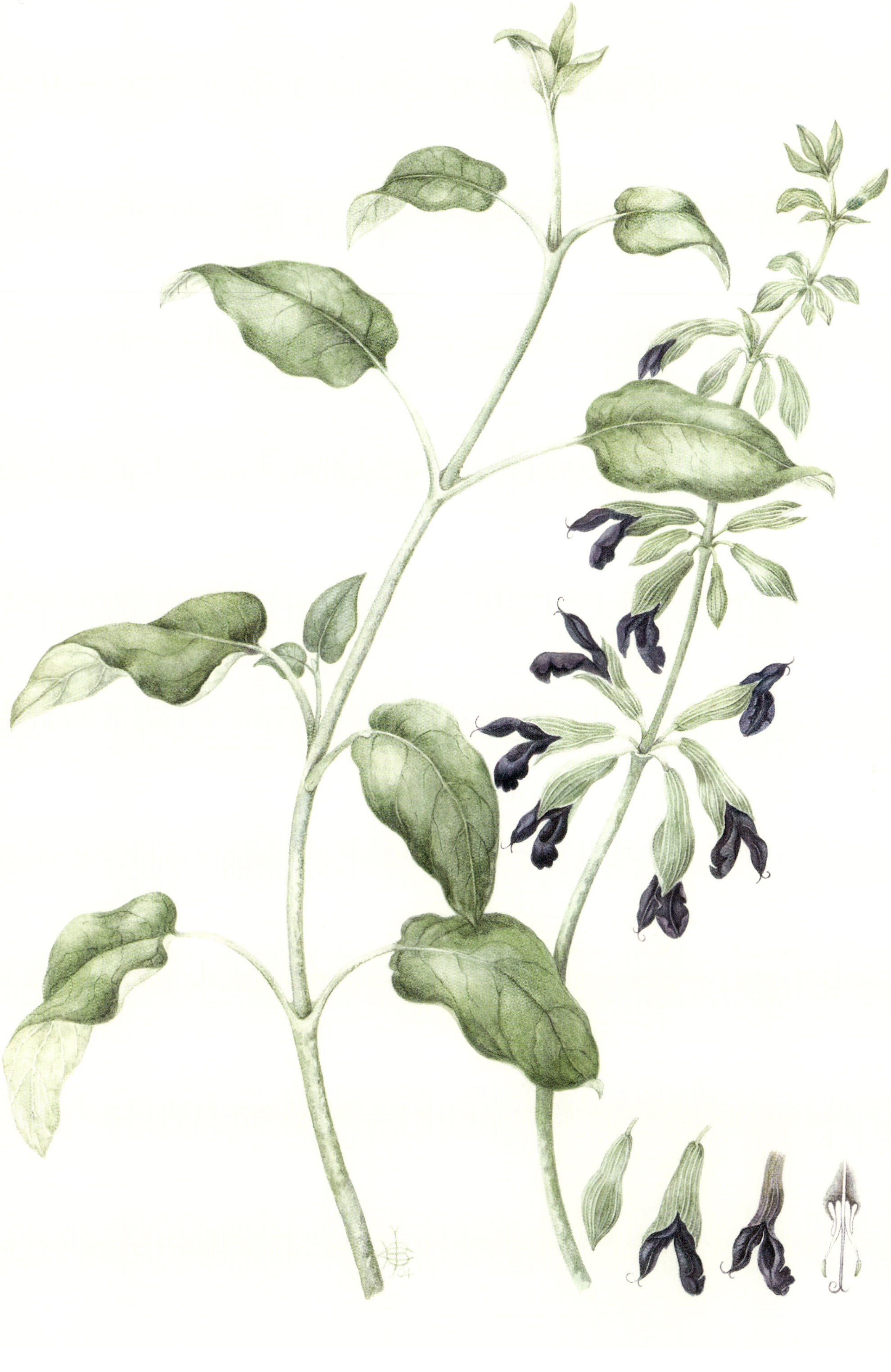

Saxifraga paniculata Miller
Family – Saxifragaceae

Loveday Gabriel-Best

According to the doctrine of signatures, plants were believed to exhibit structural characteristics which could be likened, by shape or other features, to parts of the body. Some species of *Saxifraga* have kidney-shaped leaves. This doctrine was revived by Paracelsus in the sixteenth century. He suggested that, as saxifrages grew in the crevices amongst rocks, they would be useful to break up internal stones such as gall-stones and kidney stones. However there does not appear to be any record of saxifrages actually being employed for this purpose.

Saxifraga paniculata is sometimes called the life-long saxifrage.

About the artist

Loveday began painting in her fifties. She started with oils, but soon realised that she would benefit from expert tuition. This she found at West Dean College, Chichester. Loveday discovered that she is very versatile in her work and she studied many aspects of painting at West Dean. These included botanical illustration taught by Anne-Marie Evans, who later invited Loveday to apply to join the newly-formed Chelsea Physic Garden Florilegium Society. Because of deteriorating eyesight Loveday no longer does close work, but she continues to paint still life and two of her paintings have reached the final of a national competition in 2003 and 2004.

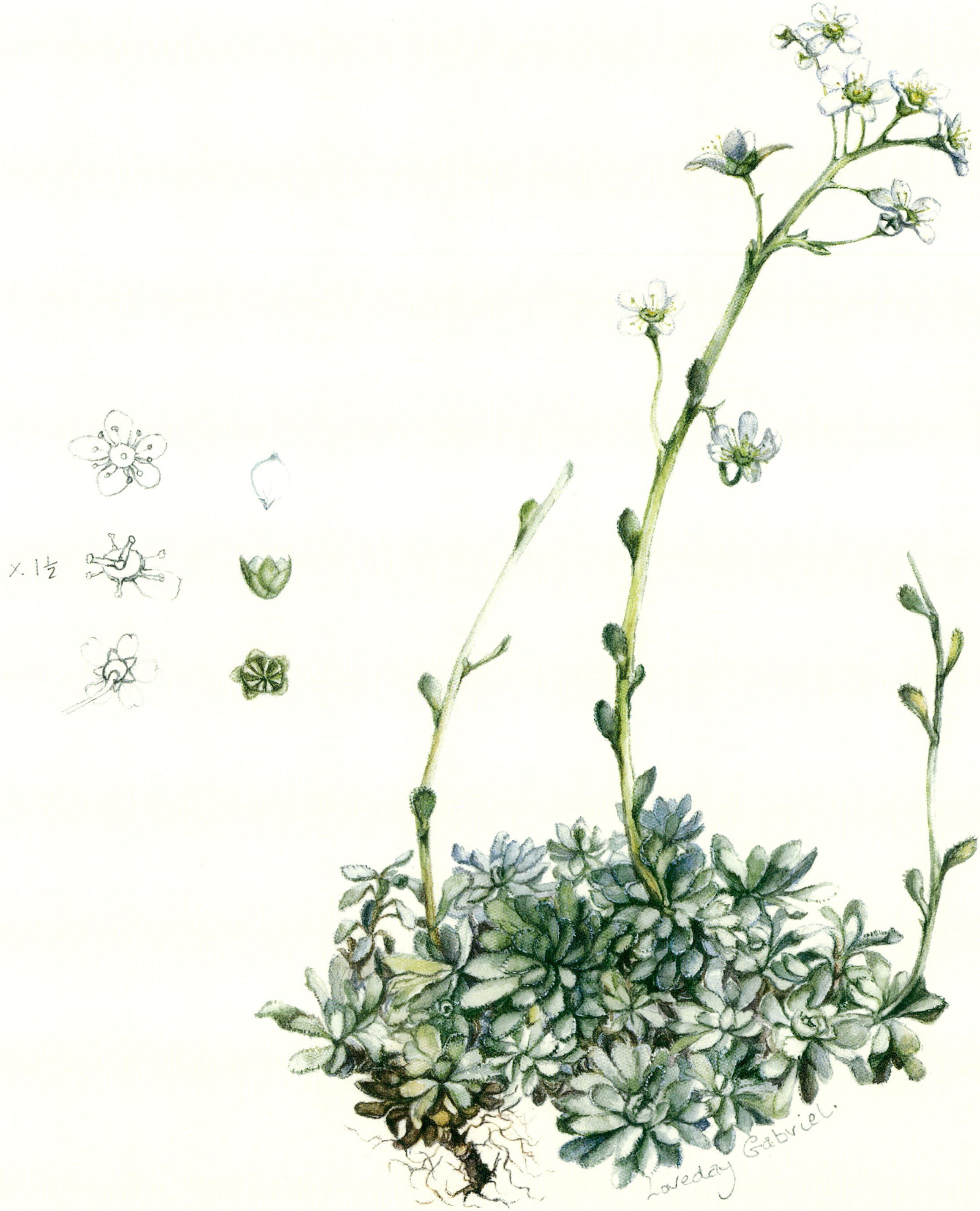
X. 1½
Loveday Gabriel.

Scopolia carniolica Jacq.
Family – Solanaceae

Sue Williams

Scopolia carniolica is a relatively unknown member of the family Solanaceae and is native to central and southeast Europe and the Russian Federation. The family includes the extremely poisonous medicinal plants deadly nightshade (*Atropa belladonna*), and thorn apple (*Datura stramonium*), both pictured in this book, as well as henbane (*Hyoscyamus niger*).

S. carniolica is also poisonous and is very similar both in structure and chemical content to these medicinal plants. It has been recognised in British Pharmacognosy as an adulterant to both the leaves and root of *Atropa belladonna*. The structure of the leaves of the two plants is so similar that they can only be safely distinguished by examination under a microscope. The content of medicinally active substances in *Scopolia* is in some cases higher than that of the material it is being used to adulterate. *Scopolia* has been used as an official source of hyoscine, a substance also obtained from *Datura stramonium*. The word scopolamine is used synonymously with hyoscine in medical literature.

The family includes many food plants, amongst them, the potato, aubergine, tomato, as well as chillies and sweet peppers. However, we do well to remember the family's inherent toxicity and to reject potato tubers that have turned green in the light. Besides making the pigment chlorophyll, the tubers will have manufactured some very toxic alkaloids.

About the artist

Sue Williams was born in India in 1942 and read Modern Languages at Oxford from 1960 to 1963. From 1966 she travelled overseas with her diplomat husband, and her language teaching gradually gave way to a passion for plants and flower painting. On leave in the UK she took short courses in botanical painting at Kew and the Victoria and Albert Museum, and in 1995 Sue became a member of the Chelsea Physic Garden Florilegium Society.

In Zimbabwe Sue was invited to paint a collection of the flowering trees and plants of that country for the National Botanic Gardens, and the proceeds of her exhibition in 1998 were donated to the Gardens' educational projects.

In New Zealand she participated in several exhibitions including, in 2001, 'Botanica' at the Adam Art Gallery; she also designed greetings cards based on the indigenous flora and fauna. New Zealand Post commissioned her to design a variety of stamp issues for the Pitcairn Islands, including the definitive botanical issue in 2000, and she was able to do much preparatory work during her visits to Pitcairn.

Since returning to the UK in 2001, apart from further exhibitions in Auckland and Tasmania and more stamp designs for Pitcairn, Sue has exhibited with the Royal Horticultural Society. She was elected to the Society of Botanical Artists in 2004.

RHS medal: Silver 2004

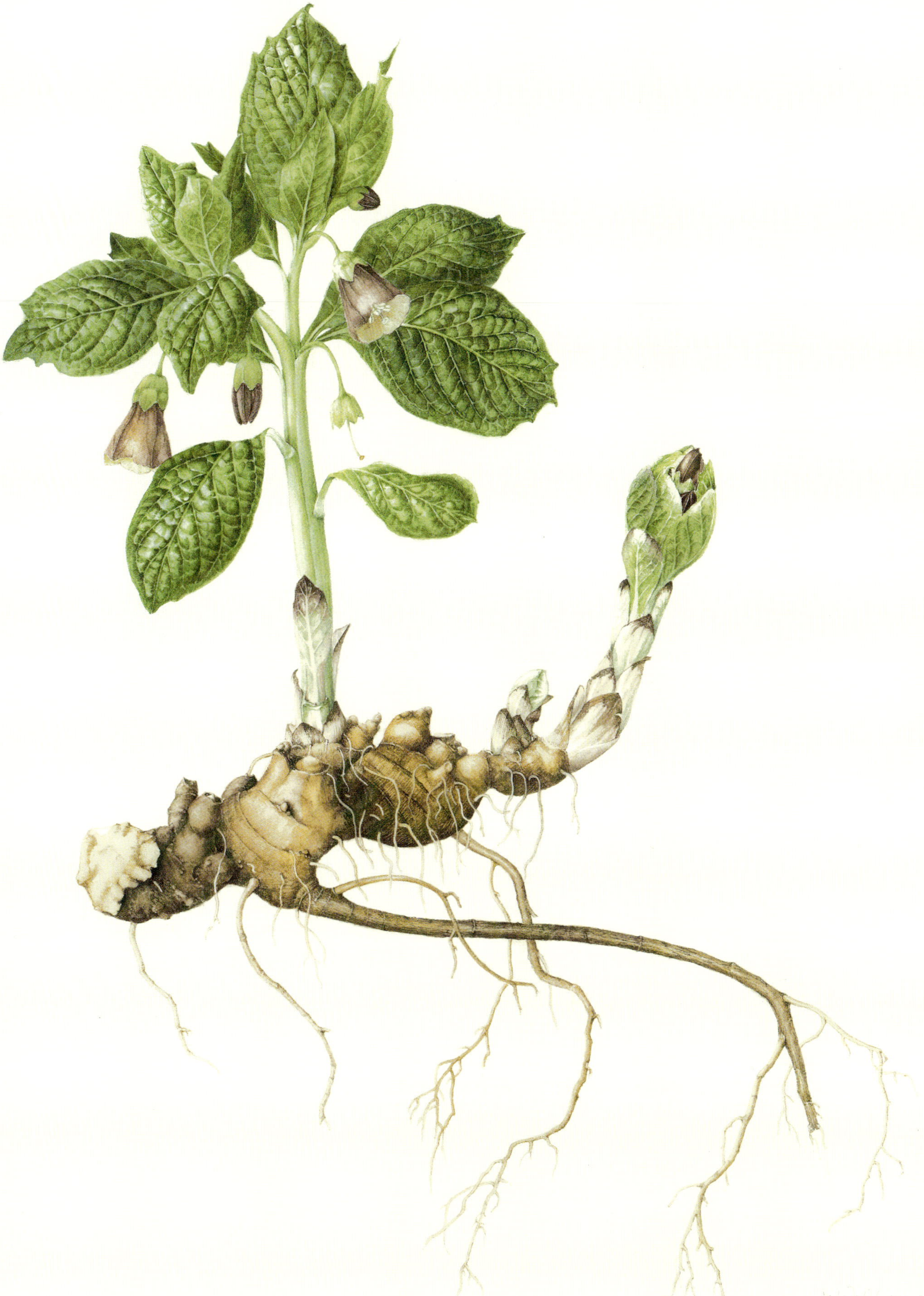

Tulipa urumiensis Stapf
Family – Liliaceae

Diana Everett

The generic name *Tulipa* is derived from the Turkish *tulbend*, a turban, from the resemblance in the shape of the flower to that of the headgear. Tulips were probably introduced to Britain in the late 1570s from material from the near East grown by Clusius (memorialised in *T. clusiana*) in Vienna.

Reputed to have been native to northwest Iran, *Tulipa urumiensis* is no longer found in the wild. It was made commercially available in 1928 by Van Tubergen, from Salmas in Azerbaijan, and was illustrated in *Curtis's Botanical Magazine* in May 1932. In 1993 it received the Award of Garden Merit (AGM) from the Royal Horticultural Society.

About the artist

Diana trained with Anne-Marie Evans at the English Gardening School in 1994. She has exhibited at the Royal Horticultural Society in London, The Society of Botanical Artists, the Ebury Galleries, London (four times) and the Ursus Gallery in New York. She has also exhibited twice at the Hunt Institute and, on the second occasion in October 2001, her portrait of *Rosa blairii* was auctioned in aid of the families of firemen who lost their lives after the terrorist raid of 11 September 2001.

For several years Diana has focused her energies on painting species of the genus *Tulipa*. Much work has been done with the collections in the alpine section at Kew, the recently-retired and renowned Head of the alpine section, Tony Hall, having been most generous with his advice and guidance. Diana has met tulip specialists from many countries and has travelled extensively in Kazakhstan and Tien Shan hunting specimens in flower to aid her studies. Diana has now illustrated 125 distinct species and forms of *Tulipa* and hopes to publish her illustrations, together with a descriptive text, in the near future. Three of the paintings were published in 2002 to decorate an information-dense article on the new industries of modern Kazakhstan in an official Kazakh government publication.

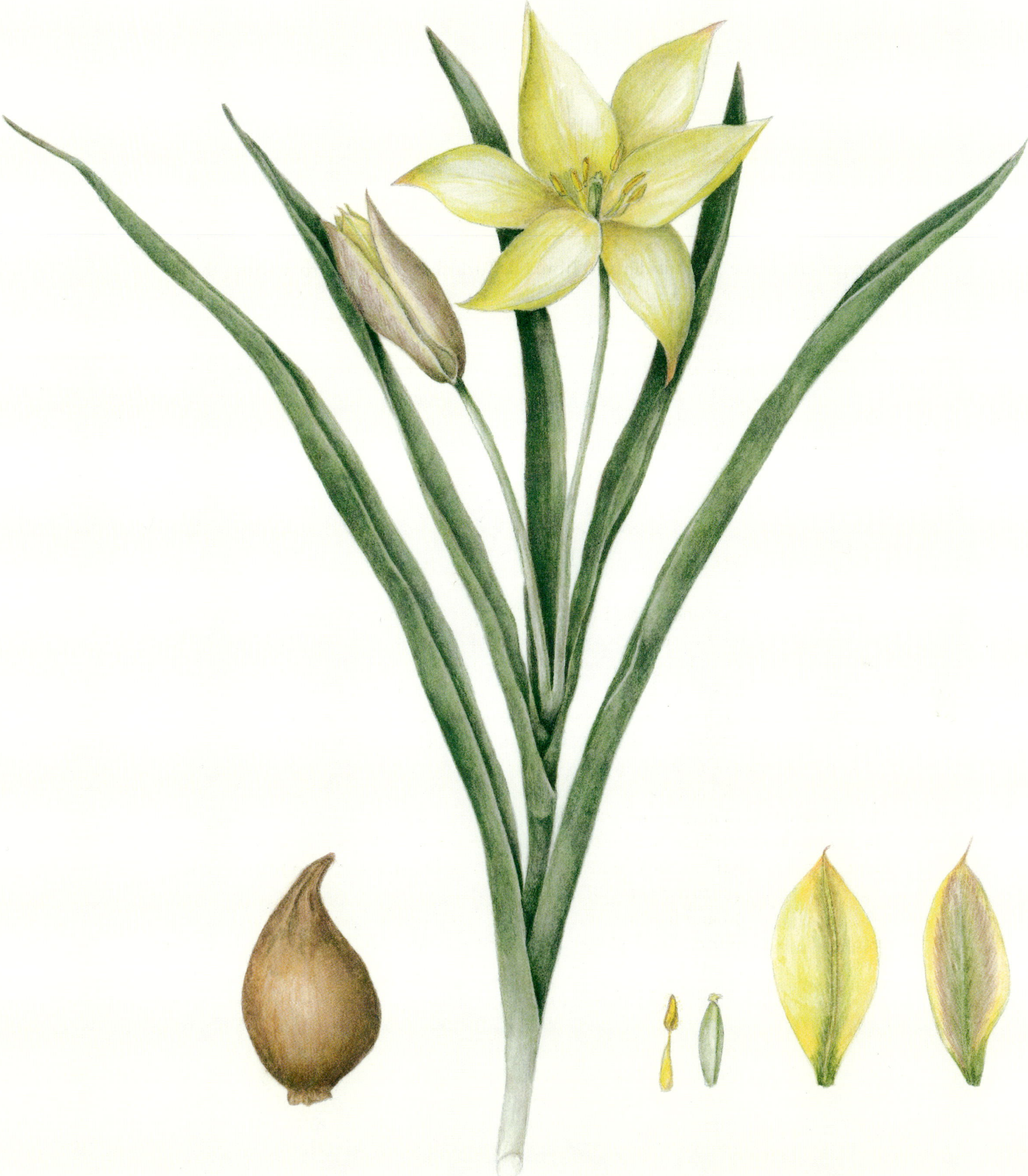

Vicia faba L. 'Crimson Flowered'
Family – Leguminosae

Judi Stone

This vegetable, known as the broad bean, has been in cultivation since at least the seventh century BC, being found in ruins of domestic properties around the Mediterranean. Seed of this crimson flowered variety was donated to the Garden in 1978 by an elderly lady whose father had grown it since the beginning of the twentieth century. *The Henry Doubleday Research Association Seed Library Catalogue* of 2000 states that crimson-flowered broad beans have been known since at least 1778.

A rare hereditary disease known as favism, a form of anaemia, has been reported in certain individuals due to inhalation of the pollen or ingestion of the bean. Culpeper, writing about beans, which he says 'are so well known, that it saves me the labour of writing any description of them' states 'if a bean be parted in two, the skin being taken away, and laid on the place where the leech hath been set that bleeds too much, stays the bleeding'.

About the artist

Judi Stone grew up in a farming family in Gloucestershire, and now lives near Sevenoaks in Kent working as a freelance botanical illustrator. She was originally trained as a biochemist, being awarded a BSc in 1967, and a PhD in 1970. She subsequently did research on novel methods of insect control.

Judi took up botanical illustration when her children were growing up and she established herself in this area by gaining honours at the Royal Horticultural Society. She now works regularly at the Royal Botanic Gardens, Kew doing both line drawings and paintings for their publications, including the prestigious *Curtis's Botanical Magazine, The Kew Bulletin*, and numerous works on orchids from all over the world.

In 1998 she had work selected for the 9th International Exhibition of Botanical Art and Illustration at the Hunt Institute. She has also recently completed several commissions for BBC *Wildlife Magazine.*

Judi's work has been exhibited widely, including the Society of Botanical Artists in Westminster, the Gilbert White Museum in Hampshire, the Sevenoaks Wildfowl Reserve and the European Patent Office, Munich. Her work is also held in private collections world-wide. She is a Fellow of the Chelsea Physic Garden Florilegium Society, where she has recently overseen the re-establishment of the Herbarium. She has also taught botanical illustration at Bromley Adult Education College as well as to visiting overseas students at the Royal Botanic Gardens, Kew.

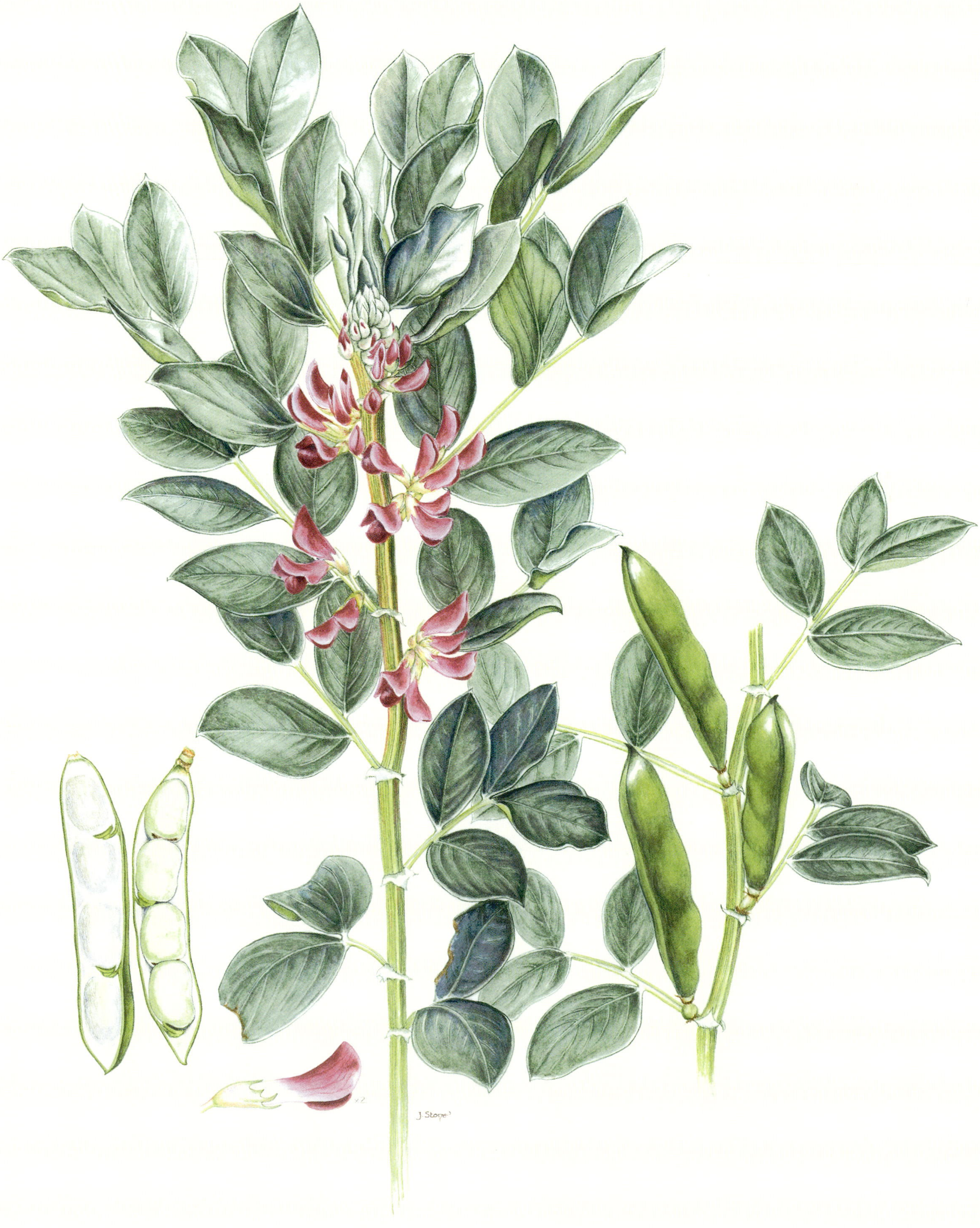
×2
J. Stone

Bibliography

This list includes both works mentioned in the text of this volume and those which were consulted in its preparation (principally for information about the uses to which the plants have been put).

Arbury, J., *Pears* (Wells and Winter, 1997)

Arbury, J., *Plums* (Beaumont Publishing Pte., 2002)

Aronson, J.K., *An Account of the Foxglove and its Medical Uses 1785–1985* (London: Oxford University Press, 1985)

Ashton, R., 'The Coinage of Rhodes 408–*c.*190 BC' in A. Meadows and K. Shipton (eds.), *Money and its Uses in the ancient Greek World* (Oxford: University Press, 2001)

Award of Garden Merit Plants 2003-2004 (London: The Royal Horticultural Society, 2004)

Barker, J., *The Medicinal Flora of Britain and Northwestern Europe* (West Wickham: Winter Press, 2001)

Bath, T., Jones, J., *The Gardener's Guide to Hardy Geraniums* (Newton Abbot: David and Charles, 1994)

Bean, W.J., *Trees and Shrubs Hardy in the British Isles* (London: John Murray, 4th edition, 1925)

Blamey, M., Grey-Wilson, C., *The Illustrated Flora of Great Britain and Northern Europe* (London: Hodder & Stoughton, 1989)

Biggs, M., *Complete Book of Vegetables* (London: Kyle Cathie, 1997)

Boyce, P., *The Genus* Arum (London: HMSO, 1993)

British National Formulary, No.43 (London: British Medical Association and The Royal Pharmaceutical Society of Great Britain, 2002)

British Pharmaceutical Codex, The (London: The Pharmaceutical Press, 1934 and 1954 Editions)

British Pharmacopoeia, The (London: Spottiswode, 1864)

British Pharmacopoeia, The (London: The Pharmaceutical Press, 1953)

British Pharmacoepoeia, The (London: HMSO, 2003)

Campbell-Culver, M., *The Origin of Plants* (London: Headline Book Publishing, 2001)

Chevalier, A., *The Encyclopedia of Medicinal Plants* (London: Dorling Kindersley, 1996)

Clebsch, B., *A Book of Salvias* (Portland: Timber Press, 2000)

Culpeper, N., *The Complete Herbal* (Birmingham: Kynoch Press, 1993). [Original 1653]

Curtis, W., *Flora Londinensis* (London, 1775-1787)

Dash, M., *La Tulipa* (J.C. Lattes, 2001)

Dean, P.M., *Pauline Dean – Portfolio of a Botanical Artist* (Guildford: Botanical Publishing, 2004)

Everard, B., Morley, B.D., *Wild Flowers of the World* (London: Peerage Books, 1970)

Fine Botanical Paintings (London: Gordon-Craig Gallery, 2000)

Gerard's Herbal The Essence thereof distilled by Marcus Woodward (London: Bracken Books, 1985) [Original 1636]
Greenish, H.G., *A Textbook of Materia Medica* (London: J & A Churchill, 1909)
Greenwood, L., Perry, F., *Flowers of the World* (London: Hamlyn Publishing, 1972)
Grieve, M., *A Modern Herbal* (London: Tiger Books International, 1992)
Guy, G.W., Whittle, B.A., Robson, P.J. (eds.) *The medicinal uses of cannabis and cannabinoids* (Pharmaceutical Press, 2004)

Heritage Seed Library Catalogue (Coventry: Henry Doubleday Research Association, published annually)
Holy Bible, The, Authorized Version, (London: Oxford University Press)
Howlett, C., *Heligan Wild* (London: Gollancz, 1999)
Huxley, A., Griffiths, M., Levy, M., *The New Royal Horticultural Society Dictionary of Gardening* (London: Macmillan, 1992)

Index Seminum (London: Chelsea Physic Garden, published annually)

Jones, J., *Hardy Geraniums for the Garden* (Hardy Plant Society, 1992, 2001)

Killick, J., Perry, R., Woodell, S.R.J., *The Flora of Oxfordshire* (Newbury: Pisces Publications, 1998)

Le Rougetel, H., *The Chelsea Gardener, Philip Miller 1691–1771* (London: Natural History Museum Publications, 1990)
Lewington, A., *Plants for People* (London: Natural History Museum Publications, 1990)
Leyens, T., *Plantas Endemicas e Avores Indiginas de Cabo Verde* (Bonn University, 1995)

Mabberley, D.J. *The Plant Book* (Cambridge: University Press, 2nd edition with corrections, 2002)
Mabey, R., *Flora Britannica* (London: Sinclair-Stevenson, 1996)
Martindale, *The Extra Pharmacopoeia* (London: The Pharmaceutical Press, 1989)
McAllen, M., Saville, R., Clematis – *Plant Portraits of Species and Selected Cultivars* (Book Guild, 2001)
Medical Dictionary, Dorland's Illustrated (London: W.B.Saunders, 25th Edition 1974)
Miller, J., *Index Horti Chelseiani* (London: 1772)
Miller, P., *Figures of the most beautiful, useful and uncommon plants described in the Gardeners Dictionary* (London: Philip Miller, 1755–1760)
Miller, P., *Gardeners Dictionary* (London, 1731)
Minter, S., *The Apothecaries' Garden* (Stroud: Sutton Publishing, 2000)
Minter, S., *Garden of World Medicine* (London: Chelsea Physic Garden, 1998)

National Gardens Scheme Book (National Gardens Scheme, 2001)
North, P., *Poisonous Plants and Fungi in Colour* (London: Blandford Press, 1967)

Pavord, A., *The Tulip* (London: Bloomsbury Publishing, 1999)
Pharmaceutical Journal, The, (151), 1943, pp.230-231 (London: Pharmaceutical Press)

Phillips, R., Foy, N., *Herbs* (London: Pan Books, 1990)
Phillips, R., Rix, M., *Perennials* (London: Pan Books, 1991)

RHS Plantfinder 2003–2004 (London: Dorling Kindersley, 2003)
Ross, I. A., *Medicinal Plants of the World* (Totowa, New Jersey: Humana Press, 1999)

Seligman, P., *Watercolour Artists' Flower Sketchbook* (Search Press, 2005)
Sherwood, S., *Contemporary Botanical Artists* (London: Weidenfeld and Nicholson, 1996)
Sherwood, S., *A Passion for Plants* (London: Cassell, 2000)
Stace, C.A., *New Flora of the British Isles* (Cambridge: University Press, 1991)
Stearn, W.T., *Dictionary of Plant Names for Gardeners* (London: Cassell, 1972)
Stevens, M., (coordinator), *Arte y Botanica* (Madrid: Lunwerg Editores, 2001)
Stevens, M., *Introduction to drawing flowers* (London: The Apple Press, 1994)
Stevens, M., (coordinator), *The Art of Botanical Painting* (London: Harper Collins, 2004)
Stockwell, C., *Nature's Pharmacy* (London: Century Hutchinson, 1988)
Stones, M., Curtis, W., *The Endemic Flora of Tasmania* (London: Ariel Press, 1967– 1978)

Turland, N.J., Chilton, L., Press, J.R., *Flora of the Cretan Area* (London: HMSO, 1993)

Vaughan, J.G., Geissler, C.A., *The New Oxford Book of Food Plants* (Oxford: University Press, 1997)

Wallis, T.E., *Textbook of Pharmacognosy* (London: J. & A. Churchill, 1955)
White, G., *The Natural History of Selborne* (London: Oxford University Press, 1951) [Original 1789]
Wren, R.C., *Potter's New Encyclopedia of Botanical Drugs and Preparations* (Saffron Walden: C.W. Daniel, 1985)

Complete Archive

W = Watercolour on paper; W/vell. = watercolour on vellum; B/W = black and white (pen and ink)

PLANT NAME	FAMILY	ARTIST	PAPER SIZE H X Wcm	IMAGE SIZE H X Wcm	MEDIUM	YEAR
Abelmoschus esculentus	Malvaceae	Ensom, Ainslie	43x32	28x26	W	1999
Abies balsamea	Pinaceae	Girling, Angie	30x42	20x30	B/W	1996
Abutilon milleri	Malvaceae	Hillelson, Judith	38x28	28x24	W	2005
Acacia dealbata	Leguminosae	McLean, Barbara	42x30	35x27	B/W	1998
Acanthus dioscoridis	Acanthaceae	Allen, Helen	58x39	39x22	W	1999
Acanthus sennii	Acanthaceae	Brown, Andrew	56x42	45x34	W	2004
Agapanthus praecox	Amaryllidaceae	Lightfoot, Chrissie	51x30	40x25	W	2000
Ajuga reptans (pink form)	Labiatae	Trickey, Julia	35x27	18x15	W	2002
Allium christophii	Liliaceae	Brown, Andrew	58x38	40x29	W	1996
Allium karataviense	Liliaceae	Brown, Andrew	57x38	36x26	W	1996
Allium sphaerocephalon	Liliaceae	Callender, Janet	39x28	36x19	W	1999
Allium subhirsutum	Liliaceae	Allen, Martin J	51x47	33x16	W	1997
Allium tuberosum	Liliaceae	Brown, Andrew	56x38	43x29	W	1996
Aloe humilis	Aloaceae	Dean, Pauline	39x29	30x16	W	1998
Aloe humilis	Aloaceae	Wilson, Judy	46x40	29x23	W	1998
Ammi visnaga	Umbelliferae	Ensom, Ainslie	41x30	36x22	B/W	2000
Antirrhinum siculum	Scrophulariaceae	McLean, Barbara	41x31	29x21	W	1998
Antirrhinum siculum	Scrophulariaceae	McLean, Barbara	30x21	28x20	B/W	1998
Arbutus unedo	Ericaceae	Hillelson, Judith	38x28	33x25	W	2005
Arbutus unedo	Ericaceae	Sasaki, Masako	26x36	18x32	W	1998
Arctostaphylos glauca	Ericaceae	Brown, Andrew	38x29	24x17	W	1999
Argemone mexicana	Papaveraceae	Barlow, Gillian	39x29	31x25	W	1999
Artemisia vulgaris	Compositae	McLean, Barbara	30x21	24x16	B/W	1997
Arum italicum	Araceae	Pinhey, Sally	57x38	48x26	W	2002
Asarina procumbens	Scrophulariaceae	Constable, Gillian	38x28	24x11	W	2005
Asarina procumbens	Scrophulariaceae	Takano, Eiko	22x30	28x24	B/W	2002
Asplenium aethiopicum	Aspleniaceae	Nicholson, Catharine	58x41	42x30	B/W	2005
Athamanta turbith	Umbelliferae	Hatherley-Champ, Margaret	38x28	26x21	W	2004
Atropa belladonna	Solanaceae	Hammond, Yvonne	28x38	20x21	B/W	2001
Atropa belladonna	Solanaceae	Hillelson, Judith	52x28	44x30	W	2000
Atropa belladonna	Solanaceae	Paige, Jane Leycester	18x25	12x19	B/W	1997
Atropa belladonna	Solanaceae	Sherras Clark, Liz	30x21	22x14	W	2000
Azara serrata	Flacourtiaceae	McLean, Barbara	38x28	28x21	B/W	2005
Azara serrata	Flacourtiaceae	McLean, Barbara	38x28	26x21	W	2005
Banksia integrifolia var. *compar*	Proteaceae	Sherras Clark, Liz	26x42	17x36	W	2002
Baptisia australis	Leguminosae	Baldwin, Mariella	58x39	49x25	W	2000
Berberis calliantha	Berberidaceae	Lundie, Joan	42x30	37x26	B/W	2005
Berberis calliantha	Berberidaceae	Lundie, Joan	41x30	37x29	W	2005
Berberis canadensis	Berberidaceae	Bruce, Jane	28x21	19x15	W	1998
Broussonetia papyrifera	Moraceae	Brown, Andrew	57x38	30x21	W	2005
Calamintha incana	Labiatae	Hatherley-Champ, Margaret	35x28	16x16	W	2002
Calandrinia grandiflora	Portulacaceae	King, Margaret	40x30	28x24	B/W	1999
Callistemon phoeniceus	Myrtaceae	Crosthwaite, Sally	39x29	27x18	W	1999
Callistemon phoeniceus	Myrtaceae	McLean, Barbara	30x42	21x29	B/W	1999
Camellia 'Cornish Snow'	Theaceae	Dawe, Peggy	38x29	20x15	W	2001
Camellia sinensis	Theaceae	Francis, Mally	38x29	34x27	W	2001
Camptotheca acuminata	Nyssaceae	Brown, Andrew	38x28	22x20	B/W	2001
Capsicum annuum var. 'Nardello'	Solanaceae	Brown, Alison F.	30x21	20x20	B/W	2000
Capsicum annuum var. 'Nardello'	Solanaceae	Brown, Alison F.	35x20	25x14	W	2000
Catharanthus roseus	Apocynaceae	Hillelson, Judith	28x19	20x11	B/W	2001
Catharanthus roseus	Apocynaceae	Hillelson, Judith	28x19	20x11	W	2001
Centaurea montana	Compositae	Lightfoot, Chrissie	39x29	24x15	W	2000
Cercis siliquastrum	Leguminosae	Stenning, Penny	51x66	24x50	W	2000
Cercis siliquastrum	Leguminosae	Stenning, Penny	35x25	28x20	B/W	2005
Cerinthe minor	Boraginaceae	Brown, Andrew	38x29	27x21	W	1998
Chamaecytisus proliferus	Leguminosae	Sasaki, Masako	50x36	41x34	W	1998
Chordospartium stevensonii	Leguminosae	Lindsay, Rosemary	40x30	25x23	W	2005

Cistus purpureus 'Alan Fradd'	Cistaceae	Hammond, Yvonne	41x30	32x22	W	1998
Citrus aurantium	Rutaceae	Page, Wendy Alexandra	42x29	28x21	B/W	2002
Citrus bergamia	Rutaceae	Stone, Judi	38x28	28x25	B/W	2004
Citrus bergamia	Rutaceae	Stone, Judi	58x38	32x28	W	2004
Citrus paradisi	Rutaceae	Francis, Mally	41x29	33x23	W	2000
Clematis alpina	Ranunculaceae	McAllen, Monica	41x31	38x21	W	1998
Clematis tibetiana	Ranunculaceae	McAllen, Monica	29x19	22x15	W	1997
Clivia miniata	Amaryllidaceae	Hammond, Yvonne	52x36	46x31	W	1999
Clivia miniata	Amaryllidaceae	Hammond, Yvonne	42x30	40x29	B/W	1999
Clivia minor	Amaryllidaceae	Hammond, Yvonne	30x24	26x16	B/W	1999
Coelogyne cristata	Orchidaceae	Stone, Judi	57x41	45x31	W	1999
Coelogyne cristata (1)	Orchidaceae	Stone, Judi	39x27	31x21	B/W	1999
Coelogyne cristata (2)	Orchidaceae	Stone, Judi	42x30	32x24	B/W	1999
Colchicum autumnale	Colchicaceae	Paige, Jane Leycester	38x29	28x18	W	2005
Colutea istria	Leguminosae	Girling, Angie	35x45	34x31	W	1997
Colutea istria	Leguminosae	Girling, Angie	29x21	17x18	B/W	1998
Colutea orientalis	Leguminosae	Hyde, June	29x24	19x17	W	1998
Coprosma robusta	Rubiaceae	Girling, Angie	24x36	16x23	B/W	1997
Coriandrum sativum	Umbelliferae	Woakes, Ruth	38x28	23x16	W	2004
Cornus amomum	Cornaceae	King, Ianthe	39x39	30x23	W	1998
Crataegus monogyna	Rosaceae	White, Charmian	38x28	32x25	W	2005
Cyclamen coum	Primulaceae	Brown, Alison F.	25x22	12x13	W/vell.	1998
Cyclamen coum	Primulaceae	Dawe, Peggy	26x33	17x19	W	2000
Cydonia oblonga	Rosaceae	King, Margaret	46x35	35x25	W	1998
Cydonia oblonga	Rosaceae	King, Margaret	30x21	22x18	B/W	1998
Cynoglossum creticum	Boraginaceae	Paige, Jane Leycester	29x22	17x12	B/W	1998
Cynoglossum creticum	Boraginaceae	Paige, Jane Leycester	38x34	28x21	W	1998
Cyrtomium fortunei	Dryopteridaceae	Nicholson, Catharine	58x38	43x26	B/W	2004
Datura innoxia	Solanaceae	King, Margaret	78x57	56x36	Pencil	2000
Datura stramonium	Solanaceae	Hall, Ruth	31x45	30x22	W	2002
Datura stramonium	Solanaceae	Nunn, Shirley Ann	57x38	36x27	W	1999
Datura stramonium	Solanaceae	Coombs, Jill	36x26	30x21	B/W	2001
Dendrobium kingianum	Orchidaceae	Stone, Judi	57x42	40x30	W	2002
Dianthus ferrugineus	Caryophyllaceae	Hammond, Yvonne	51x36	44x32	W	1998
Dianthus glacialis	Caryophyllaceae	de Folin, Angelique	41x29	32x17	W	2005
Dianthus juniperinus ssp *bauhinorum*	Caryophyllaceae	Hammond, Yvonne	55x38	32x48	W	2002
Dicentra spectabilis	Fumariaceae	Baldwin, Mariella	38x39	43x29	W	2000
Digitalis fulva	Scrophulariaceae	Callender, Janet	57x38	45x28	W	2002
Digitalis grandiflora	Scrophulariaceae	Wilson, Judy	59x45	36x25	W	1999
Digitalis lanata	Scrophulariaceae	Stone, Judi	42x30	40x17	B/W	2000
Digitalis lanata	Scrophulariaceae	Stone, Judi	58x41	46x21	W	2000
Dionaea muscipula	Droseraceae	Stone, Judi	18x25	10x13	B/W	2001
Drosera capensis	Droseraceae	Stone, Judi	15x26	8x15	B/W	2002
Dryopteris filix-mas	Polypodiaceae	Takano, Eiko	51x36	45x23	G	2002
Ecballium elaterium	Cucurbitaceae	Takano, Eiko	36x51	23x37	W	2005
Echinacea purpurea	Compositae	Brown, Andrew	58x38	44x32	B/W	1997
Eriobotrya japonica	Rosaceae	Hillelson, Judith	64x47	57x40	W	2000
Eriobotrya japonica (Flower)	Rosaceae	Hillelson, Judith	25x21	15x14	W	2004
Eriobotrya japonica (Fruit)	Rosaceae	Hillelson, Judith	25x21	17x13	W	2004
Erodium manescani	Geraniaceae	Hammerton, Sally	38x36	27x28	W	2001
Eruca sativa	Cruciferae	Hammerton, Sally	38x29	31x22	W	1997
Eryngium agavifolium	Umbelliferae	Wilson, Judy	51x38	41x33	W	1996
Eryngium bourgatii	Umbelliferae	Barlow, Gillian	38x29	36x27	W	1998
Eryngium caucasicum	Umbelliferae	Lindsay, Rosemary	42x32	33x24	W	2004
Eryngium giganteum	Umbelliferae	Leycester Paige, Jane	55x36	39x28	W	1996
Eryngium monocephalum	Apiaceae	Catchpole, Lesley	59x28	40x29	B/W	2005
Eryngium planum	Umbelliferae	Gabriel, Loveday	38x28	31x22	W	1996
Eryngium variifolium	Umbelliferae	Hammerton, Sally	44x38	35x26	W	1996
Eucalyptus leucoxylon 'Rosea'	Myrtaceae	Brown, Alison F	30x41	23x30	W	1999
Euonymus latifolius	Celastraceae	Hammond, Yvonne	46x35	37x28	W	1998
Euonymus latifolius	Celastraceae	Hammond, Yvonne	25x18	16x12	B/W	1998
Forsythia viridissima	Oleaceae	Hammond, Yvonne	38x56	31x41	W	2004
Galanthus nivalis	Amaryllidaceae	Gould, Sarah	21x16	19x12	W/vell.	2000
Galega orientalis	Leguminosae	McLean, Barbara	38x28	29x17	B/W	2004

Garrya elliptica	Garryaceae	Bolas, Valerie	29x21	17x12	B/W	1998
Gaultheria procumbens	Ericaceae	Bolas, Valerie	30x42	20x20	B/W	2000
Gaultheria procumbens	Ericaceae	Bolas, Valerie	29x32	19x20	W	2000
Geranium macrorrhizum	Geraniaceae	Ensom, Ainslie	30x39	23x32	B/W	1997
Geranium malviflorum	Geraniaceae	Brown, Alison	38x28	26x16	W	2004
Geum pyrenaicum	Rosaceae	Evans, Kate	38x40	27x23	W	1998
Geum urbanum	Rosaceae	Lightfoot, Chrissie	26x18	14x13	W	2000
Ginkgo biloba	Ginkgoaceae	Ensom, Ainslie	26x21	19x16	B/W	1997
Glaucium flavum	Papaveraceae	Searight, Jenevora	56x38	40x25	W	2004
Glaucium flavum indet. D71	Papaveraceae	Callender, Janet	50x36	40x28	W	2004
Gossypium hirsutum	Malvaceae	Ensom, Ainslie	30x21	17x17	B/W	2000
Hamamelis virginiana	Hamamelidaceae	Brown, Alison F.	30x21	19x14	B/W	1997
Hamamelis virginiana	Hamamelidaceae	Hammond, Yvonne	27x19	16x9	B/W	1997
Hebe salicifolia	Scrophulariaceae	Bridger, John	42x30	28x19	B/W	1997
Hebe salicifolia	Scrophulariaceae	Hyde, June	33x26	28x19	B/W	1997
Heliamphora nutans	Sarraceniaceae	Brown, Andrew	27x13	20x6	W	2001
Helianthemum lavandulifolium	Cistaceae	Crosthwaite, Sally	30x21	20x17	B/W	1998
Helianthemum lavandulifolium	Cistaceae	Crosthwaite, Sally	37x26	21x16	W	1998
Helianthemum nummularium	Cistaceae	Crosthwaite, Sally	30x21	20x16	B/W	1998
Helianthemum nummularium	Cistaceae	Crosthwaite, Sally	37x26	20x16	W	1998
Helleborus torquatus	Ranunculaceae	Sasaki, Masako	36x29	27x23	W	1999
Hepatica nobilis	Ranunculaceae	Dawe, Peggy	29x39	10x14	W	2002
Hermodactylus tuberosus	Iridaceae	Callender, Janet	57x39	43x28	W	1999
Hermodactylus tuberosus	Iridaceae	King, Margaret	41x31	28x21	W	1996
Hippophae rhamnoides	Elaeagnaceae	Worby, Carolyn	37x28	28x19	Pencil	2000
Hoheria lyallii	Malvaceae	Girling, Angie	37x32	26x26	W	2000
Hoheria sexstylosa	Malvaceae	Callender, Janet	41x31	38x28	W	2000
Hordeum vulgare	Gramineae	Girling, Angie	42x30	39x20	B/W	2001
Humulus lupulus	Cannabaceae	Brown, Alison	21x30	9x20	B/W	1998
Humulus lupulus	Cannabaceae	Hammond, Yvonne	31x22	14x12	B/W	1997
Humulus lupulus aureus	Cannabaceae	Ensom, Ainslie	28x29	22x24	B/W	1997
Hyoscyamus niger	Solanaceae	Nunn, Shirley Ann	58x38	33x24	W	1999
Hyoscyamus niger	Solanaceae	Pickup, Liz	34x26	28x21	B/W	2000
Ilex cornuta	Aquifoliaceae	Page, Wendy Alexandra	35x30	27x24	W	1999
Ilex cornuta	Aquifoliaceae	Page, Wendy Alexandra	30x21	16x17	B/W	1999
Ipomoea lobata	Polemoniaceae	McLean, Barbara	38x28	36x24	W	2004
Ipomoea purpurea var. *diversifolia*	Polemoniaceae	King, Margaret	41x30	35x25	B/W	1999
Iris foetidissima	Iridaceae	Worby, Carolyn	38x26	27x8	Pencil	2000
Iris orientalis	Iridaceae	Brown, Andrew	55x38	40x28	W	1998
Isoplexis canariensis	Scrophulariaceae	Girling, Angie	47x34	34x20	W	1999
Jasminum nudiflorum	Oleaceae	McAllen, Monica	43x31	36x26	W	1999
Koelreuteria paniculata	Sapindaceae	Callender, Janet	42x30	38x26	B/W	2005
Koelreuteria paniculata	Sapindaceae	Callender, Janet	38x57	33x54	W	2005
Lapageria rosea	Philesiaceae	Craig-McFeely, Joanna	41x30	38x28	W	2005
Lapageria rosea	Philesiaceae	Pinhey, Sally	31x21	23x14	W	2005
Lathyrus clymeneum `Chelsea'	Papilionaceae	Hillelson, Judith	30x21	27x19	B/W	2002
Laurentia axillaris	Campanulaceae	Girling, Angie	42x30	26x16	B/W	2004
Laurentia axillaris	Lobeliaceae	Girling, Angie	39x28	26x15	W	2002
Lavandula angustifolia	Labiatae	Bolas, Valerie	39x29	30x17	W	1998
Lavandula canariensis	Labiatae	Girling, Angie	38x28	26x21	B/W	2005
Lavandula canariensis	Labiatae	Girling, Angie	38x29	26x21	W	2005
Lavandula dentata	Labiatae	Baldwin, Mariella	38x28	28x20	W	2004
Lavandula pinnata	Labiatae	Catchpole, Lesley	26x18	19x13	B/W	2004
Lavandula pinnata	Labiatae	Catchpole, Lesley	26x18	19x13	B/W	2002
Linum bienne	Linaceae	Page, Wendy Alexandra	33x27	25x18	W/vell.	1998
Liquidambar orientalis	Hamamelidaceae	Catchpole, Lesley	41x30	26x26	W	2004
Liquidambar styraciflua	Hamamelidaceae	Barlow, Gillian	30x21	26x19	B/W	2004
Lomelosia minoana ssp *minoana*	Dipsacaceae	Sasaki, Masako	36x26	30x20	W	2002
Lomelosia minoana ssp *minoana*	Dipsacaceae	Sasaki, Masako	36x26	30x20	B/W	2004
Lonicera fragrantissima	Caprifoliaceae	Allen, Martin. J	51x37	21x18	W	1999
Luffa aegyptiaca	Cucurbitaceae	Stone, Judi	55x41	42x31	W	1998
Luffa aegyptiaca	Cucurbitaceae	Stone, Judi	42x30	27x14	B/W	1998
Lychnis coronaria atrosanguinea	Caryophyllaceae	Hillelson, Judith	38x28	32x19	W	2004
Magnolia grandiflora	Magnoliaceae	Brown, Alison F.	21x30	17x18	B/W	1998

Magnolia grandiflora	Magnoliaceae	Stones, Margaret	51x39	44x32	W	1998
Malus sylvestris	Rosaceae	Page, Wendy Alexandra	30x21	19x16	B/W	1998
Malus sylvestris	Rosaceae	Page, Wendy Alexandra	32x36	25x21	W	1998
Mandevilla suaveolens (syn. *M. laxa*)	Apocynaceae	Brown, Alison F	30x21	25x16	B/W	1999
Maurandya barclayana	Scrophulariaceae	Evans, Kate	38x29	33x24	W	2001
Melaleuca viminia	Myrtaceae	Girling, Angie	30x42	22x29	B/W	1999
Mentha piperata	Labiatae	Tanako, Eiko	38x29	30x18	W	2004
Morus alba	Moraceae	Gould, Sarah	26x21	21x18	W/vell.	1999
Muscari botryoides	Liliaceae	Page, Wendy Alexander	36x28	28x22	W	2005
Muscari comosum	Liliaceae	Paige, Jane Leycester	44x38	37x33	W	1997
Narcissus 'Le Grand Soleil'	Amaryllidaceae	Page, Wendy Alexandra	42x30	31x21	B/W	2001
Narcissus 'Grande Monarque'	Amaryllidaceae	Stenning, Penny	41x54	30x34	W	2001
Narcissus canariensis	Amaryllidaceae	Brown, Alison F	26x18	20x13	W	1998
Nerine bowdenii 'Fenwick's Variety'	Amaryllidaceae	Hammond, Yvonne	56x38	49x23	W	2005
Nicandra physalodes	Solanaceae	Allen, Helen	38x31	24x21	W	2000
Nicotiana tabacum	Solanaceae	Brown, Andrew	38x28	31x15	B/W	1997
Nicotiana tabacum	Solanaceae	Crosthwaite, Sally	42x30	37x30	B/W	1998
Nolana paradoxa	Solanaceae	Allen, Helen	39x29	28x27	W	2000
Nyssa sylvatica	Nyssaceae	Bolas, Valerie	29x38	21x29	W	
Nyssa sylvatica	Nyssaceae	Dean, Pauline	39x30	32x22	W	1997
Oenothera biennis	Onagraceae	Dawe, Peggy	39x28	29x21	W	2002
Olea europaea	Oleaceae	Baldwin, Mariella	38x28	34x20	W	2004
Ornithogalum virens Lindl.	Liliaceae	Lightfoot, Chrissie	51x36	33x25	W	2004
Papaver somniferum	Papaveraceae	King, Margaret	51x25	41x15	B/W	2001
Paphiopedilum insigne	Orchidaceae	Stone, Judi	56x38	26x22	W	2005
Paulownia tomentosa	Scrophulariaceae	Callender, Janet	30X21	28X20	B/W	1999
Paulownia tomentosa	Scrophulariaceae	Callender, Janet	55x37	48x33	W	1999
Pelargonium 'Splendide'	Geraniaceae	Hillelson, Judith	39x28	29x23	W	1999
Pelargonium alchemilloides	Geraniaceae	Brown, Andrew	38x28	30x20	B/W	1997
Pelargonium alchemilloides	Geraniaceae	Hillelson, Judith	46x34	39x26	W	1999
Pelargonium alchemilloides	Geraniaceae	McAllen, Monica	23x16	19x14	W	1996
Pelargonium ardens	Geraniaceae	Hillelson, Judith	57x39	40x29	W	1996
Pelargonium australe	Geraniaceae	Lightfoot, Chrissie	17x16	9x9	W	1999
Pelargonium cuculatum	Geraniaceae	Hillelson, Judith	57x38	48x31	W	1998
Pelargonium echinatum	Geraniaceae	Wilson, Judy	55x42	46x32	W	1997
Pelargonium graveolens	Geraniaceae	Ensom, Ainslie	32x30	20x17	B/W	1998
Pelargonium graveolens	Geraniaceae	Stone, Judi	34x25	26x20	B/W	1997
Pelargonium odoratissimum	Geraniaceae	Ensom, Ainslie	30X21	19X15	B/W	2002
Pelargonium odoratissimum	Geraniaceae	Stone, Judi	30x21	23x19	B/W	
Pelargonium odoratissimum	Geraniaceae	Stone, Judi	56x39	42x27	W	1997
Pelargonium odoratissimum	Geraniaceae	Williams, Sue	38x28	29x21	W	2005
Pelargonium papillionaceum	Geraniaceae	Wilson, Judy	50x39	34x24	W	1999
Pelargonium rapaceum	Geraniaceae	Wilson, Judy	61x46	41x32	W	1997
Pelargonium tricolor	Geraniaceae	Hillelson, Judith	38x28	33x24	W	1997
Penstemon heterophyllus	Scrophulariaceae	Dawe, Peggy	38x28	25x16	W	2004
Petrorhagia saxifraga	Caryophyllaceae	Brown, Andrew	38x28	13x19	B/W	2004
Petunia violacea	Solanaceae	Sherras Clark, Liz	38x28	26x19	W	2005
Petunia violacea	Solanaceae	Wilson, Judy	46x34	33x19	W	2001
Phlomis tuberosa	Labiatae	Bradburn, Valerie	58x38	41x21	W	1999
Phlox carolina 'Bill Baker'	Polemoniaceae	Girling, Angie	47x34	37x25	W	1999
Physalis peruviana	Solanaceae	Brown, Alison F.	30x21	24x18	B/W	1997
Pinus halepensis	Pinaceae	Callender, Janet	30x21	15x12	B/W	1998
Pinus halepensis	Pinaceae	Callender, Janet	58x38	45x31	W	1998
Platycodon grandiflorum	Campanulaceae	Sasaki, Masako	45x31	26x21	W	1999
Podophyllum hexandrum	Podophyllaceae	Sasaki, Masako	37x26	31x26	B/W	2001
Polemonium caeruleum	Polemoniaceae	Crosthwaite, Sally	43x29	38x12	B/W	2000
Polygonatum odoratum	Liliaceae	Trickey, Julia	45x36	32x22	W	2004
Primula auricula (cv unknown)	Primulaceae	Crosthwaite, Sally	38x26	16x9	W	2001
Primula auricula (cv unknown)	Primulaceae	Crosthwaite, Sally	30x21	16x9	B/W	2001
Proboscidea louisianica	Pedaliaceae	Williams, Sue	57x38	37x25	W	2005
Proboscidea louisianica (fruit)	Pedaliaceae	Williams, Sue	38x28	16x19	W	2005
Pterocarya fraxinifolia	Juglandaceae	Callender, Janet	51x37	46x36	W	2003
Pterocarya fraxinifolia	Juglandaceae	Callender, Janet	30x21	28x20	B/W	2004
Pulmonaria saccharata	Boraginaceae	Ensom, Ainslie	28x40	21x24	W	1998

Pulsatilla vernalis	Ranunculaceae	Allen, Martin. J	26x18	10x16	W	1998
Pulsatilla vulgaris	Ranunculaceae	Ensom, Ainslie	39x29	24x19	W	1998
Pulsatilla vulgaris	Ranunculaceae	Ensom, Ainslie	36x28	22x15	B/W	1998
Punica granatum	Punicaceae	Craig-McFeely, Joanna	15x20	12x17	W/vell.	2002
Punica granatum	Punicaceae	Hervey-Bathurst, Caroline	38x29	34x26	W	1997
Punica granatum	Punicaceae	Girling, Angie	24x36	13x18	B/W	1997
Punica granatum (missing)	Punicaceae	King, Margaret			B/W	1997
Punica granatum (flowers)	Punicaeae	Dawe, Peggy	35x25	21x18	W	2004
Pyracantha fortuneana	Rosaceae	Bolas, Valerie	42x30	27x20	B/W	1997
Pyracantha fortuneana	Rosaceae	Hillelson, Judith	30x21	27x18	B/W	1998
Quercus coccifera	Fagaceae	Rees-Davies, Kay	40x29	35x24	W	2005
Rhododendron 'Amoenum' (missing)	Ericaceae	Sasaki, Masako			B/W	1999
Ribes americanum	Grossulariaceae	Nunn, Shirley Ann	57x43	39x31	W	1998
Ricinus communis	Euphorbiaceae	Barlow, Gillian	37x26	30x24	B/W	1997
Romneya coulteri	Papaveraceae	Crosthwaite, Sally	42x30	26x23	B/W	
Romneya coulteri	Papaveraceae	Sherras Clark, Liz	42x30	35x24	W	2000
Rosa 'Maigold' (hips)	Rosaceae	Evans, Kate	24x18	17x11	W	1999
Rosa brunonii	Rosaceae	Page, Wendy Alexandra	33x28	23x20	W	2001
Rosa brunonii	Rosaceae	Page, Wendy Alexandra	30x21	22x16	B/W	1999
Rosa chinensis	Rosaceae	Dawe, Peggy	38x29	28x18	W	2001
Rosa damascena 'Gloire de Guilan'	Rosaceae	Page, Wendy Alexandra	42x30	31x24	B/W	1999
Rosa damascena 'Trigintipetala'	Rosaceae	Page, Wendy Alexandra	42x30	36x24	B/W	1996
Rosa rubiginosa (hips)	Rosaceae	Evans, Kate	24x17	17x11	W	1999
Rosa rugosa (hips)	Rosaceae	Evans, Kate	24x16	12x8	W	1999
Rosa 'Scabrosa'	Rosaceae	Woakes, Ruth	38x28	11x10	W	2000
Rosa sherardii	Rosaceae	Barlow, Gillian	39x29	32x24	W	1997
Rosa sherardii	Rosaceae	Ensom, Ainslie	47x29	28x19	W	1996
Rosa woodsii Lindl.	Rosaceae	Ensom, Ainslie	39x29	21x15	W	2002
Roscoea beesiana	Zingiberaceae	Bradburn, Valerie	35x48	27x14	W	2000
Ruscus aculeatus	Ruscaceae	Girling, Angie	51x36	45x24	W	1998
Ruta graveolens	Rutaceae	Allen, Martin J	37x26	20x12	B/W	1998
Ruta graveolens	Rutaceae	Bolas, Valerie	42x30	20x15	B/W	1997
Ruta graveolens	Rutaceae	Crosthwaite, Sally	42x30	21x17	B/W	1998
Ruta graveolens	Rutaceae	Page, Wendy Alexandra	42x30	17x15	B/W	1998
Salvia discolor	Labiatae	Clemence, Barbara	57x38	38x26	W	2005
Salvia guaranitica	Labiatae	Clemence, Barbara	57x38	42x30	W	2005
Salvia indica	Labiatae	Paige, Jane Leycester	44x38	39x26	W	1998
Saxifraga paniculata	Saxifragaceae	Gabriel, Loveday	38x29	18x15	W	1999
Scabiosa cretica	Dipsacaceae	Stenning, Penny	30x21	22x15	B/W	2002
Scopolia carniolica	Solanaceae	Williams, Sue	57x28	43x30	W	2005
Sempervivum tectorum	Crassulaceae	Crosthwaite, Sally	30x22	16x9	B/W	1998
Sempervivum tectorum	Crassulaceae	Page, Wendy Alexandra	42x30	14x15	B/W	1997
Silybum marianum	Compositae	Ensom, Ainslie	41x30	33x28	B/W	1997
Solanum angustifolium	Solanaceae	Francis, Mally	41x34	35x27	W	1999
Solanum aviculare	Solanaceae	King, Margaret	30x21	26x18	B/W	1997
Solanum pseudocapsicum	Solanaceae	Stenning, Penny	51x36	36x25	W	2002
Sophora tetraptera 'Gnome'	Leguminosae	Crosthwaite, Sally	51x39	34x29	B/W	2001
Sophora tetraptera 'Gnome'	Leguminosae	Crosthwaite, Sally	51x39	34x29	W	2001
Spiraea japonica var. *fortuneii*	Rosaceae	Ensom, Ainslie	30x21	18x8	B/W	1999
Taxus baccata	Taxaceae	Dean, Pauline	29x29	24x15	W	2001
Tilia cordata	Tiliaceae	Hillelson, Judith	38x28	33x23	W	1998
Tilia cordata	Tiliaceae	Sasaki, Masako	31x46	26x33	W	1999
Trifolium pratense	Leguminosae	Hammond, Yvonne	51x35	40x25	W	2000
Tulipa saxatilis	Liliaceae	Everett, Diana	38x28	30x22	W	2005
Tulipa urumiensis	Liliaceae	Everett, Diana	38x28	18x16	W	2004
Valeriana officinalis L. (missing)	Valerianaceae	McLean, Barbara	42x30	35x25	B/W	1997
Vicia faba	Leguminosae	Page, Wendy Alexandra	42x30	31x21	B/W	2001
Vicia faba 'Crimson Flowered'	Leguminosae	Stone, Judi	58x40	45x35	W	2000
Viola odorata	Violaceae	Gould, Sarah	27x27	8x9	W/vell.	2001
Viola odorata	Violaceae	Page, Wendy Alexandra	42x30	32x24	B/W	1997
Vitex agnus-castus	Verbenaceae	Brown, Andrew	51x39	36x27	W	2001
Watsonia meriana	Iridaceae	Crosthwaite, Sally	57x38	43x27	W	1998
Watsonia meriana	Iridaceae	Crosthwaite, Sally	30x21	29x15	B/W	1998
Zantedeschia aethiopica	Araceae	King, Margaret	30x21	24x17	B/W	1997

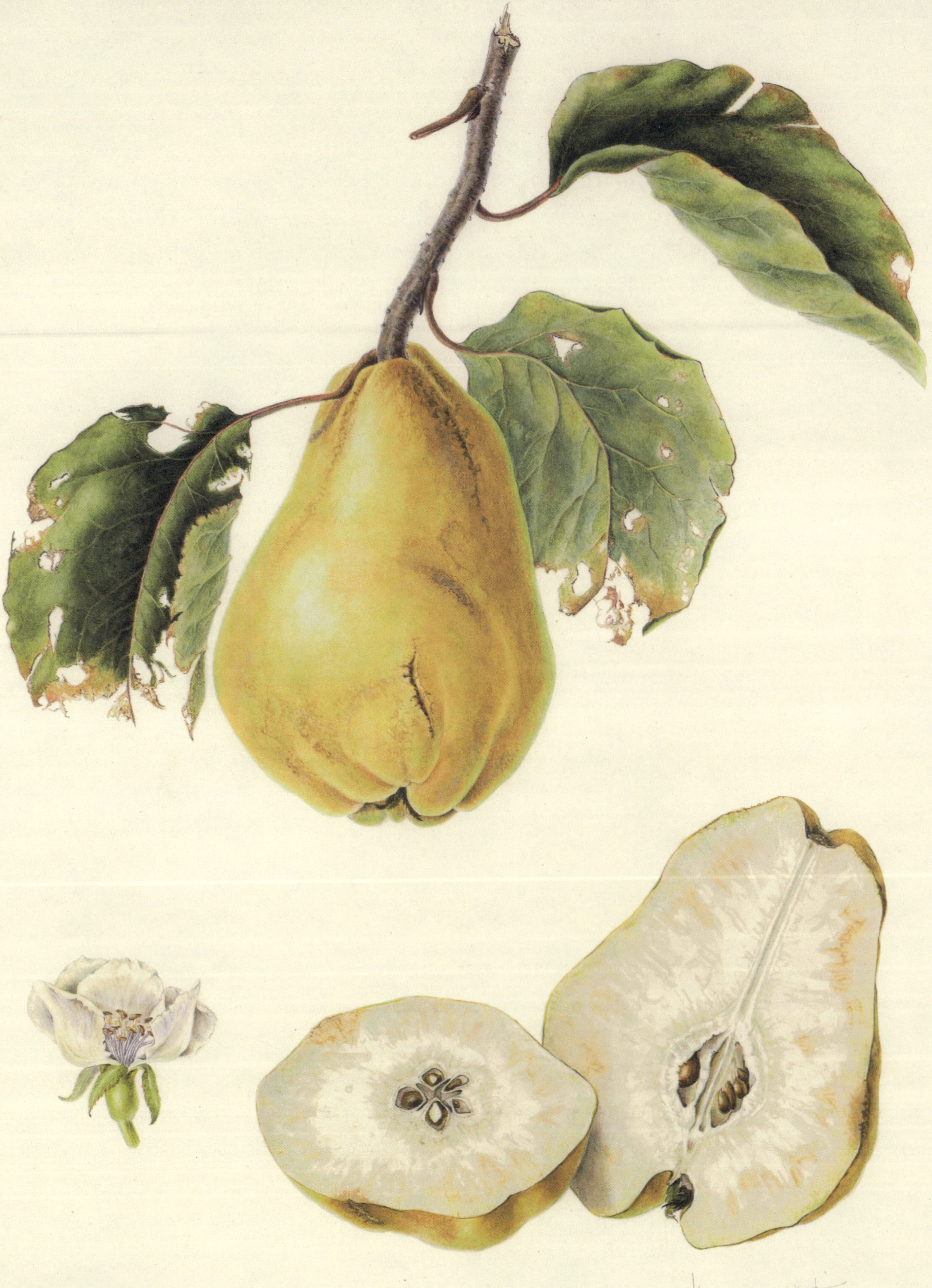